Learning Quantitative Finance with R

Implement machine learning, time-series analysis, algorithmic trading and more

Dr. Param Jeet

Prashant Vats

BIRMINGHAM - MUMBAI

Learning Quantitative Finance with R

First published: March 2017

Production reference: 1210317

Published by Packt Publishing Ltd.
Livery Place
35 Livery Street
Birmingham
B3 2PB, UK.
ISBN 978-1-78646-241-1

www.packtpub.com

Credits

About the Authors

Dr. Param Jeet is a Ph.D. in mathematics from one of India's leading technological institute in Madras (IITM), India. Dr. Param Jeet has a couple of mathematical research papers published in various international journals. Dr. Param Jeet has been into the analytics industry for the last few years and has worked with various leading multinational companies as well as consulted few of companies as a data scientist.

I would like to thank my parents, S. Dhayan Singh & Jeet Kaur, who always supported me in every phase of my life, my wife, Manpreet Kaur, who every time put herself behind me with full energy and encourage me to write book, my little boy, Kavan Singh, whose innocence and little smile always cherished me to work and all family members. I also would like to thanks my Doctorate thesis advisor, Prof. Satyajit Roy, all the mentors I've had over the years, colleagues and friends without their help this book would not have been possible. With all these, I would like to share my knowledge with everyone who is keen to learn quantitative finance using R.

Prashant Vats is a masters in mathematics from one of India's leading technological institute, IIT Mumbai. Prashant has been into analytics industry for more than 10 years and has worked with various leading multinational companies as well as consulted few of companies as data scientist across several domain.

I would like to thank my parents, Late Devendra K. Singh & Sushila Sinha, who allowed me to follow my dreams and have always supported me throughout my career. I would like to thank my wife, Namrata for standing beside me in all phases of my life and supporting me to write this book, my little boy, Aahan Vats whose smile always inspires me . I also would like to thank all the mentors I've had over the years, co-workers and friends without their help this book would not have been possible. With all these, I would like to share my knowledge with everyone who is keen to learn quantitative finance using R.

About the Reviewer

Manuel Amunategui is an applied data scientist. He has implemented enterprise predictive solutions for many industries, including healthcare, finance, and sales. Prior to that, he worked as a quantitative developer on Wall Street for 6 years for one of the largest equity-options market-making firms, and as a software developer at Microsoft for 4 years.

He holds master degrees in Predictive Analytics from Northwestern University and in International Administration from the School for International Training.

He is currently the VP of Data Science at SpringML, a startup focused on offering advanced and predictive CRM analytics advice, dashboards, and automation. SpringML's clients include Google Cloud Platform, Chevron, Yamaha, Tesoro, and Salesforce.

He is a data science advocate, blogger/vlogger (amunategui.github.io) and a trainer on Udemy.com and O'Reilly Media.

www.PacktPub.com

For support files and downloads related to your book, please visit www.PacktPub.com.

Did you know that Packt offers eBook versions of every book published, with PDF and ePub files available? You can upgrade to the eBook version at www.PacktPub.com and as a print book customer, you are entitled to a discount on the eBook copy. Get in touch with us at service@packtpub.com for more details.

At www.PacktPub.com, you can also read a collection of free technical articles, sign up for a range of free newsletters and receive exclusive discounts and offers on Packt books and eBooks.

https://www.packtpub.com/mapt

Get the most in-demand software skills with Mapt. Mapt gives you full access to all Packt books and video courses, as well as industry-leading tools to help you plan your personal development and advance your career.

Why subscribe?

- Fully searchable across every book published by Packt
- Copy and paste, print, and bookmark content
- On demand and accessible via a web browser

Customer Feedback

Thanks for purchasing this Packt book. At Packt, quality is at the heart of our editorial process. To help us improve, please leave us an honest review on this book's Amazon page at http://www.amazon.com/dp/1786462419.

If you'd like to join our team of regular reviewers, you can e-mail us at customerreviews@packtpub.com. We award our regular reviewers with free eBooks and videos in exchange for their valuable feedback. Help us be relentless in improving our products!

Table of Contents

Preface   1

Chapter 1: Introduction to R   7

  The need for R   7

  How to download/install R   8

  How to install packages   9

    Installing directly from CRAN   10

    Installing packages manually   10

  Data types   10

    Vectors   12

    Lists   13

    Matrices   14

    Arrays   14

    Factors   15

    DataFrames   15

  Importing and exporting different data types   16

    How to read and write a CSV format file   17

    XLSX   18

    Web data or online sources of data   19

    Databases   20

  How to write code expressions   21

    Expressions   21

      Constant expression   21

      Arithmetic expression   21

      Conditional expression   22

      Functional call expression   23

    Symbols and assignments   23

    Keywords   24

    Naming variables   24

  Functions   24

    Calling a function without an argument   26

    Calling a function with an argument   26

    How to execute R programs   27

    How to run a saved file through R Window   27

    How to source R script   27

  Loops (for, while, if, and if...else)   28

if statement	29
if…else statement	29
for loop	30
while loop	30
apply()	31
sapply()	31
Loop control statements	31
break	31
next	32
Questions	32
Summary	32
Chapter 2: Statistical Modeling	35
Probability distributions	35
Normal distribution	36
norm	36
pnorm	38
qnorm	38
rnorm	38
Lognormal distribution	39
dlnorm	39
plnorm	40
qlnorm	42
rlnorm	42
Poisson distribution	42
Uniform distribution	43
Extreme value theory	43
Sampling	46
Random sampling	46
Stratified sampling	47
Statistics	48
Mean	48
Median	49
Mode	49
Summary	49
Moment	49
Kurtosis	50
Skewness	50
Correlation	51
Autocorrelation	51
Partial autocorrelation	52

Cross-correlation	53
Hypothesis testing	54
Lower tail test of population mean with known variance	54
Upper tail test of population mean with known variance	56
Two-tailed test of population mean with known variance	57
Lower tail test of population mean with unknown variance	58
Upper tail test of population mean with unknown variance	59
Two tailed test of population mean with unknown variance	60
Parameter estimates	61
Maximum likelihood estimation	61
Linear model	63
Outlier detection	64
Boxplot	64
LOF algorithm	65
Standardization	67
Normalization	67
Questions	68
Summary	68
Chapter 3: Econometric and Wavelet Analysis	69
Simple linear regression	70
Scatter plot	71
Coefficient of determination	72
Significance test	72
Confidence interval for linear regression model	73
Residual plot	74
Normality distribution of errors	75
Multivariate linear regression	76
Coefficient of determination	78
Confidence interval	78
Multicollinearity	78
ANOVA	79
Feature selection	81
Removing irrelevant features	81
Stepwise variable selection	82
Variable selection by classification	83
Ranking of variables	84
Wavelet analysis	85
Fast Fourier transformation	91
Hilbert transformation	93

Questions	96
Summary	97
Chapter 4: Time Series Modeling	**99**
General time series	100
Converting data to time series	101
zoo	103
Constructing a zoo object	103
Reading an external file using zoo	104
Advantages of a zoo object	105
Subsetting the data	105
Merging zoo objects	105
Plotting zoo objects	106
Disadvantages of a zoo object	106
xts	107
Construction of an xts object using as.xts	107
Constructing an xts object from scratch	108
Linear filters	108
AR	110
MA	111
ARIMA	113
GARCH	120
EGARCH	122
VGARCH	123
Dynamic conditional correlation	125
Questions	127
Summary	127
Chapter 5: Algorithmic Trading	**129**
Momentum or directional trading	130
Pairs trading	140
Distance-based pairs trading	141
Correlation based pairs trading	147
Co-integration based pairs trading	151
Capital asset pricing model	155
Multi factor model	157
Portfolio construction	162
Questions	166
Summary	166
Chapter 6: Trading Using Machine Learning	**167**
Logistic regression neural network	168

Neural network	175
Deep neural network	183
K means algorithm	186
K nearest neighborhood	188
Support vector machine	192
Decision tree	194
Random forest	197
Questions	201
Summary	201

Chapter 7: Risk Management — 203

Market risk	203
Portfolio risk	205
VaR	209
Parametric VaR	209
Historical VaR	211
Monte Carlo simulation	213
Hedging	215
Basel regulation	216
Credit risk	217
Fraud detection	223
Liability management	225
Questions	226
Summary	226

Chapter 8: Optimization — 227

Dynamic rebalancing	228
Periodic rebalancing	228
Walk forward testing	232
Grid testing	233
Genetic algorithm	236
Questions	241
Summary	241

Chapter 9: Derivative Pricing — 243

Option pricing	243
Black-Scholes model	244
Cox-Ross-Rubinstein model	245
Greeks	248
Implied volatility	250
Bond pricing	250

Credit spread   253
Credit default swaps   256
Interest rate derivatives   257
Exotic options   258
Questions   263
Summary   263
Index   265

Preface

Learning Quantitative Finance with R explains practical examples of quantitative finance in the statistical language R. This book has been written with the intention of passing knowledge to people who are interested in learning quantitative finance with R. In this book, we have covered various topics, ranging from basic level to advance level. In particular, we have covered statistical, time series, and wavelet analysis along with their applications in algorithmic trading. We have also done our best to explain some applications of machine learning, risk management, optimization, and option pricing in this book.

What this book covers

Chapter 1, *Introduction to R*, explains basic commands in R. It starts with the installation of R and its packages and moves on to data types, DataFrames, and loops. This chapter also covers how to write and call functions and how to import data files of various formats into R. This chapter is meant to provide a basic understanding of R.

Chapter 2, *Statistical Modeling,* talks about the exploratory analysis like common distribution, correlation, measure of central tendencies, outlier detection to better understand the data. It also talks about sampling and standardization/ Normalization of the data which helps in preparing the data for analysis. Further this chapter also deals with hypothesis testing and parameter estimation.

Chapter 3, *Econometric and Wavelet Analysis*, covers simple and multivariate linear regression models, which are the backbone of every analysis. An explanation of ANOVA and feature selection adds flavor to this chapter. We also build a few models using wavelets analysis.

Chapter 4, *Time Series Modeling*, in this chapter the author presents the examples to convert data in time series using ts, zoo and xts which works as the base for forecasting models. Then the author talks about various forecasting techniques like AR, ARIMA, GARCH,VGARCH etc. and its execution in R along with examples.

Chapter 5, *Algorithmic Trading*, contains some live examples from the algorithmic trading domain, including momentum trading and pair trading using various methods. CAPM, multifactor model, and portfolio construction are also covered in this chapter.

Chapter 6, *Trading Using Machine Learning,* shows how to model a machine learning algorithm using capital market data. This covers supervised and unsupervised algorithms.

Chapter 7, *Risk Management,* in this chapter the author discusses the techniques to measure market and portfolio risk. He also captures the common methods used for calculation of VAR. He also gives examples of the best practices used in banking domain for measuring credit risk.

Chapter 8, *Optimization,* in this chapter the author demonstrates examples of optimization techniques like dynamic rebalancing, walk forward testing, grid testing, genetic algorithm in financial domain.

Chapter 9, *Derivative Pricing,* use cases of R in derivative pricing. It covers vanilla option pricing along with exotic options, bonds pricing, credit spread and credit default swaps. This chapter is complex in nature and require people to have some basic understanding of derivatives.

What you need for this book

First of all, you should make sure that R is installed on your machine. All the examples in this book have been implemented in R and can be executed on the R console. R is an open source platform and can be installed free of charge for any operating system from https ://www.r-project.org/. Installation guidelines are also found on this website. Once you have R on your machine, you can straightaway go to chapter 1 and start. Each chapter explains about the required packages, shows how to install packages, and and tells the reader how to load them into the workspace.

Who this book is for

This book is written with the intent to pass knowledge to people who are interested in learning R and its application in analytics. However, we have covered examples from finance. This book covers basic to complex finance examples, along with varying degrees of complexity of R coding. This book does not expect you to have prior R programming knowledge, however this expects you to have little bit knowledge of mathematical analytical concepts. Even if you are well versed with R, this book can still be of great help to you as it explains various live examples from the data analytics industry, in particular, capital markets.

Conventions

In this book, you will find a number of styles of text that distinguish between different kinds of information. Here are some examples of these styles, and an explanation of their meaning.

Code words in text, database table names, folder names, filenames, file extensions, pathnames, dummy URLs, user input, and Twitter handles are shown as follows: The `quantmod` package is used quite a few times."

A block of code is set as follows:

```
>getSymbols("^DJI",src="yahoo")
>dji<- DJI[,"DJI.Close"]
```

When we wish to draw your attention to a particular part of a code block, the relevant lines or items are set in bold:

```
corr<- rollapply(data,252,correlation ,by.column=FALSE)
```

For any R command we have used >, which means this command has been written on the command prompt, as >, implies command prompt.

New terms and **important words** are shown in bold. Words that you see on the screen, in menus or dialog boxes for example, appear in the text like this: "Clicking the **Next** button moves you to the next screen."

Warnings or important notes appear in a box like this.

Tips and tricks appear like this.

Reader feedback

Feedback from our readers is always welcome. Let us know what you think about this book-what you liked or disliked. Reader feedback is important for us as it helps us develop titles that you will really get the most out of. To send us general feedback, simply e-mail feedback@packtpub.com, and mention the book's title in the subject of your message. If there is a topic that you have expertise in and you are interested in either writing or contributing to a book, see our author guide at www.packtpub.com/authors.

Customer support

Now that you are the proud owner of a Packt book, we have a number of things to help you to get the most from your purchase.

Downloading the example code

You can download the example code files for this book from your account at http://www.packtpub.com. If you purchased this book elsewhere, you can visit http://www.packtpub.com/supportand register to have the files e-mailed directly to you.

You can download the code files by following these steps:

1. Log in or register to our website using your e-mail address and password.
2. Hover the mouse pointer on the **SUPPORT** tab at the top.
3. Click on **Code Downloads & Errata**.
4. Enter the name of the book in the **Search** box.
5. Select the book for which you're looking to download the code files.
6. Choose from the drop-down menu where you purchased this book from.
7. Click on **Code Download**.

Once the file is downloaded, please make sure that you unzip or extract the folder using the latest version of:

- WinRAR / 7-Zip for Windows
- Zipeg / iZip / UnRarX for Mac
- 7-Zip / PeaZip for Linux

The code bundle for the book is also hosted on GitHub at `https://github.com/PacktPubl ishing/Learning-Quantitative-Finance-with-R`. We also have other code bundles from our rich catalog of books and videos available at `https://github.com/PacktPublishing/`. Check them out!

Errata

Although we have taken every care to ensure the accuracy of our content, mistakes do happen. If you find a mistake in one of our books-maybe a mistake in the text or the code-we would be grateful if you could report this to us. By doing so, you can save other readers from frustration and help us improve subsequent versions of this book. If you find any errata, please report them by visiting `http://www.packtpub.com/submit-errata`, selecting your book, clicking on the **Errata Submission Form** link, and entering the details of your errata. Once your errata are verified, your submission will be accepted and the errata will be uploaded to our website or added to any list of existing errata under the Errata section of that title.

To view the previously submitted errata, go to `https://www.packtpub.com/books/conten t/support` and enter the name of the book in the search field. The required information will appear under the **Errata** section.

Piracy

Piracy of copyrighted material on the Internet is an ongoing problem across all media. At Packt, we take the protection of our copyright and licenses very seriously. If you come across any illegal copies of our works in any form on the Internet, please provide us with the location address or website name immediately so that we can pursue a remedy.

Please contact us at `copyright@packtpub.com` with a link to the suspected pirated material.

We appreciate your help in protecting our authors and our ability to bring you valuable content.

Questions

If you have a problem with any aspect of this book, you can contact us at `questions@packtpub.com`, and we will do our best to address the problem.

1
Introduction to R

In this chapter, we will be discussing basic R concepts. This will serve as the background for upcoming chapters. We are not going to discuss each and every concept in detail for R. This chapter is meant for people who do not have any knowledge of the R language or beginners who are looking to pursue a career in quantitative finance or want to use R for quantitative financial analysis. This chapter can give you a start in learning how to write programs in R, and for writing complex programs, you can explore other books.

This chapter covers the following topics:

- The need for R
- How to download/install R
- How to install packages
- Data types
- Import and export of different data types
- How to write code expressions
- Functions
- How to execute R programs
- Loops (for, while, if, and if...else)

The need for R

There are so many statistical packages which can be used for solving problems in quantitative finance. But R is not a statistical package but it is a language. R is a flexible and powerful language for achieving high-quality analysis.

To use R, one does not need to be a programmer or computer–subject expert. The knowledge of basic programming definitely helps in learning R, but it is not a prerequisite for getting started with R.

One of the strengths of R is its package system. It is vast. If a statistical concept exists, chances are that there is already a package for it in R. There exist many functionalities that come built in for statistics / quantitative finance.

R is extendable and provides plenty of functionalities which encourage developers in quant finance to write their own tools or methods to solve their analytical problems.

The graphing and charting facilities present in R are unparalleled. R has a strong relationship with academia. As new research gets published, the likelihood is that a package for the new research gets added, due to its open source nature, which keeps R updated with the new concepts emerging in quant finance.

R was designed to deal with data, but when it came into existence, big data was nowhere in the picture. Additional challenges dealing with big data are the variety of data (text data, metric data, and so on), data security, memory, CPU I/O RSC requirements, multiple machines, and so on. Techniques such as map-reducing, in-memory processing, streaming data processing, down-sampling, chunking, and so on are being used to handle the challenges of big data in R.

Furthermore, R is free software. The development community is fantastic and easy to approach, and they are always interested in developing new packages for new concepts. There is a lot of documentation available on the Internet for different packages of R.

Thus, R is a cost-effective, easy-to-learn tool. It has very good data handling, graphical, and charting capabilities. It is a cutting-edge tool as, due to its open nature, new concepts in finance are generally accompanied by new R packages. It is demand of time for people pursuing a career in quantitative finance to learn R.

How to download/install R

In this section, we are going to discuss how to download and install R for various platforms: Windows, Linux, and Mac.

Open your web browser and go to the following link: `https://cran.rstudio.com/`.

From the given link, you can download the required version according to the available operating system.

For the Windows version, click on **Download R for Windows,** and then select the base version and download **Download R 3.3.1 for Windows** for your Windows operating system, click on it, and select your favorite language option. Now click through the installer and it will take you through various options, such as the following:

1. Setup Wizard.
2. License Agreement.
3. Select folder location where you want to install.
4. Select the component. Select the option according to the configuration of your system; if you do not know the configuration of your system, then select all the options.
5. If you want to customize your setup, select the option.
6. Select the R launch options and desktop shortcut options according to your requirements.

R download and installation is complete for Windows.

Similarly, you click on your installer for Linux and Mac and it will take you through various options of installation.

How to install packages

R packages are a combination of R functions, compiled code, and sample data, and their storage directory is known as a library. By default, when R is installed, a set of packages gets installed and the rest of the packages you have to add when required.

A list of commands is given here to check which packages are present in your system:

```
>.libPaths()
```

The preceding command is used for getting or setting the library trees that R knows about. It gives the following result:

```
"C:/Program Files/R/R-3.3.1/library"
```

After this, execute the following command and it will list all the available packages:

```
>library()
```

There are two ways to install new packages.

Installing directly from CRAN

CRAN stands for **Comprehensive R Archive Network**. It is a network of FTP web servers throughout the globe for storing identical, up-to-date versions of code and documentation for R.

The following command is used to install the package directly from the CRAN web page. You need to choose the appropriate mirror:

```
>install.packages("Package")
```

For example, if you need to install the ggplot2 or forecast package for R, the commands are as follows:

```
>install.packages("ggplot2")
>install.packages("forecast")
```

Installing packages manually

Download the required R package manually and save the ZIP version at your designated location (let's say /DATA/RPACKAGES/) on the system.

For example, if we want to install ggplot2, then run the following command to install it and load it to the current R environment. Similarly, other packages can also be installed:

```
>install.packages("ggplot2", lib="/data/Rpackages/")
>library(ggplot2, lib.loc="/data/Rpackages/")
```

Data types

In any programming language, one needs to store various pieces of information using various variables. Variables are reserved memory locations for storing values. So by creating a variable, one is reserving some space in the memory. You may like to store various types of data types, such as character, floating point, Boolean, and so on. On the basis of data type, the operating system allocates memory and decides what can be stored in reserved memory.

All the things you encounter in R are called objects.

R has five types of basic objects, also known as atomic objects, and the rest of the objects are built on these atomic objects. Now we will give an example of all the basic objects and will verify their class:

- Character:

    We assign a character value to a variable and verify its class:

    ```
    >a <- "hello"
    >print(class(a))
    ```

    The result produced is as follows:

    ```
    [1] "character"
    ```

- Numeric:

    We assign a numeric value to a variable and verify its class:

    ```
    >a <- 2.5
    >print(class(a))
    ```

    The result produced is as follows:

    ```
    [1] "numeric"
    ```

- Integer:

    We assign an integer value to a variable and verify its class:

    ```
    >a <- 6L
    >print(class(a))
    ```

    The result produced is as follows:

    ```
    [1] "integer"
    ```

- Complex:

    We assign an integer value to a variable and verify its class:

    ```
    >a <- 1 + 2i
    >print(class(a))
    ```

The result produced is as follows:

```
[1] "complex"
```

- Logical (True/false):

  We assign an integer value to a variable and verify its class:

```
>a <- TRUE
>print(class(a))
```

  Then the result produced is as follows:

```
[1] "logical"
```

The basic types of objects in R are known as **vectors** and they consist of similar types of objects. They cannot consist of two different types of objects at the same time, such as a vector consisting of both character and numeric.

But list is an exception, and it can consist of multiple classes of objects at the same time. So a list can simultaneously contain a character, a numeric, and a list.

Now we will discuss the common data types present in R and give at least one example for each data type discussed here.

Vectors

Vectors have already been defined. If we want to construct a vector with more than one element, we can use the c() function which combines the elements into a vector, for example:

```
>a<-"Quantitative"
>b<-"Finance"
>c(a,b)
```

This produces the following result:

```
[1] "Quantitative" "Finance"
```

Similarly:

```
>Var<-c(1,2,3)
>Var
```

This produces the following result:

```
[1] 1 2 3
```

Lists

A list is an R object that consists of multiple types of objects inside it, such as vectors and even lists. For example, let's construct a list and print it using code:

```
#Create a List and print it
>List1 = list(c(4,5,6),"Hello", 24.5)
>print(List1)
```

When we execute the previous command, it produces the following result:

```
[[1]]
[1] 4 5 6
[[2]]
[1] "Hello"

[[3]]
[1] 24.5
```

We can extract the individual elements of the list according to our requirements.

For example, in the preceding case, if we want to extract the second element:

```
>print(List1[2])
```

Upon executing the preceding code, R creates the following output:

```
[[1]]
[1] "Hello"
```

One can merge the two lists using the function c(); for example:

```
>list1 <- list(5,6,7)
>list2 <- list("a","b","c")
>Combined_list <-c(list1,list2)
>print(Combined_list)
```

Upon executing the preceding command, we get the combined list:

```
[[1]]
[1] 5

[[2]]
[1] 6

[[3]]
[1] 7

[[4]]
[1] "a"

[[5]]
[1] "b"

[[6]]
[1] "c"
```

Matrices

A matrix is a two-dimensional rectangular dataset, and it is created by vector input to the matrix() function.

For example, create a matrix with two rows and three columns, and print it:

```
>M <- matrix(c(1,2,3,4,5,6), nrow = 2, ncol = 3)
>print(M)
```

When we execute the preceding code, it produces the following result:

```
     [,1] [,2] [,3]
[1,]    1    3    5
[2,]    2    4    6
```

Arrays

Matrices are confined to only two dimensions, but arrays can be of any dimension. The array() function takes a dim attribute, which creates the needed dimensions.

For example, create an array and print it:

```
>a <- array(c(4,5),dim = c(3,3,2))
>print(a)
```

When we execute the previous code, it produces the following result:

```
, , 1
      [,1] [,2] [,3]
[1,]    4    5    4
[2,]    5    4    5
[3,]    4    5    4

, , 2

      [,1] [,2] [,3]
[1,]    5    4    5
[2,]    4    5    4
[3,]    5    4    5
```

Factors

Factors are R objects that are created using a vector. It stores the vector along with the distinct elements present in the vector as labels. Labels are always in character form, irrespective of whether it is numeric, character, or Boolean.

Factors are created using the `factor()` function, and the count of levels is given by n levels; for example:

```
>a <-c(2,3,4,2,3)
>fact <-factor(a)
>print(fact)
>print(nlevels(fact))
```

When the preceding code gets executed, it generates the following results:

```
[1] 2 3 4 2 3
Levels: 2 3 4
[1] 3
```

DataFrames

DataFramesare tabular-form data objects where each column can be of different form, that is, numeric, character, or logical. Each column consists of a list of vectors having the same length.

DataFrames are generated using the function `data.frame()`; for example:

```
>data <-data.frame(
>+Name = c("Alex", "John", "Bob"),
>+Age = c(18,20,23),
>+Gender =c("M","M","M")
>+)
>print(data)
```

When the preceding code gets executed, it generates the following result:

```
  Name Age Gender
1 Alex  18     M
2 John  20     M
3  Bob  23     M
```

Importing and exporting different data types

In R, we can read the files stored from outside the R environment. We can also write the data into files which can be stored and accessed by the operating system. In R, we can read and write different formats of files, such as CSV, Excel, TXT, and so on. In this section, we are going to discuss how to read and write different formats of files.

The required files should be present in the current directory to read them. Otherwise, the directory should be changed to the required destination.

The first step for reading/writing files is to know the working directory. You can find the path of the working directory by running the following code:

```
>print (getwd())
```

This will give the paths for the current working directory. If it is not your desired directory, then please set your own desired directory by using the following code:

```
>setwd("")
```

For instance, the following code makes the folder `C:/Users` the working directory:

```
>setwd("C:/Users")
```

How to read and write a CSV format file

A CSV format file is a text file in which values are comma separated. Let us consider a CSV file with the following content from stock-market data:

Date	Open	High	Low	Close	Volume	Adj Close
14-10-2016	2139.68	2149.19	2132.98	2132.98	3.23E+09	2132.98
13-10-2016	2130.26	2138.19	2114.72	2132.55	3.58E+09	2132.55
12-10-2016	2137.67	2145.36	2132.77	2139.18	2.98E+09	2139.18
11-10-2016	2161.35	2161.56	2128.84	2136.73	3.44E+09	2136.73
10-10-2016	2160.39	2169.6	2160.39	2163.66	2.92E+09	2163.66

To read the preceding file in R, first save this file in the working directory, and then read it (the name of the file is Sample.csv) using the following code:

```
>data<-read.csv("Sample.csv")
>print(data)
```

When the preceding code gets executed, it will give the following output:

```
      Date       Open     High     Low      Close    Volume       Adj.Close
1   14-10-2016 2139.68 2149.19 2132.98 2132.98 3228150000   2132.98
2   13-10-2016 2130.26 2138.19 2114.72 2132.55 3580450000   2132.55
3   12-10-2016 2137.67 2145.36 2132.77 2139.18 2977100000   2139.18
4   11-10-2016 2161.35 2161.56 2128.84 2136.73 3438270000   2136.73
5   10-10-2016 2160.39 2169.60 2160.39 2163.66 2916550000   2163.66
```

Read.csv by default produces the file in DataFrame format; this can be checked by running the following code:

```
>print(is.data.frame(data))
```

Now, whatever analysis you want to do, you can perform it by applying various functions on the DataFrame in R, and once you have done the analysis, you can write your desired output file using the following code:

```
>write.csv(data,"result.csv")
>output <- read.csv("result.csv")
>print(output)
```

When the preceding code gets executed, it writes the output file in the working directory folder in CSV format.

XLSX

Excel is the most common format of file for storing data, and it ends with extension .xls or .xlsx.

The xlsx package will be used to read or write .xlsx files in the R environment.

Installing the xlsx package has dependency on Java, so Java needs to be installed on the system. The xlsx package can be installed using the following command:

```
>install.packages("xlsx")
```

When the previous command gets executed, it will ask for the nearest CRAN mirror, which the user has to select to install the package. We can verify that the package has been installed or not by executing the following command:

```
>any(grepl("xlsx",installed.packages()))
```

If it has been installed successfully, it will show the following output:

```
[1] TRUE
Loading required package: rJava
Loading required package: methods
Loading required package: xlsxjars
```

We can load the xlsx library by running the following script:

```
>library("xlsx")
```

Now let us save the previous sample file in .xlsx format and read it in the R environment, which can be done by executing the following code:

```
>data <- read.xlsx("Sample.xlsx", sheetIndex = 1)
>print(data)
```

This gives a DataFrame output with the following content:

```
        Date    Open    High     Low   Close      Volume  Adj.Close
1 2016-10-14 2139.68 2149.19 2132.98 2132.98 3228150000  2132.98
2 2016-10-13 2130.26 2138.19 2114.72 2132.55 3580450000  2132.55
3 2016-10-12 2137.67 2145.36 2132.77 2139.18 2977100000  2139.18
4 2016-10-11 2161.35 2161.56 2128.84 2136.73 3438270000  2136.73
5 2016-10-10 2160.39 2169.60 2160.39 2163.66 2916550000  2163.66
```

Similarly, you can write R files in `.xlsx` format by executing the following code:

```
>output<-write.xlsx(data,"result.xlsx")
>output<- read.csv("result.csv")
>print(output)
```

Web data or online sources of data

The Web is one main source of data these days, and we want to directly bring the data from web form to the R environment. R supports this:

```
URL <- "http://ichart.finance.yahoo.com/table.csv?s=^GSPC"
snp <- as.data.frame(read.csv(URL))
head(snp)
```

When the preceding code is executed, it directly brings the data for the S&P500 index into R in DataFrame format. A portion of the data has been displayed by using the `head()` function here:

```
        Date     Open     High      Low    Close      Volume   Adj.Close
1 2016-10-14 2139.68 2149.19 2132.98 2132.98 3228150000     2132.98
2 2016-10-13 2130.26 2138.19 2114.72 2132.55 3580450000     2132.55
3 2016-10-12 2137.67 2145.36 2132.77 2139.18 2977100000     2139.18
4 2016-10-11 2161.35 2161.56 2128.84 2136.73 3438270000     2136.73
5 2016-10-10 2160.39 2169.60 2160.39 2163.66 2916550000     2163.66
6 2016-10-07 2164.19 2165.86 2144.85 2153.74 3619890000     2153.74
```

Similarly, if we execute the following code, it brings the DJI index data into the R environment: its sample is displayed here:

```
>URL <- "http://ichart.finance.yahoo.com/table.csv?s=^DJI"
>dji <- as.data.frame(read.csv(URL))
>head(dji)
```

This gives the following output:

```
        Date      Open      High       Low     Close    Volume   Adj.Close
1 2016-10-14 18177.35 18261.11 18138.38 18138.38 87050000    18138.38
2 2016-10-13 18088.32 18137.70 17959.95 18098.94 83160000    18098.94
3 2016-10-12 18132.63 18193.96 18082.09 18144.20 72230000    18144.20
4 2016-10-11 18308.43 18312.33 18061.96 18128.66 88610000    18128.66
5 2016-10-10 18282.95 18399.96 18282.95 18329.04 72110000    18329.04
6 2016-10-07 18295.35 18319.73 18149.35 18240.49 82680000    18240.49
```

Please note that we will be mostly using the `snp` and `dji` indexes for example illustrations in the rest of the book and these will be referred to as `snp` and `dji`.

Databases

A relational database stores data in normalized format, and to perform statistical analysis, we need to write complex and advance queries. But R can connect to various relational databases such as MySQL Oracle, and SQL Server, easily and convert the data tables into DataFrames. Once the data is in DataFrame format, doing statistical analysis is easy to perform using all the available functions and packages.

In this section, we will take the example of MySQL as reference.

R has a built-in package, `RMySQL`, which provides connectivity with the database; it can be installed using the following command:

```
>install.packages("RMySQL")
```

Once the package is installed, we can create a connection object to create a connection with the database. It takes username, password, database name, and localhost name as input. We can give our inputs and use the following command to connect with the required database:

```
>mysqlconnection = dbConnect(MySQL(), user = '...', password = '...',
dbname = '..',host = '.....')
```

When the database is connected, we can list the table that is present in the database by executing the following command:

```
>dbListTables(mysqlconnection)
```

We can query the database using the function `dbSendQuery()`, and the result is returned to R by using function `fetch()`. Then the output is stored in DataFrame format:

```
>result = dbSendQuery(mysqlconnection, "select * from <table name>")
>data.frame = fetch(result)
>print(data.fame)
```

When the previous code gets executed, it returns the required output.

We can query with a filter clause, update rows in database tables, insert data into a database table, create tables, drop tables, and so on by sending queries through `dbSendQuery()`.

How to write code expressions

In this section, we will discuss how to write various basic expressions which are the core elements of writing a program. Later, we will discuss how to create user-defined functions.

Expressions

R code consists of one or more expressions. An expression is an instruction to perform a particular task.

For example, the addition of two numbers is given by the following expression:

```
>4+5
```

It gives the following output:

```
[1] 9
```

If there is more than one expression in a program, they get executed one by one, in the sequence they appear.

Now we will discuss basic types of expressions.

Constant expression

The simplest form of expression are constant values, which may be character or numeric values.

For example, 100 is a numeric value expression of a constant value.

`Hello World` is a character form expression of a constant expression.

Arithmetic expression

The R language has standard arithmetic operators and using these, arithmetic expressions can be written.

R has the following arithmetic operators:

Operands	Operators
+	Addition
−	Subtraction
*	Multiplication
/	Division
^	Exponentiation

Using these arithmetic operations, one can generate arithmetic expressions; for example:

```
4+5
4-5
4*5
```

R follows the BODMAS rule. One can use parentheses to avoid ambiguity in creating any arithmetic expression.

Conditional expression

A conditional expression compares two values and returns a logical value in the form of True or False.

R has standard operators for comparing values and operators for combining conditions:

Operands	Operators
==	Equality
> (>=)	Greater than (greater than equal to)
< (<=)	Less than (less than equal to)
!=	Inequality
&&	Logical AND
||	Logical OR
!	Logical NOT

For example:

`10>5`, when executed, returns `True`.

`5>10`, when executed, returns `False`.

Functional call expression

The most common and useful type of R expression is calling functions. There are a lot of built-in functions in R, and users can built their own functions. In this section, we will see the basic structure of calling a function.

A function call consists of a function name followed by parentheses. Within the parentheses, arguments are present, separated by commas. Arguments are expressions that provide the necessary information to the functions to perform the required tasks. An example will be provided when we discuss how to construct user-defined functions.

Symbols and assignments

R code consists of keywords and symbols.

A symbol is the label for an object stored in RAM, and it gets the stored value from the memory when the program gets executed.

R also stores many predefined values for predefined symbols, which is used in the program as required and gets automatically downloaded.

For example, the `date()` function produces today's date when executed.

The result of an expression can be assigned to a symbol, and it is assigned by using the assignment operator `<-`.

For example, the expression `value <-4+6` assigns the symbol value with value `10` and is stored in memory.

Keywords

Some symbols are used to represent special values and cannot be reassigned:

- NA: This is used to define missing or unknown values
- Inf: This is used to represent infinity. For example, 1/0 produces the result infinity
- NaN: This is used to define the result of arithmetic expression which is undefined. For example, 0/0 produces NaN
- NULL: This is used to represent empty result
- TRUE and FALSE: These are logical values and are generally generated when values are compared

Naming variables

When writing R code, we need to store various pieces of information under many symbols. So we need to name these symbols meaningfully as that will make the code easy to understand. Symbols should be self-explanatory. Writing short symbol name will make the code tougher to understand.

For example, if we represent date of birth information by DateOfBirth or DOB, then the first option is better as it is self-explanatory.

Functions

In this section, we will provide some examples of built-in functions that already exist in R and also construct a user-defined function for a specific task.

A function is a collection of statements put together to do a specific task.

R has a lot of built-in functions and users can define their own functions.

According to their requirement, in R, the interpreter passes control to the function object along with the arguments required for the accomplishment of the task designated for the function. After completing the task, the function returns the control to the interpreter.

The syntax for defining a function is as follows:

```
>function_name<-function(arg1, arg2,...){
>+function body
>+}
```

Here:

- **Function name**: This is the name of the defined function and is stored as an object with this name.
- **Arguments**: Arguments are the required information needed for the function to accomplish its task. Arguments are optional.
- **Function body**: This is a collection of statements that does the designated task for the function.
- **Return value**: The return value is the last expression of a function which is returned as an output value of the task performed by the function.

Please find here an example of some of the inbuilt functions along with their results when executed:

```
>print(mean(25:82))
[1] 53.5
>print(sum(41:68))
[1] 1526
```

Now we will look at how to build the user-defined functions. Here we are trying to find the square of a given sequence.

The name of the function is `findingSqrFunc` and takes the argument value, which must be an integer:

```
>findingSqrFunc<-function(value){
>+for(j in 1:value){
>+sqr<-j^2
>+print(sqr)
>+}
>+}
```

Once the preceding code gets executed, we call the function:

```
>findingSqrFunc(4)
```

We get the following output:

```
[1]  1
[1]  4
[1]  9
[1]  16
```

Calling a function without an argument

Construct a function without an argument:

```
>Function_test<-function(){
>+ for(i in 1:3){
>+ print(i*5)
>+ }
>+ }
>Function_test()
```

On executing the preceding function without arguments, the following output gets printed:

```
[1]  5
[1]  10
[1]  15
```

Calling a function with an argument

The arguments to a function can be supplied in the same sequence as the way it has been defined. Otherwise the arguments have to be given in any order but assigned to their name. Given here are the steps for creating and calling the functions:

1. First create a function:

   ```
   >Function_test<-function(a,b,c){
   >+ result<-a*b+c
   >+ print(result)
   >+ }
   ```

2. Call the function by providing the arguments in the same sequence. It gives the following output:

   ```
   >Function_test(2,3,4)
   [1]  10
   ```

3. Call the function by names of arguments in any sequence:

```
>Function_test(c=4,b=3,a=4)
```

This gives the following output:

```
[1] 16
```

How to execute R programs

In this section, we will discuss different ways of executing R programs.

How to run a saved file through R Window

For running a program in the R workspace, follow these steps:

1. Open R (double-click on the desktop icon or open the program from **Start**).
2. Click on **File** and open the script.
3. Select the program you want to run; it will appear in an R Editor window.
4. Right-click and **Select All** (or type *Ctrl + A*).
5. Right-click and **Run Line** or **Selection** (or type *Ctrl + R*).
6. The output will appear in the R console window.

How to source R script

Please perform the following steps for sourcing the R code:

1. First check your working directory. It can be checked by the following code:

```
>print(getwd())
```

2. On running the preceding code, if it gives the path of the designated folder, it is fine. Otherwise, change the working directory by using the following code:

```
>setwd("D:/Rcode")
```

3. Change the destination directory according to your need and then run the required code using the following code:

```
>Source('firstprogram.r')
```

For example, let's say the program `firstprogram.r` has the following code in it:

```
a<-5
print(a)
```

Upon sourcing, it will generate the output 5 at the console.

When you want to tell R to execute a number of lines of code without waiting for instructions, you can use the `source` function to run the saved script. This is known as sourcing a script.

It's better to write the entire code in Studio Editor and then save it and source the entire script. If you want to print an output in source script then please use the `print` function to get the desired output. However, in the interactive editor, you do not need to write print. It will give it by default.

In other operating systems, the command for running the program remains the same.

Comments are parts of a program that are ignored by the interpreter while executing the actual program.

Comments are written using #; for example:

```
#this is comment in my program.
```

Loops (for, while, if, and if...else)

Loops are instructions for automating a multistep process by organizing sequences of actions by grouping the parts which need to be repeated. All the programming languages come up with built-in constructs, which allow the repetition of instructions or blocks of instructions. In programming languages, there are two types of loops.

Decision-making is one of the significant components of programming languages. This can be achieved in R programming by using the conditional statement `if...else`. The syntax, along with an example, is given here.

Let us first discuss `if` and `else` conditional statements and then we will discuss loops.

if statement

Let us first see how `if` and `else` work in R. The general syntax for an `if` clause is given here:

```
if (expression) {
    statement
}
```

If an expression is correct then the statement gets executed else nothing happens. An expression can be a logical or numeric vector. In the case of numeric vectors, 0 is taken as `False` and the rest are taken as `True`, for example:

```
>x<-5
>if(x>0)
>+ {
>+ print(" I am Positive")
>+ }
```

When the preceding code gets executed then it prints `I am Positive`.

if...else statement

Now let us see how the if and else conditions work in R. Here is the syntax:

```
if(expression){
    statement1
} else {
    statement2
}
```

The `else` part is evaluated in case if the `if` part is `False`, for example:

```
> x<--5
> if(x>0)
>+ {
>+ print(" I am Positive")
>+ }else
>+{
>+ print(" I am Negative")
>+}
```

When the preceding code gets executed, it prints `I am Negative`.

for loop

These loops are executed for a defined number of times and are controlled by a counter or index and incremented at each cycle. Please find here the syntax of the `for` loop construct:

```
for (val in sequence) {
    statement
}
```

Here is an example:

```
>Var <- c(3,6,8,9,11,16)
>counter <- 0
>for (val in Var) {
>+    if(val %% 2 != 0)  counter = counter+1
>+}
print(counter)
```

When the preceding code gets executed, it counts the number of odd numbers present in vector `c`, that is, 3.

while loop

`while` loops are the loops which are set at onset for verifying the logical condition. The logical condition is tested at the start of the loop construct. Here is the syntax:

```
while (expression) {
    statement
}
```

Here, the expression is evaluated first and, if it is true, the body of the `for` loop gets executed. Here is an example:

```
>Var <- c("Hello")
>counter <- 4
>while (counter < 7) {
>+    print(Var)
>+    counter = counter+ 1
>+}
```

Here, first the expression gets evaluated and, if it is true, the body of the loop gets executed and it keeps executing till the expression returns `False`.

apply()

apply() is a function in R used for quick operations on a matrix, vector, or array and can be executed on rows, columns, and on both together. Now let us try to find the sum of rows of a matrix using the apply function. Let us execute the following code:

```
> sample = matrix(c(1:10), nrow = 5 , ncol = 2)
> apply(sample, 1,sum)
```

It generates the sum row-wise.

sapply()

sapply() operates over a set of data such as a list or vector, and calls the specified function for each item. Let us execute the following code to check the example:

```
> sapply(1:5, function(x) x^3)
```

It computes cubes for 1 to 5.

Loop control statements

There are control statements that can change the normal sequence of execution. break and next are loop control statements, and we will briefly discuss these control statements here.

break

break terminates the loop and gives control to the next following statement of the loop; for example:

```
>Vec <- c("Hello")
>counter <- 5
>repeat {
>+    print(Vec)
>+    counter <- counter + 1
>+    if(counter > 8) {
>+        break
>+    }
>+}
```

As a result of the `break` statement, when the preceding statement gets executed, it prints `Hello` four times and then leaves the loop. `repeat` is another loop construct that keeps executing unless a stop condition is specified.

next

`next` does not terminate the loop, but skips the current iteration of the flow and goes to the next iteration. See the following example:

```
>Vec <- c(2,3,4,5,6)
>for ( i in Vec) {
>+    if (i == 4) {
>+        next
>+    }
>+    print(i)
>+}
```

In the preceding example, when the iteration goes to the third element of vector `Vec`, then the control skips the current iteration and goes back to the next iteration. So, when the preceding statement gets executed, it prints vector elements 2, 3, 5, and 6, and skips 4.

Questions

1. What are the various atomic objects of R?
2. What is a vector in R?
3. What is the difference between a vector and a list?
4. What is the difference between arrays and matrices?
5. What is a DataFrame and what is its significance in R?
6. How do you read and write CSV and XLSX files in R?
7. How do you read and write stock-market data in R?
8. Explain the process of connecting R with any relational database.
9. What is a function and what is its significance in R?
10. What is an assignment operator in R?
11. How do you call a function in R?
12. How do you source a script in R?
13. What is the difference between `for` and `while` loops in R?

Summary

Now let us recap what we have learned so far in this chapter:

- How it is very important for analysts pursuing their career in financial analytics to learn R
- Installation of R and its packages
- The basic objects in R are character, numeric, integer, complex, and logical
- Commonly used data types in R are lists, matrices, arrays, factors, and DataFrames
- Reading files from external data files such as CSV and XLSX, and particularly from online sources and databases in R
- Writing files to CSV and XLSX from R
- Writing different types of expression, such as constant, arithmetic, logical, symbols, assignments, and so on
- Write user-defined functions
- Ways of calling of user defined functions and inbuilt functions
- Running R programs from the console window and by sourcing saved files
- The use of conditional decision-making by using if and else statements
- The use of loops such as `for` and `while`

2
Statistical Modeling

In this chapter, we are going to discuss statistical modeling, which will be the first step in learning quantitative finance in R as the concepts of statistical modeling are the driving force for quantitative finance. Before starting this chapter, the assumption is that learners are familiar with basic programming in R and have a sound knowledge of statistical concepts. We will not be discussing statistical concepts in this chapter. We will be discussing how to do the statistical modeling in R.

This chapter covers the following topics:

- Probability distributions
- Sampling
- Statistics
- Correlation
- Hypothesis testing
- Parameter estimation
- Outlier detection
- Standardization
- Normalization

Probability distributions

Probability distributions determine how the values of random variables are spread. For example, the set of all the possible outcomes of the tossing of a sequence of coins gives rise to binomial distribution. The means of large samples of the data population follow normal distribution, which is the most common and useful distribution.

The features of these distributions are very well known and can be used to extract inferences about the population. We are going to discuss in this chapter some of the most common probability distributions and how to compute them.

Normal distribution

Normal distribution is the most widely used probability distribution in the financial industry. It is a bell-shaped curve and mean, median mode is the same for normal distribution. It is denoted by $N(\mu, \sigma^2)$, where μ is the mean and σ^2 is the variance of the sample. If the mean is 0 and variance is 1 then the normal distribution is known as standard normal distribution N(1, 0).

Now let us discuss the main functions to compute the important features associated with normal distribution. Please note we will be using the dataset `DataChap2.csv` for all the calculations in this chapter. A sample is displayed in the following table. Let the imported dataset in R be `Sampledata`.

In the given sample, `Date` is the time when the data has been captured. `Open`, `High`, `Low`, and `Close` are the the opening, highest, lowest, and closing price of the day, respectively. `Adj.Close` is the adjusted prices of the day and `return` is the return calculated using the `Adj.Close` price of today and yesterday. `Flag` and `Sentiments` are the dummy variables created for the purpose of analysis:

Date	Open	High	Low	Close	Volume	Adj.Close	Return	Flag	Sentiments
12/14/2016	198.74	203	196.76	198.69	4144600	198.69	0	1	Good
12/13/2016	193.18	201.28	193	198.15	6816100	198.15	0.03	1	Bad
12/12/2016	192.8	194.42	191.18	192.43	615800	192.43	0	1	Good
12/9/2016	190.87	193.84	190.81	192.18	2719600	192.18	0	0	Bad
12/8/2016	192.05	192.5	189.54	192.29	3187300	192.29	0	0	Good

norm

`norm` returns the height of the normal distribution and the function is defined by the following:

```
dnorm(x, mean, sd)
```

Here, x is the vector of numbers and sd is the standard deviation.

When we execute the following code, it generates the given plot showing the height of all the points:

```
> y <- dnorm(Sampledata$Return, mean = mean(Sampledata$Return), sd
=sd(Sampledata$Return, na.rm = FALSE))
> plot(Sampledata$Return,y)
```

The graphical representation is as follows:

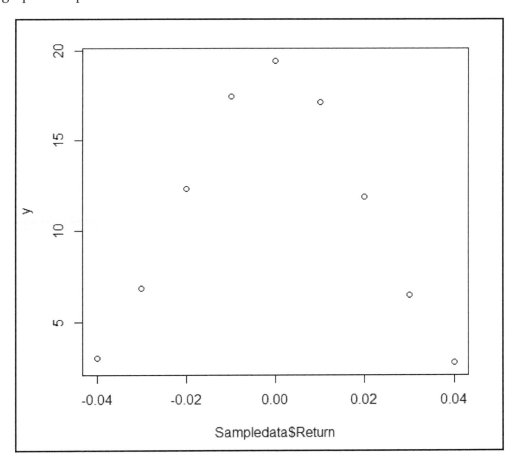

Figure 2.1: Plot showing height of normal distribution

pnorm

`pnorm` is known as the cumulative distribution function and it gives the probability of a random variable less than a given value of a random variable and is given by the following:

```
pnorm(x, mean, sd)
```

We execute the following code:

```
>  pnorm(.02, mean = mean(Sampledata$Return), sd = sd(Sampledata$Return,
na.rm = FALSE))
```

This yields `0.159837` and can be interpreted as there is a 16% probability of getting a return greater than 2%.

qnorm

`qnorm` takes the probability value and returns a number for which the cumulative value matches the probability and the function is defined as follows:

```
qnorm(x, mean, sd)
```

Here, `x` is the probability value.

We execute the following code:

```
> qnorm(0.159837, mean = mean(Sampledata$Return), sd =
+sd(Sampledata$Return, na.rm = FALSE),lower.tail=FALSE)
```

This gives the output `0.02`, which means that for the return of greater than equal 2% the probability is 16%.

rnorm

`rnorm` is used to generate the random number whose distribution is normal. It is given by the following:

```
qnorm(x, mean, sd)
```

Here, x is the number of random variables to be generated.

If we run the following code, it will generate five random values with the mean and standard deviation of the return:

```
>rnorm(5, mean = mean(Sampledata$Return), sd = +sd(Sampledata$Return, na.rm
= FALSE))
```

When this code gets executed, it generates five normal random variables with the specified mean and standard deviation.

Lognormal distribution

In a financial time series, the lognormal distribution plays a more critical role than normal distribution. Just like normal distribution, we will be discussing the same features for lognormal distribution.

dlnorm

dlnorm is used to find the density function of the lognormal distribution. The general syntax for computing the density function is given by the following:

```
dlnorm(x, meanlog, sdlog)
```

Let us find the density function of the volume of the sample data, which can be done by executing the following code:

```
> y <- dlnorm(Sampledata$Volume, meanlog = mean(Sampledata$Volume), sdlog=
sd(Sampledata$Volume, na.rm = FALSE))> plot(Sampledata$Volume,y)
```

The graphical representation is as follows:

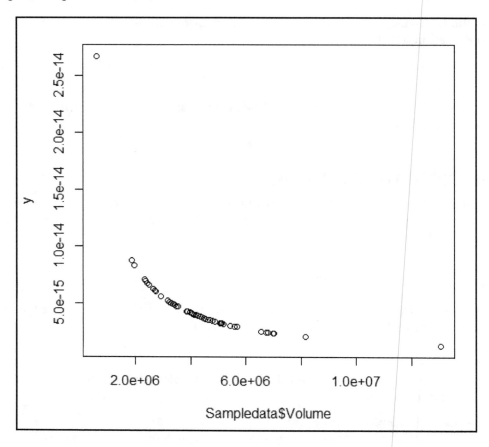

Figure 2.2: Plot showing density function of lognormal distribution

plnorm

plnorm gives the cumulative probability distribution function of lognormal distribution. The general syntax is given here:

```
>dlnorm(x, meanlog, sdlog)
```

Now let us find the `cdf` for volume, which is given by the following code:

```
> y <- plnorm(Sampledata$Volume, meanlog = mean(Sampledata$Volume), sdlog=
sd(Sampledata$Volume, na.r=FALSE))> plot(Sampledata$Volume,y)
```

This gives the `cdf` plot as shown here:

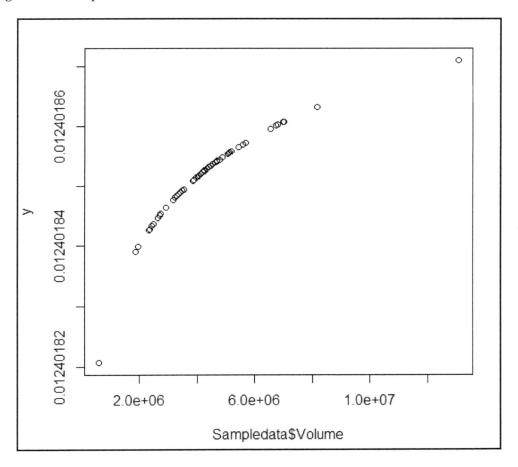

Figure 2.3: Plot showing cumulative distribution function of lognormal distribution

qlnorm

qlnorm is used to generate p quantiles of the lognormal distribution, which can be done by using the following syntax:

```
qlnorm(p, mean, standard deviation)
```

rlnorm

rlnorm generates a dataset with a given mean and standard deviation. The syntax is as follows:

```
rlnorm((n, mean , standard dev)
```

Poisson distribution

Poisson distribution is the probability distribution of the occurrence of independent events in an interval. If λ is the mean occurrence per interval, then the probability of having x occurrences within a given interval is given by the following:

$$F(x) = \lambda x \ e\text{-}\lambda/x!$$

Here, $x = 0, 1, 2, 3.....$

If there are, on average, 10 stocks whose return per minute is getting positive, we can find the probability of having 15 stocks whose returns are getting positive in a particular minute by using the following code:

```
>ppois(15, lambda=10)
```

This gives the output value 0.9512596.

Hence the lower tail probability of getting returns of 15 stocks positive is 0.95.

Similarly, we can find the upper tail probability by executing the following code:

```
>ppois(15, lambda=10, lower=FALSE)
```

Uniform distribution

Continuous uniform distribution is the probability distribution of a random number selection from the continuous interval between *a* and *b*. Its density function is given as follows:

F(x) = 1/(b-a)

Here $a \leq x \leq b$ and

F(x) = 0 if x≤a or x≥b

Now let us generate 10 random numbers between 1 and 5. It can be given by executing the following code:

```
>runif(10, min=1, max=5)
```

This generates the following output:

```
3.589514 2.979528 3.454022 2.731393 4.416726 1.560019 4.592588 1.500221
4.067229 3.515988.
```

Extreme value theory

Most of the commonly known statistical distributions are focused on the center of distributions and do not bother about the tails of distributions, which contain the extreme/outlier values. One of the toughest challenges for a risk manager is to develop risk models which can take care of rare and extreme events. **Extreme value theory (EVT)** attempts to provide the best possible estimate of the tail area of a distribution.

There are two types of models for estimating extreme values, that is, block maxima models fitted with the **generalized extreme value (GEV)** distribution and **peaks over threshold (POT)** models fitted with the **generalized Pareto distribution (GPD)**. Generally, POT is used these days so we will be giving an example of POT in this chapter. Let us use a subset of the dataset available in the POT package as an example.

To find the tail distribution, first we need to find a threshold point, which can be done by executing the following code:

```
> data(ardieres)
> abc<-ardieres[1:10000,]
> events <- clust(abc, u = 1.5, tim.cond = 8/365, clust.max = TRUE)
> par(mfrow = c(2, 2))
> mrlplot(events[, "obs"])
> diplot(events)
> tcplot(events[, "obs"], which = 1)
> tcplot(events[, "obs"], which = 2)
```

This gives the following plot:

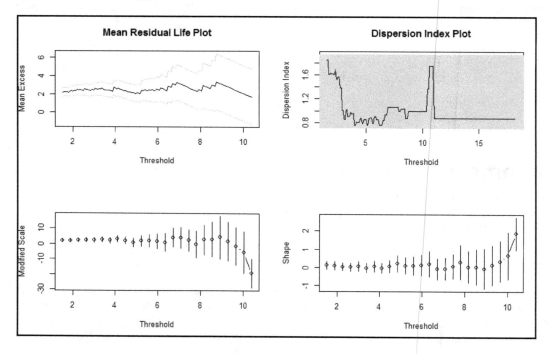

Figure 2.4: Analysis for threshold selection for EVT

After analyzing these plots, the threshold point can be set and the parameters of GPD models can be estimated. This is done by executing the following code:

```
>obs <- events[,"obs"]
>ModelFit <- fitgpd(obs, thresh = 5, "pwmu")
>ModelFit
```

This gives the parameter estimates of the GPD model:

```
Estimator: PWMU

Varying Threshold: FALSE

  Threshold Call: 7
    Number Above: 10
Proportion Above: 0.07692

Estimates
   scale       shape
 3.67073   -0.14746

Standard Error Type:

Standard Errors
  scale      shape
1.76817   0.38432

Asymptotic Variance Covarianc
        scale       shape
scale   3.12641   -0.56227
shape  -0.56227    0.14770

Correlation
        scale       shape
scale   1.00000   -0.82742
shape  -0.82742    1.00000

Optimization Information
   Convergence: NA
   Function Evaluations: NA
```

Figure 2.5: Parameter estimates of GPD model for EVT

Sampling

When building any model in finance, we may have very large datasets on which model building will be very time-consuming. Once the model is built, if we need to tweak the model again, it is going to be a time-consuming process because of the volume of data. So it is better to get the random or proportionate sample of the population data on which model building will be easier and less time-consuming. So in this section, we are going to discuss how to select a random sample and a stratified sample from the data. This will play a critical role in building the model on sample data drawn from the population data.

Random sampling

Select the sample where all the observation in the population has an equal chance. It can be done in two ways, one without replacement and the other with replacement.

A random sample without replacement can be done by executing the following code:

```
> RandomSample <- Sampledata[sample(1:nrow(Sampledata), 10,
>+ replace=FALSE),]
```

This generates the following output:

```
      Date     Open   High    Low    Close  Volume  Adj.Close Return Flag Sentiments
9   12/2/2016 182.88 184.88 180.00 181.47 4037200    181.47   0.00   0    Good
13 11/28/2016 195.48 199.35 194.55 196.12 4487100    196.12   0.00   0    Good
27  11/7/2016 193.59 194.29 190.05 193.21 3852000    193.21   0.01   1    Good
5   12/8/2016 192.05 192.50 189.54 192.29 3187300    192.29   0.00   0    Good
30 11/2/2016 190.70 192.70 187.51 188.02 4208700    188.02  -0.01   0    Bad
26  11/8/2016 193.79 197.49 191.26 194.94 3251400    194.94   0.01   1    Bad
12 11/29/2016 195.56 196.73 189.50 189.57 4431200    189.57  -0.03   0    Bad
35 10/26/2016 201.00 203.19 200.10 202.24 4647800    202.24   0.00   0    Good
17 11/21/2016 185.04 188.89 184.41 184.52 4344600    184.52   0.00   0    Good
3  12/12/2016 192.80 194.42 191.18 192.43  615800    192.43   0.00   1    Good
```

Figure 2.6: Table shows random sample without replacement

A random sample with replacement can be done by executing the following code. Replacement means that an observation can be drawn more than once. So if a particular observation is selected, it is again put into the population and it can be selected again:

```
> RandomSample <- Sampledata[sample(1:nrow(Sampledata), 10,
>+ replace=TRUE),]
```

This generates the following output:

```
          Date     Open    High     Low   Close      Volume  Adj.Close  Return  Flag  Sentiments
45    10/12/2016  200.95  203.88  200.42  201.51     1970700     201.51    0.01     1        Good
30     11/2/2016  190.05  192.70  187.51  188.02     4208700     188.02   -0.01     0         Bad
34    10/27/2016  211.34  213.70  201.65  204.01    13066400     204.01    0.01     1         Bad
34.1  10/27/2016  211.34  213.70  201.65  204.01    13066400     204.01    0.01     1         Bad
11    11/30/2016  191.00  191.89  187.50  189.40     3535000     189.40    0.00     0        Good
40    10/19/2016  199.74  206.66  198.06  203.56     6991200     203.56    0.02     1         Bad
45.1  10/12/2016  200.95  203.88  200.42  201.51     1970700     201.51    0.01     1        Good
32    10/31/2016  202.49  202.49  195.81  197.73     4685100     197.73   -0.01     0         Bad
30.1   11/2/2016  190.05  192.70  187.51  188.02     4208700     188.02   -0.01     0         Bad
10     12/1/2016  188.25  188.53  181.00  181.88     5112100     181.88   -0.04     0         Bad
```

Figure 2.7: Table showing random sampling with replacement

Stratified sampling

In stratified sampling, we divide the population into separate groups, called strata. Then, a probability sample (often a simple random sample) is drawn from each group. Stratified sampling has several advantages over simple random sampling. With stratified sampling, it is possible to reduce the sample size in order to get better precision.

Now let us see how many groups exist by using `Flag` and `Sentiments` as given in the following code:

```
>library(sampling)
>table(Sampledata$Flag,Sampledata$Sentiments)
```

The output is as follows:

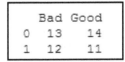

```
    Bad  Good
0    13    14
1    12    11
```

Figure 2.8: Table showing the frequencies across different groups

Now you can select the sample from the different groups according to your requirement:

```
>Stratsubset=strata(Sampledata,c("Flag","Sentiments"),size=c(6,5, >+4,3),
method="srswor")
> Stratsubset
```

The output is as follows:

	Flag	Sentiments	ID_unit	Prob	Stratum
1	1	Good	1	0.5454545	1
19	1	Good	19	0.5454545	1
21	1	Good	21	0.5454545	1
23	1	Good	23	0.5454545	1
27	1	Good	27	0.5454545	1
41	1	Good	41	0.5454545	1
6	1	Bad	6	0.4166667	2
14	1	Bad	14	0.4166667	2
16	1	Bad	16	0.4166667	2
34	1	Bad	34	0.4166667	2
38	1	Bad	38	0.4166667	2
10	0	Bad	10	0.3076923	3
12	0	Bad	12	0.3076923	3
24	0	Bad	24	0.3076923	3
36	0	Bad	36	0.3076923	3
17	0	Good	17	0.2142857	4
29	0	Good	29	0.2142857	4
43	0	Good	43	0.2142857	4

Figure 2.9: Table showing output for stratified sampling

Statistics

In a given dataset, we try to summarize the data by the central position of the data, which is known as measure of central tendency or summary statistics. There are several ways to measure the central tendency, such as mean, median, and mode. Mean is the widely used measure of central tendency. Under different scenarios, we use different measures of central tendency. Now we are going to give an example of how to compute the different measures of central tendency in R.

Mean

mean is the equal weightage average of the sample. For example, we can compute the mean of Volume in the dataset Sampledata by executing the following code, which gives the arithmetic mean of the volume:

```
mean(Sampledata$Volume)
```

Median

Median is the mid value of the matrix when it is arranged in a sorted way, which can be computed by executing the following code:

```
median(Sampledata$Volume)
```

Mode

Mode is the value present in the attribute which has maximum frequency. For mode, there does not exist an inbuilt function so we will write a function to compute mode:

```
findmode <- function(x) {
    uniqx <- unique(x)
    uniqx[which.max(tabulate(match(x, uniqx)))]
}
findmode(Sampledata$return)
```

Executing the preceding code gives the mode of the return attribute of the dataset.

Summary

We can also generate basic statistics of a column by executing the following code:

```
summary(Sampledata$Volume)
```

This generates the mean, median, minimum, maximum, Q1, and Q2 quartiles.

Moment

Moment gives the characteristics such as variance, skewness, and so on of the population, which is computed by the following code. The code gives the third order moment of the attribute Volume. Once can change the order to get the relevant characteristics. However before that, we need to install package e1071:

```
moment(Sampledata$Volume, order=3, center=TRUE)
```

Kurtosis

Kurtosis measures whether the data is heavy-tailed or light-tailed relative to a normal distribution. Datasets with high kurtosis tend to have heavy tails, or outliers. Datasets with low kurtosis tend to have light tails, and fewer outliers. The computed value of kurtosis is compared with the kurtosis of normal distribution and the interpretation is made on the basis of that.

The `kurtosis` of `Volume` is given by the following code:

```
kurtosis(Sampledata$Volume)
```

It gives value `5.777117`, which shows the distribution of volume as leptokurtic.

Skewness

Skewness is the measure of symmetry of the distribution. If the mean of data values is less than the median then the distribution is said to be left-skewed and if the mean of the data values is greater than the median, then the distribution is said to be right-skewed.

The `skewness` of `Volume` is computed as follows in R:

```
skewness(Sampledata$Volume)
```

This gives the result `1.723744`, which means it is right-skewed.

 For computing `skewness` and `kurtosis`, we need to install the package `e1071`.

Correlation

Correlation plays a very important role in quant finance. It not only determines the relation between the financial attributes but also plays a crucial role in predicting the future of financial instruments. Correlation is the measure of linear relationship between the two financial attributes. Now let us try to compute the different types of correlation in R using Sampledata, which is used in identifying the orders of components of predictive financial models.

Correlation can be computed by the following code. Let's first subset the data and then run the function for getting correlation:

```
x<-Sampledata[,2:5]
rcorr(x, type="pearson")
```

This generates the following correlation matrix, which shows the measure of linear relationship between the various daily level prices of a stock:

	Open	High	Low	Close
Open	1	0.962062	0.934174	0.878553
High	0.962062	1	0.952676	0.945434
Low	0.934174	0.952676	1	0.960428
Close	0.878553	0.945434	0.960428	1

Autocorrelation

Autocorrelation is the correlation of the series with its past or future values. It is also known as serial correlation and lagged correlation. It plays a critical role in time series prediction modeling. The function acf computes estimates of the autocorrelation function.

The following code when executed gives the autocorrelation of the series with its lagged values:

```
acf(Sampledata$Volume)
```

The graph is as follows:

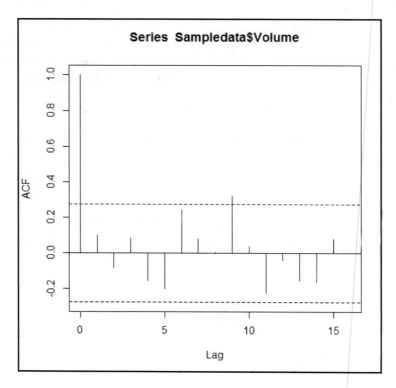

Figure 2.10: Plot showing autocorrelation of series with its lag

This gives the plot of autocorrelations of the series with its lagged values. There are other options in functions such as `lag.max`, `plot`, and so on.

Partial autocorrelation

Partial autocorrelation of a time series is the correlation with its own lagged values, controlling for the values of the time series at all shorter lags. It is also used in time series modeling for identifying the orders of the components of forecasting techniques. It is computed by using the following code:

```
pacf(Sampledata$Volume)
```

It also contains other options such as how many lags you want to use and plot. The preceding code gives the following plot:

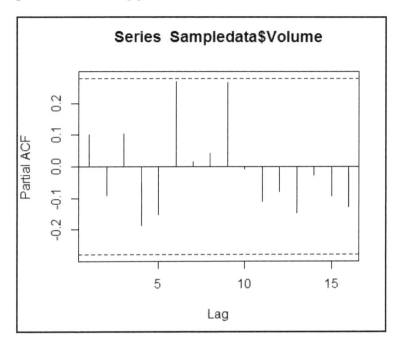

Figure 2.11: Plot showing partial autocorrelation of series with its lag

Cross-correlation

Cross-correlation is a measure of the similarity of two series as a function of the displacement of one relative to the other. Just like `acf` and `pacf`, it also plays a crucial role in time series forecasting. It can be computed by using the following function:

```
ccf(Sampledata$Volume,Sampledata$High, main = "ccf plot")
```

When the preceding code gets executed, it generates the following plot:

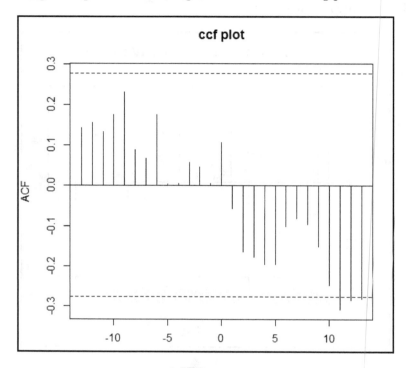

Figure 2.12: Plot showing cross-correlation of two series

Hypothesis testing

Hypothesis testing is used to reject or retain a hypothesis based upon the measurement of an observed sample. We will not be going into theoretical aspects but will be discussing how to implement the various scenarios of hypothesis testing in R.

Lower tail test of population mean with known variance

The null hypothesis is given by $\mu \geq \mu_0$, where μ_0 is the hypothesized lower bound of the population mean.

Let us assume a scenario where an investor assumes that the mean of daily returns of a stock since inception is greater than $10. The average of 30 days' daily return sample is $9.9. Assume the population standard deviation is 0.011. Can we reject the null hypothesis at .05 significance level?

Now let us calculate the test statistics z which can be computed by the following code in R:

```
> xbar= 9.9
> mu0 = 10
> sig = 1.1
> n = 30
> z = (xbar-mu0)/(sig/sqrt(n))
> z
```

Here:

- xbar: Sample mean
- mu: Hypothesized value
- sig: Standard deviation of population
- n: Sample size
- z: Test statistics

This gives the value of z the test statistics:

```
[1] -0.4979296
```

Now let us find out the critical value at 0.05 significance level. It can be computed by the following code:

```
> alpha = .05
> z.alpha = qnorm(1-alpha)
> -z.alpha
```

This gives the following output:

```
[1] -1.644854
```

Since the value of the test statistics is greater than the critical value, we fail to reject the null hypothesis claim that the return is greater than $10.

In place of using the critical value test, we can use the `pnorm` function to compute the lower tail of Pvalue test statistics. This can be computed by the following code:

```
> pnorm(z)
```

This gives the following output:

```
[1] 0.3092668
```

Since the Pvalue is greater than `0.05`, we fail to reject the null hypothesis.

Upper tail test of population mean with known variance

The null hypothesis is given by $\mu \leq \mu_0$, where μ_0 is the hypothesized upper bound of the population mean.

Let us assume a scenario where an investor assumes that the mean of daily returns of a stock since inception is at most $5. The average of 30 days' daily return sample is $5.1. Assume the population standard deviation is 0.25. Can we reject the null hypothesis at `.05` significance level?

Now let us calculate the test statistics z, which can be computed by the following code in R:

```
> xbar= 5.1
> mu0 = 5
> sig = .25
> n = 30
> z = (xbar-mu0)/(sig/sqrt(n))
> z
```

Here:

- `xbar`: Sample mean
- `mu0`: Hypothesized value
- `sig`: Standard deviation of population
- `n`: Sample size
- `z`: Test statistics

It gives `2.19089` as the value of test statistics. Now let us calculate the critical value at `.05` significance level, which is given by the following code:

```
> alpha = .05
> z.alpha = qnorm(1-alpha)
> z.alpha
```

This gives `1.644854`, which is less than the value computed for the test statistics. Hence we reject the null hypothesis claim.

Also, the Pvalue of the test statistics is given as follows:

```
>pnorm(z, lower.tail=FALSE)
```

This gives `0.01422987`, which is less than `0.05` and hence we reject the null hypothesis.

Two-tailed test of population mean with known variance

The null hypothesis is given by $\mu=\mu_0$, where μ_0 is the hypothesized value of the population mean.

Let us assume a scenario where the mean of daily returns of a stock last year is $2. The average of 30 days' daily return sample is $1.5 this year. Assume the population standard deviation is .2. Can we reject the null hypothesis that there is not much significant difference in returns this year from last year at `.05` significance level?

Now let us calculate the test statistics z, which can be computed by the following code in R:

```
> xbar= 1.5
> mu0 = 2
> sig = .1
> n = 30
> z = (xbar-mu0)/(sig/sqrt(n))
> z
```

This gives the value of test statistics as `-27.38613`.

Now let us try to find the critical value for comparing the test statistics at .05 significance level. This is given by the following code:

```
>alpha = .05
>z.half.alpha = qnorm(1-alpha/2)
>c(-z.half.alpha, z.half.alpha)
```

This gives the value $-1.959964, 1.959964$. Since the value of test statistics is not between the range $(-1.959964, 1.959964)$, we reject the claim of the null hypothesis that there is not much significant difference in returns this year from last year at .05 significance level.

The two-tailed Pvalue statistics is given as follows:

```
>2*pnorm(z)
```

This gives a value less than .05 so we reject the null hypothesis.

In all the preceding scenarios, the variance is known for population and we use the normal distribution for hypothesis testing. However, in the next scenarios, we will not be given the variance of the population so we will be using t distribution for testing the hypothesis.

Lower tail test of population mean with unknown variance

The null hypothesis is given by $\mu \geq \mu_0$, where μ_0 is the hypothesized lower bound of the population mean.

Let us assume a scenario where an investor assumes that the mean of daily returns of a stock since inception is greater than $1. The average of 30 days' daily return sample is $.9. Assume the population standard deviation is 0.01. Can we reject the null hypothesis at .05 significance level?

In this scenario, we can compute the test statistics by executing the following code:

```
> xbar= .9
> mu0 = 1
> sig = .1
> n = 30
> t = (xbar-mu0)/(sig/sqrt(n))
> t
```

Here:

- xbar: Sample mean
- mu0: Hypothesized value
- sig: Standard deviation of sample
- n: Sample size
- t: Test statistics

This gives the value of the test statistics as -5.477226. Now let us compute the critical value at $.05$ significance level. This is given by the following code:

```
> alpha = .05
> t.alpha = qt(1-alpha, df=n-1)
> -t.alpha
```

We get the value as -1.699127. Since the value of the test statistics is less than the critical value, we reject the null hypothesis claim.

Now instead of the value of the test statistics, we can use the Pvalue associated with the test statistics, which is given as follows:

```
>pt(t, df=n-1)
```

This results in a value less than .05 so we can reject the null hypothesis claim.

Upper tail test of population mean with unknown variance

The null hypothesis is given by $\mu \leq \mu_0$, where μ_0 is the hypothesized upper bound of the population mean.

Let us assume a scenario where an investor assumes that the mean of daily returns of a stock since inception is at most \$3. The average of 30 days' daily return sample is \$3.1. Assume the population standard deviation is $.2$. Can we reject the null hypothesis at $.05$ significance level?

Now let us calculate the test statistics t which can be computed by the following code in R:

```
> xbar= 3.1
> mu0 = 3
> sig = .2
> n = 30
> t = (xbar-mu0)/(sig/sqrt(n))
> t
```

Here:

- xbar: Sample mean
- mu0: Hypothesized value
- sig: Standard deviation of sample
- n: Sample size
- t: Test statistics

This gives the value 2.738613 of the test statistics. Now let us find the critical value associated with the .05 significance level for the test statistics. It is given by the following code:

```
> alpha = .05
> t.alpha = qt(1-alpha, df=n-1)
> t.alpha
```

Since the critical value 1.699127 is less than the value of the test statistics, we reject the null hypothesis claim.

Also, the value associated with the test statistics is given as follows:

```
>pt(t, df=n-1, lower.tail=FALSE)
```

This is less than .05. Hence the null hypothesis claim gets rejected.

Two tailed test of population mean with unknown variance

The null hypothesis is given by $\mu = \mu_0$, where μ_0 is the hypothesized value of the population mean.

Let us assume a scenario where the mean of daily returns of a stock last year is $2. The average of 30 days' daily return sample is $1.9 this year. Assume the population standard deviation is .1. Can we reject the null hypothesis that there is not much significant difference in returns this year from last year at .05 significance level?

Now let us calculate the test statistics t, which can be computed by the following code in R:

```
> xbar= 1.9
> mu0 = 2
> sig = .1
> n = 30
> t = (xbar-mu0)/(sig/sqrt(n))
> t
```

This gives −5.477226 as the value of the test statistics. Now let us try to find the critical value range for comparing, which is given by the following code:

```
> alpha = .05
> t.half.alpha = qt(1-alpha/2, df=n-1)
> c(-t.half.alpha, t.half.alpha)
```

This gives the range value (−2.04523, 2.04523). Since this is the value of the test statistics, we reject the claim of the null hypothesis.

Parameter estimates

In this section, we are going to discuss some of the algorithms used for parameter estimation.

Maximum likelihood estimation

Maximum likelihood estimation (MLE) is a method for estimating model parameters on a given dataset.

Now let us try to find the parameter estimates of a probability density function of normal distribution.

Let us first generate a series of random variables, which can be done by executing the following code:

```
> set.seed(100)
> NO_values <- 100
> Y <- rnorm(NO_values, mean = 5, sd = 1)
> mean(Y)
```

This gives 5.002913.

```
> sd(Y)
```

This gives 1.02071.

Now let us make a function for `log` likelihood:

```
LogL <- function(mu, sigma) {
+       A = dnorm(Y, mu, sigma)
+       -sum(log(A))
+   }
```

Now let us apply the function `mle` to estimate the parameters for estimating mean and standard deviation:

```
> library(stats4)
> mle(LogL, start = list(mu = 2, sigma=2))
```

`mu` and `sigma` have been given initial values.

This gives the output as follows:

```
Call:
mle(minuslogl = LogL, start = list(mu = 2, sigma = 2))

Coefficients:
      mu    sigma
5.002926 1.015619
Warning messages:
1: In dnorm(Y, mu, sigma) : NaNs produced
2: In dnorm(Y, mu, sigma) : NaNs produced
3: In dnorm(Y, mu, sigma) : NaNs produced
4: In dnorm(Y, mu, sigma) : NaNs produced
5: In dnorm(Y, mu, sigma) : NaNs produced
6: In dnorm(Y, mu, sigma) : NaNs produced
7: In dnorm(Y, mu, sigma) : NaNs produced
8: In dnorm(Y, mu, sigma) : NaNs produced
9: In dnorm(Y, mu, sigma) : NaNs produced
10: In dnorm(Y, mu, sigma) : NaNs produced
```

Figure 2.13: Output for MLE estimation

NaNs are produced when negative values are attempted for the standard deviation.

This can be controlled by giving relevant options, as shown here. This ignores the warning messages produced in the output displayed in *Figure 2.13*:

```
> mle(LogL, start = list(mu = 2, sigma=2), method = "L-BFGS-B",
+   lower = c(-Inf, 0),
+       upper = c(Inf, Inf))
```

This, upon execution, gives the best possible fit, as shown here:

```
Call:
mle(minuslogl = LogL, start = list(mu = 2, sigma = 2), method = "L-BFGS-B",
    lower = c(-Inf, 0), upper = c(Inf, Inf))

Coefficients:
      mu    sigma
5.002913 1.015595
```

Figure 2.14: Revised output for MLE estimation

Linear model

In the linear regression model, we try to predict dependent/response variables in terms of independent/predictor variables. In the linear model, we try to fit the best possible line, known as the regression line, though the given points. The coefficients for the regression lines are estimated using statistical software. An intercept in the regression line represents the mean value of the dependent variable when the predictor variable takes the value as zero. Also the response variable increases by the factor of estimated coefficients for each unit change in the predictor variable. Now let us try to estimate parameters for the linear regression model where the dependent variable is Adj.Close and independent variable is Volume of Sampledata. Then we can fit the linear model as follows:

```
> Y<-Sampledata$Adj.Close
> X<-Sampledata$Volume
> fit <- lm(Y ~ X)
> summary(fit)
```

Upon executing the preceding code, the output is generated as given here:

```
Call:
lm(formula = Y ~ X)

Residuals:
    Min       1Q    Median       3Q      Max
-12.3053  -5.1630   -0.4186   5.9110  14.2786

Coefficients:
              Estimate Std. Error t value Pr(>|t|)
(Intercept)  1.945e+02  2.427e+00  80.146   <2e-16 ***
X           -1.880e-07  5.057e-07  -0.372    0.712
---
Signif. codes:  0 '***' 0.001 '**' 0.01 '*' 0.05 '.' 0.1 ' ' 1

Residual standard error: 6.926 on 48 degrees of freedom
Multiple R-squared:  0.002871,  Adjusted R-squared:  -0.0179
F-statistic: 0.1382 on 1 and 48 DF,  p-value: 0.7117
```

Figure 2.15: Output for linear model estimation

The `summary` display shows the parameter estimates of the linear regression model. Similarly, we can estimate parameters for other regression models such as multiple or other forms of regression models.

Outlier detection

Outliers are very important to be taken into consideration for any analysis as they can make analysis biased. There are various ways to detect outliers in R and the most common one will be discussed in this section.

Boxplot

Let us construct a `boxplot` for the variable volume of the `Sampledata`, which can be done by executing the following code:

```
> boxplot(Sampledata$Volume, main="Volume", boxwex=0.1)
```

The graph is as follows:

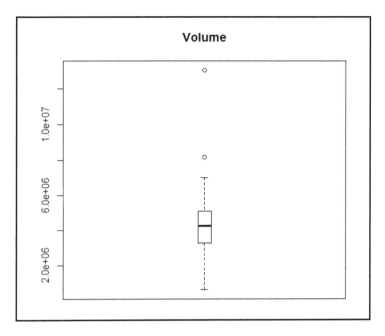

Figure 2.16: Boxplot for outlier detection

An outlier is an observation which is distant from the rest of the data. When reviewing the preceding boxplot, we can clearly see the outliers which are located outside the fences (whiskers) of the boxplot.

LOF algorithm

The **local outlier factor** (**LOF**) is used for identifying density-based local outliers. In LOF, the local density of a point is compared with that of its neighbors. If the point is in a sparser region than its neighbors then it is treated as an outlier. Let us consider some of the variables from the Sampledata and execute the following code:

```
> library(DMwR)
> Sampledata1<- Sampledata[,2:4]
> outlier.scores <- lofactor(Sampledata1, k=4)
> plot(density(outlier.scores))
```

Here, k is the number of neighbors used in the calculation of the local outlier factors.

The graph is as follows:

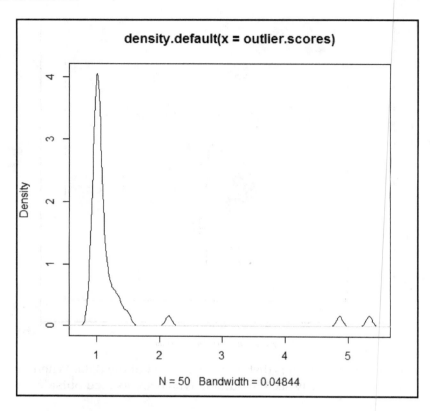

Figure 2.17: Plot showing outliers by LOF method

If you want the top five outliers then execute the following code:

```
> order(outlier.scores, decreasing=T)[1:5]
```

This gives an output with the row numbers:

```
[1] 50 34 40 33 22
```

Standardization

In statistics, standardization plays a crucial role as we have various attributes for modeling and all of them have different scales. So for comparison purposes, we need to standardize the variables to bring them on the same scale. Centering the values and creating the z scores is done in R by the `scale()` function. It takes the following arguments:

- `x`: A numeric object
- `center`: If TRUE, the object's column means are subtracted from the values in those columns (ignoring NAs); if FALSE, centering is not performed
- `scale`: If TRUE, the centered column values are divided by the column's standard deviation (when center is also TRUE; otherwise, the root mean square is used); if FALSE, scaling is not performed

If we want to center the data of `Volume` in our dataset, we just need to execute the following code:

```
>scale(Sampledata$Volume, center=TRUE, scale=FALSE)
```

If we want to standardize the data of volume in our dataset, we just need to execute the following code:

```
>scale(Sampledata$Volume, center=TRUE, scale=TRUE)
```

Normalization

Normalization is done using the `minmax` concept to bring the various attributes on the same scale. It is calculated by the formula given here:

normalized = (x-min(x))/(max(x)-min(x))

So if we want to normalize the volume variable, we can do it by executing the following code:

```
> normalized = (Sampledata$Volume-
+min(Sampledata$Volume))/(max(Sampledata$Volume)-+min(Sampledata$Volume))
> normalized
```

Questions

1. Construct examples of normal, Poisson, and uniform distribution in R.
2. How do you do random and stratified sampling in R?
3. What are the different measures of central tendency and how do you find them in R?
4. How do you compute kurtosis and skewness in R?
5. How do you do hypothesis testing in R with known/unknown variance of population in R?
6. How do you detect outliers in R?
7. How do you do parameter estimates for a linear model and MLE in R?
8. What is standardization and normalization in R and how do you perform it in R?

Summary

In this chapter, we have discussed the most commonly used distributions in the finance domain and associated metrics computations in R; sampling (random and stratified); measures of central tendencies; correlations and types of correlation used for model selections in time series; hypothesis testing (one-tailed/two-tailed) with known and unknown variance; detection of outliers; parameter estimation; and standardization/normalization of attributes in R to bring attributes on comparable scales.

In the next chapter, analysis done in R associated with simple linear regression, multivariate linear regression, ANOVA, feature selection, ranking of variables, wavelet analysis, fast Fourier transformation, and Hilbert transformation will be covered.

3
Econometric and Wavelet Analysis

In financial analytics, we need techniques to do predictive modeling for forecasting and finding the drivers for different target variables. In this chapter, we will discuss types of regression and how we can build a regression model in R for building predictive models. Also we will discuss, how we can implement a variable selection method and other aspects associated with regression. This chapter will not contain theoretical description but will just guide you in how to implement a regression model in R in the financial space. Regression analysis can be used for doing forecast on cross-sectional data in the financial domain. We will also cover frequency analysis of the data, and how transformations such as Fast Fourier, wavelet, Hilbert, haar transformations in time, and frequency domains help to remove noise in the data.

This chapter covers the following topics:

- Simple linear regression
- Multivariate linear regression
- Multicollinearity
- ANOVA
- Feature selection
- Stepwise variable selection
- Ranking of variables
- Wavelet analysis
- Fast Fourier transformation
- Hilbert transformation

Simple linear regression

In simple linear regression, we try to predict one variable in terms of a second variable called a predictor variable. The variable we are trying to predict is called the dependent variable and is denoted by y, and the independent variable is denoted by x. In simple linear regression, we assume a linear relationship between the dependent attribute and predictor attribute.

First we need to plot the data to understand the linear relationship between the dependent variable and independent variable. Here our, data consists of two variables:

- YPrice: Dependent variable
- XPrice: Predictor variable

In this case, we are trying to predict Yprice in terms of XPrice. StockXprice is the independent variable and StockYprice is the dependent variable. For every element of StockXprice, there is an element of StockYprice, which implies one-to-one mapping between elements of StockXprice and StockYprice.

A few lines of data used for the following analysis are displayed using the following code:

```
>head(Data)
```

	StockYPrice	StockXPrice
1	80.13	72.86
2	79.57	72.88
3	79.93	71.72
4	81.69	71.54
5	80.82	71
6	81.07	71.78

Scatter plot

First we will plot scatter plot between y and x, to understand the type of linear relationship between x and y. The following code, when executed, gives the following scatter plot:

```
> YPrice = Data$StockYPrice
> XPrice = Data$StockXPrice
> plot(YPrice, XPrice,        xlab="XPrice",
ylab="YPrice")
```

Here, our dependent variable is `YPrice` and predictor variable is `Xprice`. Please note this example is just for illustration purposes:

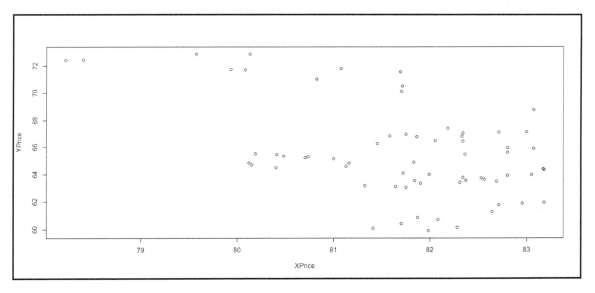

Figure 3.1: Scatter plot of two variables

Once we have examined the relationship between the dependent variable and predictor variable, we try fit the best straight line through the points which represent the predicted Y value for all the given predictor variables. A simple linear regression is represented by the following equation describing the relationship between the dependent and predictor variables:

$$Y = \alpha + \beta x + \varepsilon$$

Here α and β are parameters and ε is the error term. α is also known as the intercept and β as the coefficient of the predictor variable; it is obtained by minimizing the sum of squares of the error term ε. All the statistical software gives the option of estimating the coefficients and so does R.

We can fit the linear regression model using the `lm` function in R as shown here:

```
> LinearR.lm = lm(YPrice ~ XPrice, data=Data)
```

Here, `Data` is the input data given and `Yprice` and `Xprice` are the dependent and predictor variables respectively. Once we have fitted the model, we can extract our parameters using the following code:

```
> coeffs = coefficients(LinearR.lm); coeffs
```

The preceding result gives the value of the intercept and coefficient:

```
(Intercept)        XPrice
92.7051345  -0.1680975
```

So now we can write our model as follows:

```
> YPrice = 92.7051345 + -0.1680975*(Xprice)
```

This can give the predicted value for any given `Xprice`.

Also, we can execute the following code to get the predicted value using the fitted linear regression model on any other data, say `OutofSampleData`, by executing the following code:

```
> predict(LinearR.lm, OutofSampleData)
```

Coefficient of determination

We have fitted our model but now we need to test how good the model is fitting to the data. There are a few measures available for it but the main one is the coefficient of determination. This is given by the following code:

```
> summary(LinearR.lm)$r.squared
```

By definition, it is a proportion of the variance in the dependent variable that is explained by the independent variable and is also known as R2.

Significance test

Now, we need to examine whether the relationship between the variables in the linear regression model is significant or not, at 0.05 significance level.

We execute the following code:

```
> summary(LinearR.lm)
```

It gives all the relevant statistics of the linear regression model as shown here:

```
Call:
lm(formula = YPrice ~ XPrice, data = Data)

Residuals:
     Min      1Q   Median      3Q     Max
-2.31151 -0.70341  0.07678  0.79348 1.91989

Coefficients:
            Estimate Std. Error t value Pr(>|t|)
(Intercept) 92.70513    2.31592  40.030  < 2e-16 ***
XPrice      -0.16810    0.03528  -4.764 1.13e-05 ***
---
Signif. codes:  0 '***' 0.001 '**' 0.01 '*' 0.05 '.' 0.1 ' ' 1

Residual standard error: 0.9644 on 64 degrees of freedom
Multiple R-squared:  0.2618,    Adjusted R-squared:  0.2503
F-statistic:  22.7 on 1 and 64 DF,  p-value: 1.129e-05
```

Figure 3.2: Summary of linear regression model

If the **Pvalue** associated with `Xprice` is less than **0.05** then the predictor is explaining the dependent variable significantly at **0.05** significance level.

Confidence interval for linear regression model

One of the important issues for the predicted value is to find the confidence interval around the predicted value. So let us try to find a 95% confidence interval around the predicted value of the fitted model. This can be achieved by executing the following code:

```
> Predictdata = data.frame(XPrice=75)
> predict(LinearR.lm, Predictdata, interval="confidence")
```

Here we are estimating the predicted value for the given value of `Xprice = 75` and then we try to find the confidence interval around the predicted value.

The output generated by executing the preceding code is shown in the following screenshot:

```
        fit        lwr        upr
1 80.09782  79.39094  80.8047
```

Figure 3.3: Prediction of confidence interval for linear regression model

Residual plot

Once we have fitted the model then we compare it with the observed value and find the difference, which is known as the residual. Then we plot the residual against the predictor variable to see the performance of the model visually. The following code can be executed to get the residual plot:

```
> LinearR.res = resid(LinearR.lm)
> plot(XPrice, LinearR.res,
ylab="Residuals", xlab="XPrice",
main="Residual Plot")
```

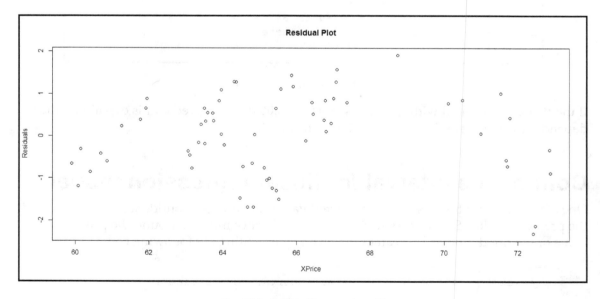

Figure 3.4: Residual plot of linear regression model

We can also plot the residual plot for the standardized residuals by just executing the following code in the previously mentioned code:

```
> LinearRSTD.res = rstandard(LinearR.lm)
> plot(XPrice, LinearRSTD.res,
ylab="Standardized Residuals", xlab="XPrice",
main="Residual Plot")
```

Normality distribution of errors

One of the assumptions of linear regression is that errors are normally distributed, and after fitting the model, we need to check that errors are normally distributed.

This can be checked by executing the following code and can be compared with theoretical normal distribution:

```
> qqnorm(LinearRSTD.res,
ylab="Standardized Residuals",
xlab="Normal Scores",
main="Error Normal Distribution plot")
> qqline(LinearRSTD.res)
```

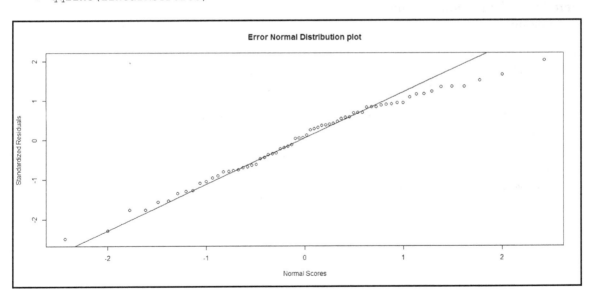

Figure 3.5: QQ plot of standardized residuals

Further details of the `summary` function for the linear regression model can be found in the R documentation. The following command will open a window which has complete information about the linear regression model, that is, `lm()`. It also has information about each and every input variable, including their data type, what all the variables this function returns are, and how output variables can be extracted, along with the examples:

```
> help(summary.lm)
```

Multivariate linear regression

In multiple linear regression, we try to explain the dependent variable in terms of more than one predictor variable. The multiple linear regression equation is given by the following formula:

$$Y = \alpha + \sum \beta_k x_k + \varepsilon$$

Here $\alpha, \beta_1 \ldots \beta_k$ are multiple linear regression parameters and can be obtained by minimizing the sum of squares, which is also known as the OLS method of estimation.

Let us an take an example where we have the dependent variable `StockYPrice` and we are trying to predict it in terms of independent variables `StockX1Price`, `StockX2Price`, `StockX3Price`, and `StockX4Price`, which are present in the dataset `DataMR`.

Now let us fit the multiple regression model and get parameter estimates of multiple regression:

```
> MultipleR.lm = lm(StockYPrice ~  StockX1Price + StockX2Price +
StockX3Price + StockX4Price,  data=DataMR)
> summary(MultipleR.lm)
```

When we execute the preceding code, it fits the multiple regression model on the data and gives the basic summary of statistics associated with multiple regression:

```
Call:
lm(formula = StockYPrice ~ StockX1Price + StockX2Price + StockX3Price +
    StockX4Price, data = DataMR)

Residuals:
    Min      1Q   Median      3Q     Max
-2.2436 -0.6599  0.1809  0.7148  1.6833

Coefficients:
             Estimate Std. Error t value Pr(>|t|)
(Intercept)  88.42137    6.54845  13.503  < 2e-16 ***
StockX1Price -0.16625    0.03649  -4.556 2.55e-05 ***
StockX2Price -0.00468    0.04169  -0.112    0.911
StockX3Price  0.03497    0.04442   0.787    0.434
StockX4Price  0.02713    0.04346   0.624    0.535
---
Signif. codes:  0 '***' 0.001 '**' 0.01 '*' 0.05 '.' 0.1 ' ' 1

Residual standard error: 0.9788 on 61 degrees of freedom
Multiple R-squared:  0.2753,    Adjusted R-squared:  0.2278
F-statistic: 5.793 on 4 and 61 DF,  p-value: 0.0005107
```

Figure 3.6: Summary of multivariate linear regression

Just like the simple linear regression model, the lm function estimates the coefficients of the multiple regression model, as shown in the previous summary, and we can write our prediction equation as follows:

```
> StockYPrice = 88.42137 +(-0.16625)*StockX1Price
+ (-0.00468) * StockX2Price + (.03497)*StockX3Price+ (.02713)*StockX4Price
```

For any given set of independent variables, we can find the predicted dependent variable by using the previous equation.

For any out of sample data, we can obtain the forecast by executing the following code:

```
> newdata = data.frame(StockX1Price=70, StockX2Price=90, StockX3Price=60,
StockX4Price=80)
> predict(MultipleR.lm, newdata)
```

This gives the output 80.63105 as the predicted value of the dependent variable for the given set of independent variables.

Coefficient of determination

For checking the adequacy of a model, the main statistics are the coefficient of determination and adjusted coefficient of determination, which have been displayed in the summary table as R-squared and adjusted R-squared matrices.

We can also obtain them using the following code:

```
> summary(MultipleR.lm)$r.squared
> summary(MultipleR.lm)$adj.r.squared
```

From the summary table, we can see which variables are becoming significant. If the Pvalue associated with the variables in the summary table is <0.05 then the specific variable is significant, otherwise it is insignificant.

Confidence interval

We can find the prediction interval for the 95% confidence interval for the predicted value by the multiple regression model by executing the following code:

```
> predict(MultipleR.lm, newdata, interval="confidence")
```

The preceding code generates the following output:

```
          fit      lwr      upr
1 80.63105 79.84809 81.41401
```

Figure 3.7: Prediction of confidence interval for multiple regression model

Multicollinearity

If the predictor variables are correlated then we need to detect multicollinearity and treat it. Recognition of multicollinearity is crucial because two or more variables are correlated, which shows a strong dependence structure between those variables, and we are using correlated variables as independent variables, which end up having a double effect of these variables on the prediction because of the relation between them. If we treat the multicollinearity and consider only variables which are not correlated then we can avoid the problem of double impact.

We can find multicollinearity by executing the following code:

```
> vif(MultipleR.lm)
```

This gives the multicollinearity table for the predictor variables:

```
StockX1Price  StockX2Price  StockX3Price  StockX4Price
    1.038288      1.039964      1.014838      1.025872
```

Figure 3.8: VIF table for multiple regression model

Depending upon the values of VIF, we can drop the irrelevant variable.

ANOVA

ANOVA is used to determine whether there are any statistically significant differences between the means of three or more independent groups. In the case of only two samples, we can use the t-test to compare the means of the samples, but in the case of more than two samples, it may be very complicated. We are going to study the relationship between quantitative dependent variable returns and single qualitative independent variable stock. We have five levels of stock: stock1, stock2, .. stock5.

We can study the five levels of stock by means of a box plot and we can compare by executing the following code:

```
> DataANOVA = read.csv("C:/Users/prashant.vats/Desktop/Projects/BOOK
R/DataAnova.csv")
>head(DataANOVA)
```

This displays a few lines of the data used for analysis in tabular format:

	Returns	Stock
1	1.64	Stock1
2	1.72	Stock1
3	1.68	Stock1
4	1.77	Stock1
5	1.56	Stock1
6	1.95	Stock1

```
>boxplot(DataANOVA$Returns ~ DataANOVA$Stock)
```

This gives the following output and box plots it:

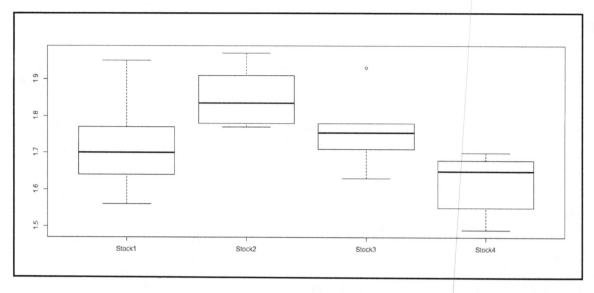

Figure 3.9: Box plot of different levels of stock

The preceding box plot shows that level stock has higher returns. If we repeat the procedure, we are most likely going to get different returns. It may be possible that all the levels of stock give similar numbers and we are just seeing random fluctuation in one set of returns. Let us assume that there is no difference at any level and it is our null hypothesis. Using ANOVA, let us test the significance of the hypothesis:

```
> oneway.test(Returns ~ Stock, var.equal=TRUE)
```

Executing the preceding code gives the following outcome:

```
        One-way analysis of means

data:  Returns and Stock
F = 5.4063, num df = 3, denom df = 20, p-value = 0.006876
```

Figure 3.10: Output of ANOVA for different levels of stock

Since the **Pvalue** is less than **0.05**, the null hypothesis gets rejected. The returns at the different levels of stock are not similar.

Feature selection

Feature selection is one of the toughest parts of financial model building. Feature selection can be done statistically or by having domain knowledge. Here we are going to discuss only a few of the statistical feature selection methods in the financial space.

Removing irrelevant features

Data may contain highly correlated features and the model does better if we do not have highly correlated features in the model. The Caret R package gives the method for finding a correlation matrix between the features, which is shown by the following example.

A few lines of data used for correlation analysis and multiple regression analysis are displayed here by executing the following code:

```
>DataMR = read.csv("C:/Users/prashant.vats/Desktop/Projects/BOOK
R/DataForMultipleRegression.csv")
>head(DataMR)
```

	StockYPrice	StockX1Price	StockX2Price	StockX3Price	StockX4Price
1	80.13	72.86	93.1	63.7	83.1
2	79.57	72.88	90.2	63.5	82
3	79.93	71.72	99	64.5	82.8
4	81.69	71.54	90.9	66.7	86.5
5	80.82	71	90.7	60.7	80.8
6	81.07	71.78	93.1	62.9	84.2

The preceding output shows five variables in `DataMR` named `StockYPrice`, `StockX1Price`, `StockX2Price`, `StockX3Price`, and `StockX4Price`. Here `StockYPrice` is dependent and all the other four variables are independent variables. Dependence structure is very important to study for going deep into the analysis.

The following command calculates the correlation matrix between the first four columns, which are `StockYPrice`, `StockX1Price`, `StockX2Price`, and `StockX3Price`:

```
> correlationMatrix<- cor(DataMR[,1:4])
```

```
            StockYPrice StockX1Price StockX2Price StockX3Price
StockYPrice  1.00000000  -0.51167435   0.08791618   0.10493970
StockX1Price -0.51167435  1.00000000  -0.17845772  -0.02198223
StockX2Price  0.08791618  -0.17845772   1.00000000   0.04577783
StockX3Price  0.10493970  -0.02198223   0.04577783   1.00000000
```

Figure 3.11: Correlation matrix table

The preceding correlation matrix shows which variables are highly correlated and, accordingly, the feature will be selected in such a way that highly correlated features are not in the model.

Stepwise variable selection

We can use stepwise variable selection (forward, backward, both) in predictive models using the `stepAIC()` function for feature selection.

This can be done by executing the following code:

```
> MultipleR.lm = lm(StockYPrice ~
StockX1Price + StockX2Price + StockX3Price + StockX4Price,
data=DataMR)
> step <- stepAIC(MultipleR.lm, direction="both")
> step$anova
```

Here, we are using the dataset used for multiple regression as the input dataset. One can also use all-subsets regression using the `leaps()` function from the leaps package.

Variable selection by classification

We can use classification techniques such as decision tree or random forest to get the most significant predictors. Here we are using random forest (code is given) to find the most relevant features. All the four attributes in the dataset `DataForMultipleRegression1` have been selected in the following example and the plot shows the accuracy of different subset sizes comparing across all the subsets:

```
>library(mlbench)
>library(caret)
>DataVI = read.csv("C:/Users/prashant.vats/Desktop/Projects/BOOK
R/DataForMultipleRegression1.csv")
>head(DataVI)
```

It displays a few lines of the data used for analysis, as shown in the following table:

	PortfolioYDirection	StockX1Price	StockX2Price	StockX3Price	StockX4Price
1	0	72.86	93.1	63.7	83.1
2	1	72.88	90.2	63.5	82
3	0	71.72	99	64.5	82.8
4	0	71.54	90.9	66.7	86.5
5	1	71	90.7	60.7	80.8
6	0	71.78	93.1	62.9	84.2

Execute the following code to do the required analysis:

```
>control<- rfeControl(functions=rfFuncs, method="cv", number=10)
>Output <- rfe(DataVI[,1:4], DataVI[,0:1], sizes=c(1:4),
rfeControl=control)
>predictors(Output)
>plot(Output, type=c("g", "o"))
```

It generates the following plot, showing the accuracy of different subset sizes comparing across all the subsets:

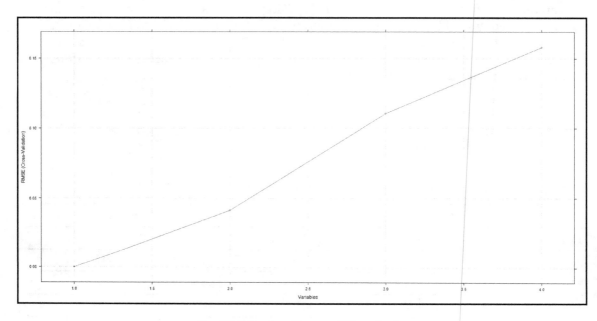

Figure 3.12: Plot showing model accuracy of different subset sizes

We have given some of the examples of feature selection. Some of the other feature selection methods such as classification techniques and information value for predictive modeling are also available.

Ranking of variables

After fitting a regression/predictive model, we need to understand what the relative ranking of significant attributes is on a comparative scale. This is explained by Beta parameter estimates. Beta, or standardized coefficients, are the slopes we get if all the variables are on the same scale, which is done by converting them to z-scores before doing the predictive modeling (regression). Beta coefficients allow a comparison of the approximate relative importance of the predictors and hence the variables can be ranked, which neither the unstandardized coefficients nor the Pvalues can. Scaling, or standardizing, the data vectors can be done using the `scale()` function. Once the scaled variables are created, the regression is redone using them. The resulting coefficients are the beta coefficients.

Wavelet analysis

Time series information is not always sufficient to get insight into the data. Sometimes the frequency content of the data also contains important information about the data. In the time domain, Fourier transformation (FT) captures the frequency-amplitude of the data but it does not show when in time this frequency has happened. In the case of stationary data, all frequency components exist at any point in time but this is not true for non-stationary data. So, FT does not fit for non-stationary data. **Wavelet transformation (WT)** has the capacity to provide time and frequency information simultaneously in the form of time-frequency. WT is important to analyze financial time series as most of the financial time series are non-stationary. In the remainder of this chapter, wavelet analysis (WT), I will help you understand how to solve non-stationary data in R using wavelets analysis. Stock price/index data requires certain techniques or transformations to obtain further information about the series which raw data does not show. The daily closing price for the **Dow Jones Industrial Average (DJIA)** and **S&P500** index from January 1, 2010 to December 31, 2015 has been used for illustration purposes. I am going to use the wavelets package for this:

1. Before starting to work with wavelets transformation, you have to install the package named Wavelets:

    ```
    >   install.packages('wavelets')
    ```

2. Once you install it or you already have this package in your machine then you just have to load it into the workspace:

    ```
    > library(wavelets)
    ```

3. To get a first impression of the data, we plot the dji and snp time series and their reture:

    ```
    >   par(mfrow=c(2,1))
    >   plot(dji,type="l")
    >   plot(ret_dji,type="l")
    ```

The first line is used to divide the plot into a two-by-one matrix, so the plot can have two plots in one figure, and the next two commands plot the Dow Jones price and its return series, which can be seen in *Figure 3.13*:

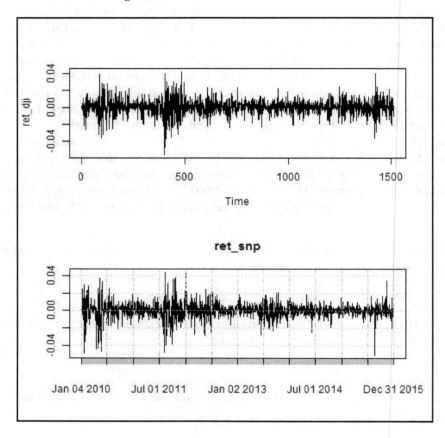

Figure 3.13: Price and return series for Dow Jones Index (DJI)

The dji and snp time series are non-stationary. We use head and tail to look at the first and last part of the time series:

```
>head (dji)
           DJI.Close
2010-01-04 10583.96
2010-01-05 10572.02
2010-01-06 10573.68
2010-01-07 10606.86
2010-01-08 10618.19
2010-01-11 10663.99
```

```
>tail (dji)
          DJI.Close
2015-12-23 17602.61
2015-12-24 17552.17
2015-12-28 17528.27
2015-12-29 17720.98
2015-12-30 17603.87
2015-12-31 17425.03
```

Now we apply **discrete wavelets transformation (DWT)** on the dji data and decompose it using various filters. It requires data in time series, matrix, or data frame format. We look at the dji variable format which is xts and zoo object. So we need to convert it into an acceptable format:

```
dji<- as.ts (dji)
```

Now it is ready to be used in discrete wavelets transformation's R function. We also need to provide other parameters, such as the type of filter you will be using and the number of levels you want your data to be decomposed into:

```
model<- dwt (dji, filter="la8", n.levels=3)
```

It saves the output in the variable called model. You can write model on the command prompt and it will display the output in the command prompt:

```
>model
```

It generates output which consists of various information matrices such as wavelet coefficients, scaling coefficients, type of filter used, and number of levels used. You can extract any individual information as well. To extract wavelet coefficients, you have to write the following command on the command prompt:

```
>model
```

It generates output which consists of various information matrices such as wavelet coefficients, scaling coefficients, type of filter used, and number of levels used. You can extract any individual information as well. To extract wavelet coefficients, you have to write the following command on the command prompt:

```
>model@W          # to extract wavelets coefficients
>model@V          # to extract scaling coefficients
```

These commands generate a relative list of wavelets and scaling coefficients. To get an individual component of wavelets, you have to mention the following:

```
> model@W$W1      # to extract first level of wavelet coefficients
> model@V$V1      # to extract first level of scaling coefficients
```

We can also use the plot command to visualize data series, wavelets, and scaling coefficients:

```
> plot (model)
```

Figure 3.14 will plot the price and its various level coefficients and help us to visualize and understand the data clearly:

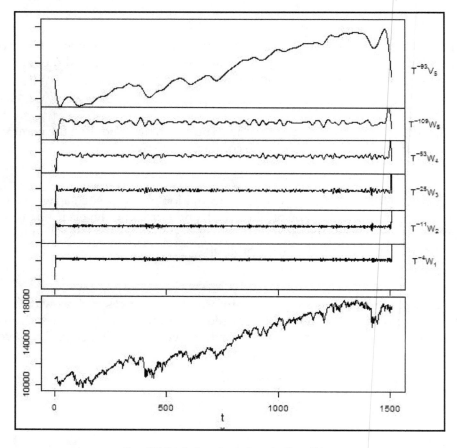

Figure 3.14: Plots for time series, wavelets, and scaling coefficients

You can also use the discrete wavelet transformation function for the `haar` filter:

```
model<- dwt (dji, filter="haar", n.levels=3)
> plot (model)
```

It will plot the data series, wavelets, and scaling coefficients using the `haar` filter.

To compute inverse discrete wavelet transformation, you have to use a wavelet object, as defined using discrete wavelet transformation. The variable model is a wavelet object using the `haar` filter:

```
imodel<- idwt(model, fast=TRUE)
```

Sometimes it is necessary to know the class of the R objects, for example, `model` and `imodel`.

We can use the following commands for this:

```
> class(model)
[1] "dwt"
attr(,"package")
[1] "wavelets"
>   class(imodel)
[1] "ts"
```

The variable `imodel` is created using inverse wavelet transformation and it generates an original time series object.

Multiresolution analysis (**MRA**) is another widely useful wavelet method for time series analysis. Financial markets generate large quantities of data, which is analyzed to generate algorithmic trading signals. Wavelet multi-resolution analysis is increasingly being applied to these datasets because it enables traders to focus on a particular time scale where trading patterns are considered important. The la8 filter is used in the following example and the `haar` filter also can replaced for `la8`:

```
> model <- mra(dji, filter="la8", n.levels=3)
```

For the analysis of market data, **maximal overlap discrete wavelet transform** (**MODWT**) is preferred.

As an example, I considered the case of Dow Jones Index time series, `dji`, as input to the `modwt` function:

```
> model <- modwt(dji, filter="la8", n.levels=5)
```

The preceding function decomposes the time series in detailed wavelets and scaled coefficients, which can be seen in *Figure 3.15*. The `plot.modwt()` function can be used to plot this `modwt` output:

```
>plot.modwt(model)
```

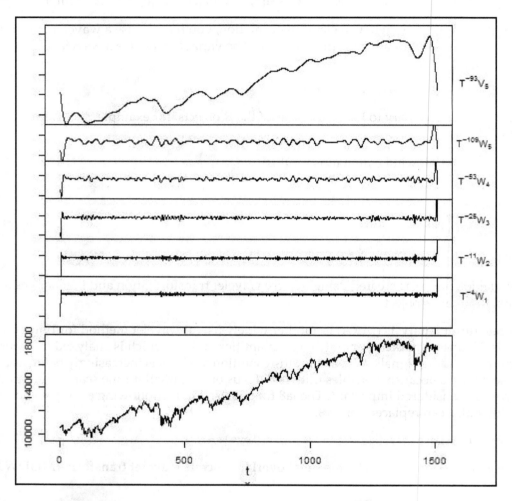

Figure 3.15: Plot of Maximal Overlap Discrete wavelets transform

A few jumps in the time series can be seen as jumps in smaller coefficients such as **W1** and **W2**, and smooth coefficients such as **W6** show movement about some mean for the time period. Wavelets and scaled coefficients in *Figure 3.15* clearly show price data at different time scales.

Wavelet analysis provides an important tool in quantitative finance, with applications ranging from short-term prediction and the calculation of variance in relation to specific time scales.

Fast Fourier transformation

Fast Fourier transformation (FFT) is used for calculating the Fourier transform of discrete time series. You need to install the relevant package `fft` for FFT with the help of the following code:

```
install.packages('fft')
```

Once you install the package, you have to load this into the workspace by using the following code:

```
library(fft)
```

Fast Fourier transform of time series can be calculated using `fft`, and it accepts real or complex numbers series.

In the following example, `dji` is a real number time series:

```
> model<- fft(dji)
```

The variable `model` is a transformed series which basically consists of complex numbers, and the real and imaginary parts can be extracted using the following code:

```
>rp = Re(model)
>ip = Im(model)
```

The following command calculates the absolute value of the model:

```
>absmodel<- abs(model)
```

Let me plot this and see what information the absolute value of `fft` has for me:

```
>plot(absmodel)
```

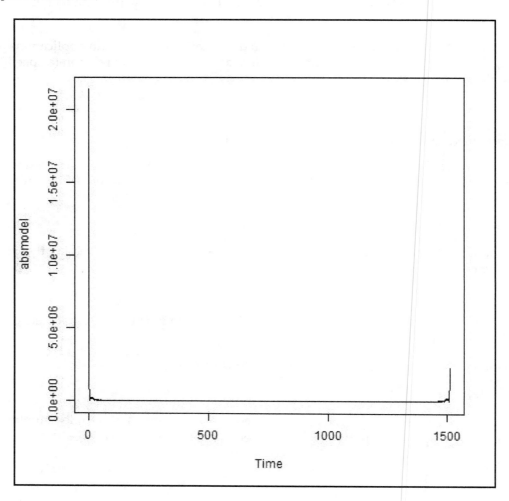

Figure 3.16: Plot for absolute value of FFT modeled series

Figure 3.16 shows spikes at both ends of the data. FFT can accept complex inputs, when the input is real (as with most real-world cases). The output for bins greater than $N/2$ is redundant and does not provide additional spectral information. So, we can remove the values for bins > $N/2$. This arises from lack of normalization.

Results need to be normalized for the sample size. As the input data is real-valued, data greater than *N/2* is removed and we normalize the data by *N/2*:

```
>norm_absmodel<- absmodel[1:(length(dji)/2)]
```

The angle between the real and imaginary parts of the Fourier transformed series is calculated as follows:

```
Angle = atan2(ip, rp)
```

Sometimes it is important to analyze the spectrum density of the time series and this can be calculated in R using the following code:

```
>spec_density<- spectrum(dji, method = c("pgram", "ar"))
```

It accepts two methods: periodogram and autoregressive. You can choose either of these methods. This function returns the vector of frequencies at which spectral densities are estimated, as well as the vector of estimated spectral densities at frequency. It also returns some other parameters which are useful to multivariate analysis, such as coherence level and phase between multivariate series.

Hilbert transformation

Hilbert transformation is another technique to transform time series and R uses the `seewave` package for this. This package can be installed using `install.packages()` and loaded into the workspace using the `library()` command:

```
> model <-  hilbert(dji, 1)
```

The first parameter is the time series object which you would like to transform, and the second parameter is the sampling frequency of the wave. In the preceding example, I used `dji` as time series and sampling frequency as 1 to calculate the Hilbert transformation.

If you would like to know the output of the model then you should use the following code:

```
> summary(model)
      V1
 Length:2555
 Class :complex
 Mode  :complex
```

The preceding output mentions the length of input data series is 2555 and the type of output variable named `model` is complex.

As the output is complex, we can extract real and imaginary values using the following code:

```
>rp<- Re(model)
>ip<- Im(model)
```

Here, the real part is the original time series, which is `dji` in our case, and the imaginary part is the Hilbert transformed series of the original series. `ifreq()` returns the phase or instantaneous frequency, depending upon what output we want:

```
>ifreq(dji,1,ylim=c(0,0.00001))
```

The preceding code will generate instantaneous frequency:

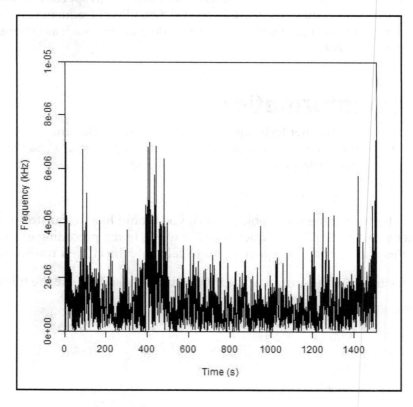

Figure:3.17. Instantaneous frequency of time series using Hilbert transformation

However, if we would like to generate phases then we have to explicitly mention
PHASE=TRUE in the function:

```
>ifreq(dji, 1 ,phase="TRUE",ylim=c(-0.5,1))
```

Figure 3.18 shows the phases with respect to time variations. As time progresses, phases also increase with the increase in time:

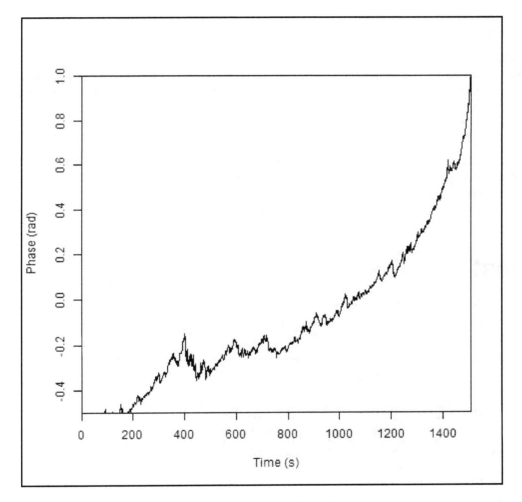

Figure 3.18: Phases of time series using Hilbert transformation

By default, the plot is true. If we say `PLOT=FALSE`, then it will not generate a plot and only generate variables in the workspace:

```
> output = ifreq(dji, 1 ,plot=FALSE)
```

The output variable is in the form of a list which contains both instantaneous frequency and phase and can be extracted using the following:

```
>freq<- output$f
>phase<- output$p
```

Sometimes we analyze a pair of time series and then calculating phase difference is crucial rather than looking at the phase of univariate series. So, phase difference can be calculated by simply calculating phases of individual series and then subtracting the phase of one series from the other series:

```
>phase_difference<- phase1 - phase2
```

There is another package, `waveslim`, which has all these transformations, such as discrete wavelet transformation, fast Fourier transformation, and Hilbert transformation, in one. In fact, there are many more packages which contain these transformations. You can use whichever you are comfortable with and find easy to use.

Questions

1. Define regression and how you can implement in R.
2. How do you find the coefficient of determination for linear regression / multiple regression in R?
3. How do you find the confidence interval for a prediction fitted with linear regression / multiple regression in R?
4. How will you detect multicollinearity in R in multiple regression?
5. What is the significance of ANOVA and how will you use it to compare the results of two linear regression models?
6. How do you perform feature selection in R for multiple linear regression?
7. How do you rank significance attributes in a multiple linear regression model in R?
8. How do you install the `waveslim` package and load it into the R workspace?
9. How do you plot a time series and extract the head and tail of the time series?

10. How would you know the class of a variable created by the `fft` function?
11. How do you use the dwt function using any given filter and take inverse dwt?
12. How do you extract the real and imaginary parts of a series?
13. How would you use fast Fourier transformation and Hilbert transformation?

Summary

Regression is the backbone of any analysis and the reader cannot go ahead without touching on it. In this chapter, I have presented linear regression and multivariate regression and how they are used for prediction. The R function `lm()` is used to implement both simple and multivariate linear regression. I also presented significance testing along with residual calculations and the normality plot, which tests residuals for normality using a qq plot. **Analysis of variance** (**ANOVA**) is used to select the difference means of two or more samples. Multivariate linear regression involves many variables, and the coefficient of each variable is different, which varies the importance of each variable and is ranked accordingly. Stepwise regression is used to select variables which are important in the regression. Time series analysis does not represent the complete information sometimes. It becomes necessary to explore frequency analysis, which can be done with wavelet, fast Fourier and Hilbert transformation. All the methods are implemented in R for frequency analysis. I have also explained how results can be seen and plotted wherever it is necessary.

In the next chapter, I will explain time series analysis and prediction techniques.

4
Time Series Modeling

Time series forecasting analysis is one of the most important components of quantitative finance. R software gives a lot of time series and forecasting packages to support time series analysis. There are sufficient packages in R to convert the equally spaced and unequally spaced series in time series. Also, there are sufficient packages in R to build forecasting models such as autoregressive integrated moving average and generalized autoregressive conditional heteroscedasticity. In this chapter, we are going to give brief flavors of converting any series into time series and forecasting models.

In this chapter, we are going to cover the following topics:

- General time series
- Converting data to time series
- zoo
- xts
- Linear filters
- AR
- MA
- ARIMA
- GARCH
- EGARCH
- VGARCH
- Dynamic conditional correlation

General time series

A time series is the sequence of data usually collected at regular intervals. There are a lot of domains where information is stored in time series form and needs to be analyzed for future planning.

For example, in the financial domain, we have the daily/monthly data available for unemployment, GDP, daily exchange rates, share prices, and so on. So all the investors or the people working in financial institutions need to plan their future strategy and so they want to analyze the time series data. Thus time series play a crucial role in the financial domain.

Time series data is very unpredictable in nature and to understand the data we need to decompose the time series data into various components, as given here:

- **Trend**: This is a pattern of long-term movements in the mean of time series data. The trend may be linear or nonlinear and keeps changing across time. There is no sure process to identify the exact trend but if it is behaving monotonously then it is possible to estimate with a certain acceptable degree of error.
- **Seasonal effects**: These are cyclical fluctuations related to the periodical cycle. So, for example, the sale of a particular product spikes during a particular month/quarter of the year. The seasonality can be identified by plotting the series and inspecting it.
- **Cycles (Ct)**: Apart from seasonal cycles, there are certain cycles which are associated with business cycles which need to be taken care of when doing time series analysis.
- **Residuals**: Time series consist of systematic patterns and random noise (error), which makes it difficult to identify the pattern. Generally, time series techniques involve certain ways of filtering the noise in order to make the pattern more salient.

In some of the techniques of forecasting, the time series is assumed to be stationary. The stationarity is required because for forecasting we are assuming the mean and variance to be static as that will be required for future forecasting analysis. If the series is nonstationary then we difference it to first make it stationary and then proceed further.

Converting data to time series

A time series is a sequence of data points where each data point is associated with a particular time.

For example, the adjusted close of a stock is the closing price of a stock on a particular day. The time series data is stored in an R object called a time series object and it is created by using the function `ts()` in R.

The basic syntax of `ts` is given here:

```
ts(data, start, end, frequency)
```

Here:

- `data`: It is a vector or matrix containing the data values
- `start`: It is the starting point or time of first observation
- `end`: It is the time point of last observation
- `frequency`: It is the number of data points per unit time

Let us consider a vector which is given by the following code:

```
> StockPrice<
-c(23.5,23.75,24.1,25.8,27.6,27,27.5,27.75,26,28,27,25.5)
> StockPrice
```

Now convert it into a time series object, which can be done with the following code:

```
> StockPricets<- ts(StockPrice,start = c(2016,1),frequency = 12)
> StockPricets
```

The output is as follows:

	Jan	Feb	Mar	Apr	May	Jun	Jul	Aug	Sep	Oct	Nov	Dec
2016	23.50	23.75	24.10	25.80	27.60	27.00	27.50	27.75	26.00	28.00	27.00	25.50

Figure 4.1: Table showing time series object

Let us plot this data by using the following code:

```
> plot(StockPricets)
```

This generates the following output plot:

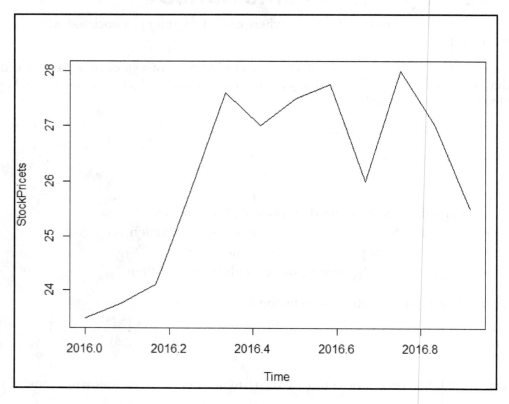

Figure 4.2: Time series plot using ts object

The frequency parameter in the `ts()` function identifies at which time the interval data is measured:

- Frequency = 12 means that data is at monthly level
- Frequency = 4 means that data is at quarterly level
- Frequency = 6 means data points for every 10 minutes of an hour
- Frequency = 5 means that data is at daily level business days

ZOO

The `ts` object has its limitations in representing the time series. It is used for representing equally spaced data. It cannot be used to represent the daily level stock prices as stock prices are equally spaced between Monday to Friday, but it is not the same case for Friday to Monday and in case there is market holidays on weekdays. This type of unequally spaced data cannot be represented by a `ts` object.

`zoo` is flexible and fully equipped to handle unequally spaced data, equally spaced data, and numerically indexed data.

Let us first install and load the `zoo` library. This can be done by executing the following code:

```
> install.packages("zoo")
> library(zoo)
```

Now we will discuss how to represent different time series scenarios using `zoo`.

Please note we will be using a common dataset for all the examples.

Constructing a zoo object

In order to create a `zoo` object, an ordered time index and data are required. So we are going to construct a `zoo` object.

Let us first import a few rows of our sample dataset, which can be done with the following code:

```
>StockData <- read.table("DataChap4.csv",header = TRUE, sep = ",",nrows=3)
```

This gives the following output:

Date	Volume	Adj.Close	Return
12/14/2016	4144600	198.69	0.27
12/13/2016	6816100	198.15	2.97
12/12/2016	615800	192.43	0.13

Now let us try to convert this DataFrame into a `zoo` object. This can be done by executing the following code:

```
> dt = as.Date(StockData$Date, format="%m/%d/%Y")
>Stockdataz = zoo(x=cbind(StockData$Volume,StockData$Adj.Close),
order.by=dt)
> colnames(Stockdataz) <- c("Volume","Adj.Close")
> Stockdataz
```

Upon execution, it generates the following `zoo` object:

	Volume	Adj.Close
12/12/2016	615800	192.43
12/13/2016	6816100	198.15
12/14/2016	4144600	198.69

Reading an external file using zoo

The function `read.zoo` is a wrapper which can be used to read an external dataset, which assumes that the first column is the index and rest of the columns are data.

Now let us read a dataset using `zoo` which has the following format:

Date	Volume	Adj Close	Return
12/14/2016	4144600	198.69	0.27

We execute the following code:

```
>StockData <- read.zoo("DataChap4.csv",header = TRUE, sep =
",",format="%m/%d/%Y")
```

This gives us an output with the following format:

	Volume	Adj.Close	Return
2016-12-14	4144600	198.69	0.27

Advantages of a zoo object

Here are some of the examples that show the advantageous behavior of a zoo object.

Subsetting the data

Subsetting can be done on an index using the `window()` function by executing the following code:

```
>window(StockData, start=as.Date("2016/11/1"), end=as.Date("2016/11/3"))
```

This gives the following output:

	Volume	Adj.Close	Return
11/1/2016	7014900	190.79	-3.51
11/2/2016	4208700	188.02	-1.45
11/3/2016	2641400	187.42	-0.32

Merging zoo objects

Let us form two zoo objects with a common index and then merge them. This can be done by executing the following code:

```
> StockData <- read.table("DataChap4.csv",header = TRUE, sep = ",",nrows=3)
> zVolume <-zoo(StockData[,2:2],as.Date(as.character(StockData[, 1]),
format="%m/%d/%Y"))
> zAdj.Close <-zoo(StockData[,3:3],as.Date(as.character(StockData[, 1]),
format="%m/%d/%Y"))
> cbind(zVolume, zAdj.Close)
```

The final output is given in the following table:

	zVolume	zAdj.Close
12/12/2016	615800	192.43
12/13/2016	6816100	198.15
12/14/2016	4144600	198.69

Plotting zoo objects

You can plot your data across time. A sample is shown here:

```
>plot(StockData$Adj.Close)
```

This generates the following plot:

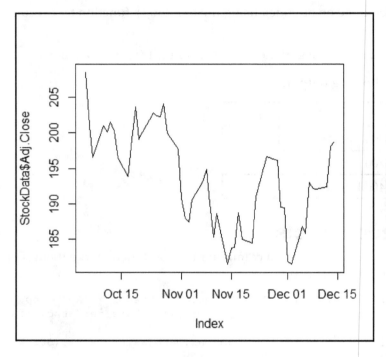

Figure 4.3: Time series plot using zoo object

Disadvantages of a zoo object

An index in a `zoo` object cannot have `Date` classed variables, whereas the index of an `xts` object has to be a known and supported `time` or `Date` class. Also, in `zoo`, we cannot add arbitrary attributes which can be done in `xts`.

xts

xts is an extensible time series object which carries all the features of a zoo object. It consists of a matrix and index which has to be time-based. There are two ways of constructing xts objects: one is by calling as.xts and another is constructing the xts object from scratch.

Construction of an xts object using as.xts

Let us read a few lines of our sample data through zoo and construct the xts object by executing the following code:

```
> StockData <- read.zoo("DataChap4.csv",header = TRUE, sep =
",",format="%m/%d/%Y",nrows=3)
> matrix_xts <- as.xts(StockData,dateFormat='POSIXct')
> matrix_xts
```

This gives the following output:

	Volume	Adj.Close	Return
12/12/2016	615800	192.43	0.13
12/13/2016	6816100	198.15	2.97
12/14/2016	4144600	198.69	0.27

The composition of the xts object can be given by the following code:

```
> str(matrix_xts)
```

This generates the following output:

An xts object on 2016-12-12/2016-12-14 contains the following:

```
  Data: num [1:3, 1:3] 615800 6816100 4144600 192 198 ...
 - attr(*, "dimnames")=List of 2
  ..$ : NULL
  ..$ : chr [1:3] "Volume" "Adj.Close" "Return"
  Indexed by objects of class: [Date] TZ: UTC
  xts Attributes:
List of 1
 $ dateFormat: chr "POSIXct"
```

Constructing an xts object from scratch

Let us first form a matrix and date sequence of same order and then convert it into an `xts` object. This can be done by executing the following code:

```
> x<-matrix(5:8, ncol =2, nrow =2)
> dt<-as.Date(c("2016-02-02","2016-03-02"))
> xts_object<-xts(x,order.by=dt)
> colnames(xts_object) <- c("a","b")
> xts_object
```

This gives the `xts` object, as displayed here:

	a	b
2/2/2016	5	7
3/2/2016	6	8

The special aspects of an `xts` object is that it behaves like a matrix with time associated with each observation. The subsets will always preserve the matrix form and the attributes of the `xts` objects are always retained. Also, since `xts` is a subclass of `zoo`, it gets all the power of the `zoo` library.

Linear filters

The first step in time series analysis is to decompose the time series in trend, seasonality, and so on.

One of the methods of extracting trend from the time series is linear filters.

One of the basic examples of linear filters is moving average with equal weights.

Examples of linear filters are weekly average, monthly average, and so on.

The function used for finding filters is given as follows:

```
Filter(x,filter)
```

Here, x is the time series data and `filter` is the coefficients needed to be given to find the moving average.

Now let us convert the `Adj.Close` of our `StockData` in time series and find the weekly and monthly moving average and plot it. This can be done by executing the following code:

```
> StockData <- read.zoo("DataChap4.csv",header = TRUE, sep =
",",format="%m/%d/%Y")
>PriceData<-ts(StockData$Adj.Close, frequency = 5)
> plot(PriceData,type="l")
> WeeklyMAPrice <- filter(PriceData,filter=rep(1/5,5))
> monthlyMAPrice <- filter(PriceData,filter=rep(1/25,25))
> lines(WeeklyMAPrice,col="red")
> lines(monthlyMAPrice,col="blue")
```

This generates the following plot:

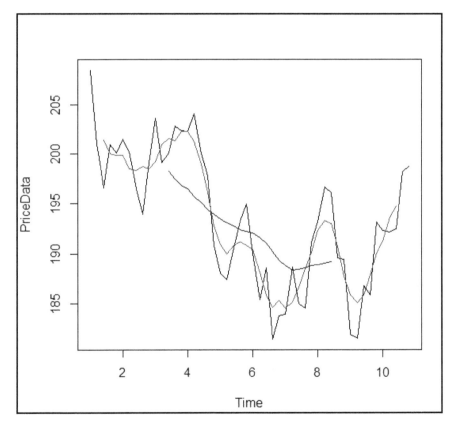

Figure 4.4: Example of moving average using linear filter

AR

AR stands for **autoregressive model**. Its basic concept is that future values depend on past values and they are estimated using a weighted average of the past values. The order of the AR model can be estimated by plotting the autocorrelation function and partial autocorrelation function of the series. In time series autocorrelation function measures correlation between series and it's lagged values. Whereas partial autocorrelation function measures correlation of a time series with its own lagged values, controlling for the values of the time series at all shorter lags. So first let us plot the `acf` and `pcf` of the series. Let us first plot the `acf` plot by executing the following code:

```
> PriceData<-ts(StockData$Adj.Close, frequency = 5)
> acf(PriceData, lag.max = 10)
```

This generates the autocorrelation plot as displayed here:

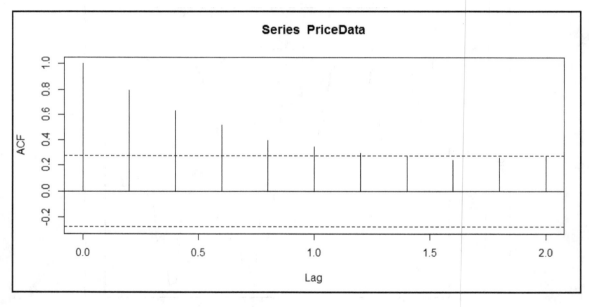

Figure 4.5: acf plot of price

Now let us plot `pacf` by executing the following code:

```
> pacf(PriceData, lag.max = 10)
```

This generates the partial autocorrelation plot as shown here:

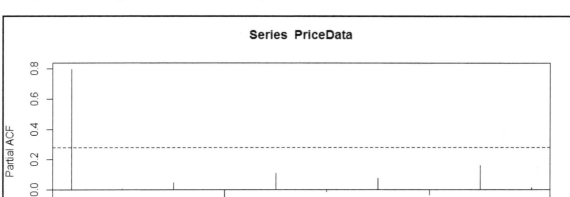

Figure 4.6: pacf plot of price

The preceding plots are autocorrelation and partial autocorrelation plots of the series considered. Now let us come to identify the order of AR. Since here there is no differencing and `acf` is decaying slowly, whereas `pacf` cuts off after one lag, so the order of AR is 1. Similarly, if `pacf` cuts off after second lag and `acf` is decaying slowly, then the order of AR is 2.

MA

MA stands for **moving average** and in MA modeling we do not take into account the past values of the actual series. We consider the moving average of the past few forecast errors in this process. For identifying the orders of MA, we also need to plot `acf` and `pacf`. So let us plot the `acf` and `pacf` of the volume of `StockData` to evaluate the order of MA. `acf` can be plotted by executing the following code:

```
> VolumeData<-ts(StockData$Volume, frequency = 5)
> acf(VolumeData, lag.max = 10)
```

This gives the following `acf` plot:

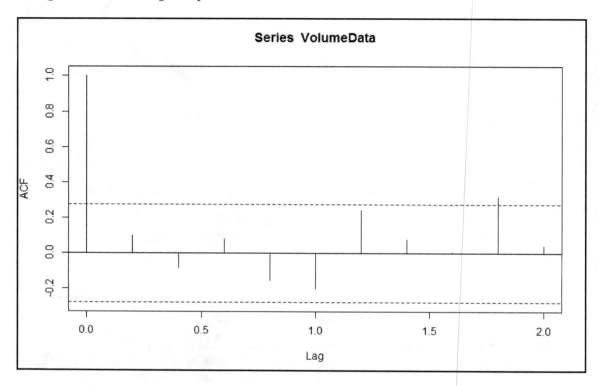

Figure 4.7: acf plot of volume

Let us plot the `pacf` plot of volume by executing the following code:

```
> pacf(VolumeData, lag.max = 10)
```

This gives the following plot:

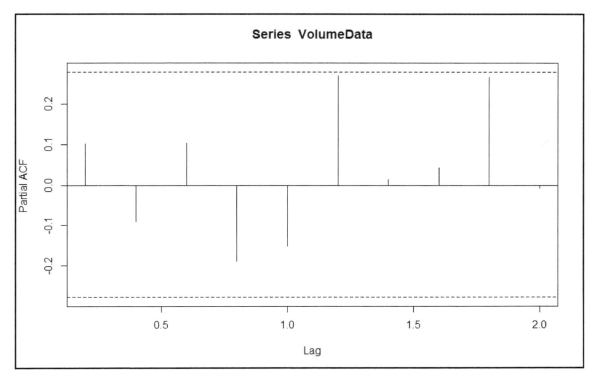

Figure 4.8: pacf plot of volume

After evaluating the preceding plots, the `acf` cuts sharply after `lag1` so the order of MA is 1.

ARIMA

ARIMA stands for **autoregressive integrated moving average** models. Generally, it is defined by the equation **ARIMA**(p, d, q).

Here,

- p is the order of the autoregressive model
- d is the order required for making the series stationary
- q is the order of moving average

The very first step in ARIMA is to plot the series, as we need a stationary series for forecasting.

So let us first plot the graph of the series by executing the following code:

```
> PriceData<-ts(StockData$Adj.Close, frequency = 5)
> plot(PriceData)
```

This generates the following plot:

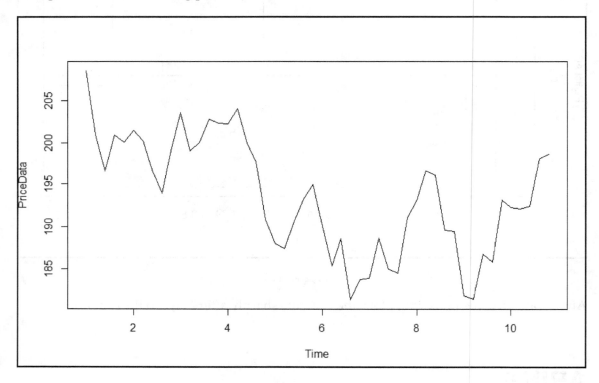

Figure 4.9: Plot of price data

Clearly, upon inspection, the series seems to be nonstationary, so we need to make it stationary by differencing. This can be done by executing the following code:

```
> PriceDiff <- diff(PriceData, differences=1)
> plot(PriceDiff)
```

This generates the following plot for the differenced series:

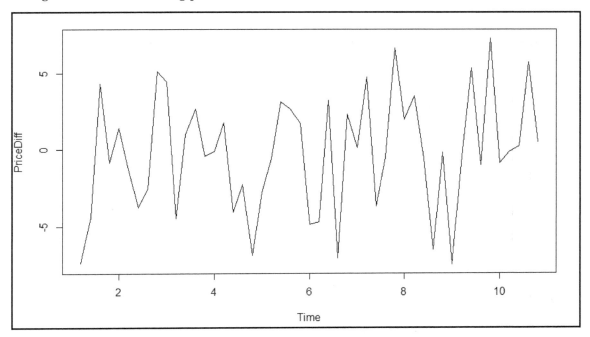

Figure 4.10: Plot of differenced price data

This is a stationary series, as the means and variance seem to be constant across time. Also, we can check the stationarity using the `Dickey-Fuller` test. Thus we have identified the value of d for our ARIMA model, which is 1. Now let us plot the autocorrelation function and partial autocorrelation function of the differenced series for identifying the values of p and q.

The `acf` plot is given by executing the following code:

```
> acf(PriceDiff, lag.max = 10)
```

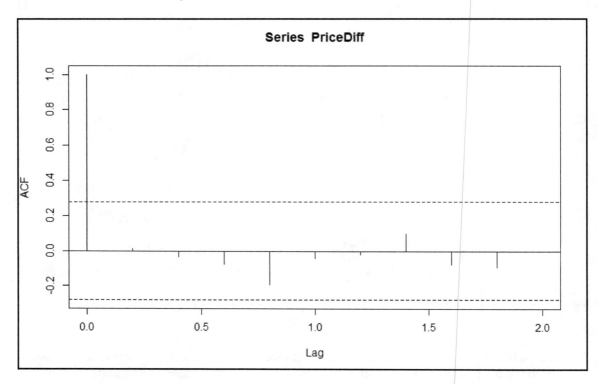

Figure 4.11: acf plot of differenced series

The `pacf` plot is given by executing the following code:

```
> pacf(PriceDiff, lag.max = 10)
```

This generates the `pacf` plot for the differenced series:

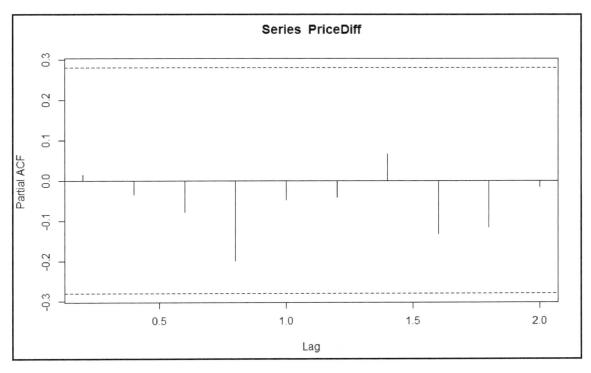

Figure 4.12: pacf plot of differenced series

This clearly shows that the AR and MA order is 0 and 1 respectively and hence the best candidate model is ARIMA(0,1,1).

Now let us estimate the coefficients of the identified ARIMA model, which can be done by executing the following code:

```
>PriceArima <- arima(PriceData, order=c(0,1,1))
>PriceArima
```

This generates coefficients of the identified ARIMA model as follows:

```
Call:
arima(x = PriceData, order = c(0, 1, 1))

Coefficients:
         ma1
      0.0177
s.e.  0.1512

sigma^2 estimated as 14.66:  log likelihood = -135.31,  aic = 274.62
```

Figure 4.13: Fitted summary of ARIMA (0,1,1)

Now let us try to predict the forecast and plot it, which can be done by executing the following code:

```
> library(forecast)
> FutureForecast<-forecast.Arima(PriceArima,h=5)
> FutureForecast
```

This generates the following output:

	Point Forecast	Lo 80	Hi 80	Lo 95	Hi 95
11.0	198.6978	193.7912	203.6043	191.1938	206.2017
11.2	198.6978	191.6972	205.6983	187.9914	209.4042
11.4	198.6978	190.0989	207.2967	185.5469	211.8486
11.6	198.6978	188.7542	208.6413	183.4904	213.9051
11.8	198.6978	187.5709	209.8247	181.6806	215.7149

Figure 4.14: The future forecast with confidence interval

Now plot the forecasted value along with the confidence interval by executing the following code:

```
> plot.forecast(FutureForecast)
```

This generates the following plot:

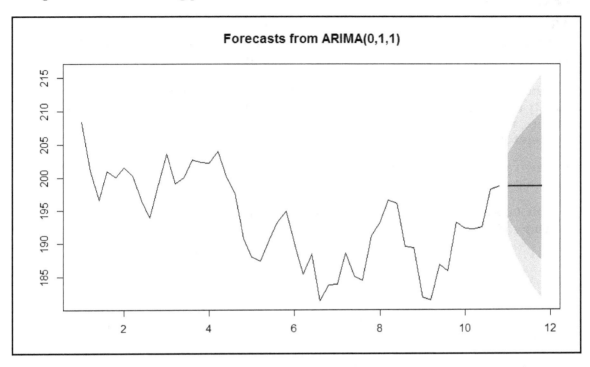

Figure 4.15: Plot of forecasted value along with the confidence interval

Model adequacy can be checked by executing the following code:

```
>Box.test(FutureForecast$residuals, lag=20, type="Ljung-Box")
```

This generates the following output:

```
        Box-Ljung test

data:  FutureForecast$residuals
X-squared = 17.386, df = 20, p-value = 0.6278
```

Figure 4.16: Model adequacy check statistics for fitted model

Since the Pvalue is greater than 0.05, there is no significant autocorrelation in the residuals at lags 1-20:

GARCH

GARCH stands for **generalized autoregressive conditional heteroscedasticity**. One of the assumptions in OLS estimation is that variance of error should be constant. However, in financial time series data, some periods are comparatively more volatile, which contributes to rise in strengths of the residuals, and also these spikes are not randomly placed due to the autocorrelation effect, also known as volatility clustering, that is, periods of high volatility tend to group together. This is where GARCH is used to forecast volatility measures, which can be used to forecast residuals in the model. We are not going to go into great depth but we will show how GARCH is executed in R.

There are various packages available in R for GARCH modeling. We will be using the `rugarch` package.

Let us first install and load the `rugarch` package, which can be done by executing the following code:

```
>install.packages("rugarch")
>Library(rugarch)
 >snp <- read.zoo("DataChap4SP500.csv",header = TRUE, sep =
",",format="%m/%d/%Y")
```

Now let us define the specs for the GARCH model and try to estimate the coefficients by running the following code:

```
> gspec.ru <- ugarchspec(mean.model=list( armaOrder=c(0,0)),
distribution="std")
> gfit.ru <- ugarchfit(gspec.ru, snp$Return)
> coef(gfit.ru)
```

This gives the following output:

mu	omega	alpha1	beta1	shape
1.937922e-04	8.406716e-07	2.204731e-01	7.291160e-01	4.756128e+00

Figure 4.17: Summary of coefficients estimate of GARCH

The main arguments for GARCH modeling are as follows:

- **Variance model**: List containing the variance model specifications, especially which GARCH model to use and what should be the orders of p and q in ARCH (q) and GARCH (p).
- **Mean model**: List containing the mean model specifications: arma order the autoregressive (AR) and moving average (MA) orders.
- **Distribution model**: The conditional density to use for the innovations. Valid choices are `norm` for the normal distibution, `snorm` for the skew-normal distribution, `std` for the student $-t$, and so on.

Now we can generate our forecast according to our requirement, which is given by the following code:

```
> FutureForecast=ugarchforecast(gfit.ru, n.ahead = 5)
> FutureForecast
```

The output is as follows:

```
*------------------------------------*
*           GARCH Model Forecast     *
*------------------------------------*
Model: sGARCH
Horizon: 5
Roll Steps: 0
Out of Sample: 0

0-roll forecast [T0=2016-12-28]:
         Series      Sigma
T+1  0.0001938   0.002681
T+2  0.0001938   0.002769
T+3  0.0001938   0.002850
T+4  0.0001938   0.002924
T+5  0.0001938   0.002993
```

Figure 4.18: GARCH model forecast

There are a lot of options in the GARCH model and we can use it according to our requirement.

EGARCH

EGARCH stands for exponential GARCH. EGARCH is an improved form of GARCH and models some of the market scenarios better.

For example, negative shocks (events, news, and so on) tend to impact volatility more than positive shocks.

This model differs from the traditional GARCH in structure due to the log of variance.

Let us take an example to show how to execute EGARCH in R. First define `spec` for EGARCH and estimate the coefficients, which can be done by executing the following code on the `snp` data:

```
> snp <- read.zoo("DataChap4SP500.csv",header = TRUE, sep =
",",format="%m/%d/%Y")
> egarchsnp.spec =
ugarchspec(variance.model=list(model="eGARCH",garchOrder=c(1,1)),
+                 mean.model=list(armaOrder=c(0,0)))
> egarchsnp.fit = ugarchfit(egarchsnp.spec, snp$Return)
> egarchsnp.fit
> coef(egarchsnp.fit)
```

This gives the coefficients as follows:

mu	omega	alpha1	beta1	gamma1
-0.0002229209	-0.2473967968	-0.2120878918	0.9772788064	-0.1046940426

Figure 4.19: Parameter estimates of EGARCH

Now let us try to forecast, which can be done by executing the following code:

```
> FutureForecast=ugarchforecast(egarchsnp.fit, n.ahead = 5)
> FutureForecast
```

This gives the following output:

```
*------------------------------------------*
*            GARCH Model Forecast          *
*------------------------------------------*
Model: eGARCH
Horizon: 5
Roll Steps: 0
Out of Sample: 0

0-roll forecast [T0=2016-12-28]:
          Series     Sigma
T+1 -0.0002229  0.002348
T+2 -0.0002229  0.002381
T+3 -0.0002229  0.002413
T+4 -0.0002229  0.002445
T+5 -0.0002229  0.002477
```

Figure 4.20: Forecast prediction of EGARCH

VGARCH

VGARCH stands for vector GARCH or multivariate GARCH. In the financial domain, the assumption is that financial volatilities move together over time across assets and markets. Acknowledging this aspect through a multivariate modeling framework leads to a better model separate univariate model. It helps in making better decision tools in various areas, such as asset pricing, portfolio selection, option pricing, and hedging and risk management. There are multiple options in R for building in multivariate mode.

Let us consider an example of multivariate GARCH in R for the last year of data from the S&P500 and DJI index:

```
>install.packages("rmgarch")
>install.packages("PerformanceAnalytics")
>library(rmgarch)
>library(PerformanceAnalytics)
>snpdji <- read.zoo("DataChap4SPDJIRet.csv",header = TRUE, sep =
",",format="%m/%d/%Y")
>garch_spec = ugarchspec(mean.model = list(armaOrder =
c(2,1)),variance.model = list(garchOrder = c(1,1), model = "sGARCH"),
distribution.model = "norm")
> dcc.garch_spec = dccspec(uspec = multispec( replicate(2, garch_spec) ),
```

```
      dccOrder = c(1,1), distribution = "mvnorm")
    > dcc_fit= dccfit(dcc.garch_spec,data = snpdji)
    > fcst=dccforecast(dcc_.fit,n.ahead=5)
    > fcst
```

This gives the following output:

```
*----------------------------------*

Distribution          :  mvnorm
Model                 :  DCC(1,1)
Horizon               :  5
Roll Steps            :  0
------------------------------------

0-roll forecast:
, , 1

         [,1]     [,2]
[1,]   1.0000 -0.1026
[2,]  -0.1026  1.0000

, , 2

         [,1]     [,2]
[1,]   1.0000 -0.1026
[2,]  -0.1026  1.0000

, , 3

         [,1]     [,2]
[1,]   1.0000 -0.1026
[2,]  -0.1026  1.0000

, , 4

         [,1]     [,2]
[1,]   1.0000 -0.1026
[2,]  -0.1026  1.0000

, , 5

         [,1]     [,2]
[1,]   1.0000 -0.1026
[2,]  -0.1026  1.0000
```

Figure 4.21: Future prediction of multivariate GARCH

Dynamic conditional correlation

Multivariate GARCH models, which are linear in squares and cross products of the data, are generally used to estimate the correlations changing with time. Now this can be estimated using **dynamic conditional correlation** (**DCC**), which is a combination of a univariate GARCH model and parsimonious parametric models for the correlation. It has been observed that they perform well in a variety of situations. This method has the flexibility of univariate GARCH and does not have the complexity of multivariate GARCH.

Now let us see how to execute DCC in R.

First we need to install and load the packages `rmgarch` and `PerformanceAnalytics`. This can be done by executing the following code:

```
install.packages("rmgarch")
install.packages("PerformanceAnalytics")
library(rmgarch)
library(PerformanceAnalytics)
```

Now let us consider returns of the last year for the `S&P 500` and DJI indexes and try to get DCC for these returns.

Now let us set the specification for DCC by executing the following code:

```
snpdji <- read.zoo("DataChap4SPDJIRet.csv",header = TRUE, sep =
",",format="%m/%d/%Y")
> garchspec = ugarchspec(mean.model = list(armaOrder = c(0,0)),
+                variance.model = list(garchOrder = c(1,1),
+                model = "sGARCH"), distribution.model = "norm")
>
> dcc.garchsnpdji.spec = dccspec(uspec = multispec( replicate(2, garchspec)
), dccOrder = c(1,1), distribution = "mvnorm")
```

Now let us fit the model, which can be done by executing the following code:

```
> dcc_fit = dccfit(dcc.garchsnpdji.spec , data = snpdji,
fit.control=list(scale=TRUE))
> dcc_fit
```

This gives the following output:

```
*----------------------------------*
*          DCC GARCH Fit           *
*----------------------------------*

Distribution          :  mvnorm
Model                 :  DCC(1,1)
No. Parameters        :  11
[VAR GARCH DCC UncQ]  :  [0+8+2+1]
No. Series            :  2
No. Obs.              :  251
Log-Likelihood        :  2176.442
Av.Log-Likelihood     :  8.67

Optimal Parameters
------------------------------------
                     Estimate   Std. Error   t value   Pr(>|t|)
[ReturnSP500].mu     0.000195   0.000198   0.987099   0.32359
[ReturnSP500].omega  0.000002   0.000002   1.030038   0.30299
[ReturnSP500].alpha1 0.233722   0.065514   3.567521   0.00036
[ReturnSP500].beta1  0.643125   0.085516   7.520516   0.00000
[returnDji].mu       0.000289   0.000185   1.562649   0.11814
[returnDji].omega    0.000002   0.000001   1.599731   0.10966
[returnDji].alpha1   0.271243   0.070150   3.866605   0.00011
[returnDji].beta1    0.583464   0.099683   5.853191   0.00000
[Joint]dcca1         0.000000   0.000021   0.000301   0.99976
[Joint]dccb1         0.921866   0.149733   6.156745   0.00000

Information Criteria
--------------------

Akaike         -17.255
Bayes          -17.100
Shibata        -17.258
Hannan-Quinn   -17.192
```

Figure 4.22: Fitted summary of DCC

Since the forecast has been already shown in the most topic, there is no point discussing it again here.

Questions

1. Please give an example of converting a data series into a time series using the `ts()` function.
2. How are `zoo` and `xts` different from the `ts()` function? Give an example of constructing `xts` and `zoo` objects.
3. How do you read a file using `zoo`?
4. How do you check stationarity in time series?
5. How do you identify an AR(2) model in R?
6. How do you identify an MA(2) model in R?
7. Provide an example for the given below model and execute it in R.

   GARCH,

   EGARCH,

   VGARCH

8. How do you identify an ARIMA(1,1,1) model in R?
9. Provide an example for the given model and execute it in R.

Summary

In this chapter, we have discussed how to decompose a time series into its various components, such as trend, seasonality, cyclicity, and residuals. Also, I have discussed how to convert any series into a time series in R and how to execute the various forecasting models, such as linear filters, AR, MA, ARMA, ARIMA, GARCH, EGARCH, VGARCH, and DCC, in R and make forecast predictions.

In the next chapter, different concepts of trading using R will be discussed, starting with trend, followed by strategy, followed by pairs trading using three different methods. Capital asset pricing, the multi factor model, and portfolio construction will also be discussed. Machine learning technologies for building trading strategy will also be discussed.

5
Algorithmic Trading

Algorithmic trading is defined as the buying and selling of financial instruments using predefined rules called algorithms. Traders use predictive modeling, time series modeling, and machine learning to predict the price, return, or direction of movement of the asset.

Algorithms are developed by quantitative traders or quantitative researchers and tested on historical data. Algorithms go through rigorous testing before they are used for live trading. Technical indicator-based trading can also come under algorithm trading if it is fully automated. However, sometimes quantitative traders also use fundamental data such as market capitalization, cash flow, debt to equity ratio, and so on to define rules for algorithms. People are free to use any technique to define rules for algorithms. Very recently, investment or trading firms have started to dive deep into machine learning methods to predict price, return, or direction movement.

I will be covering machine learning-based trading in the next chapter.

In this chapter, I will be covering some trading strategies that are commonly used in the industry, along with their implementation. Specifically, I will cover the following topics:

- Momentum or directional trading
- Pairs trading
- Capital asset pricing model
- Multi factor model
- Portfolio construction

For this, I will require specific R packages such as quantmod, tseries, xts, zoo, and PerformanceAnalytics, which you can install using the following command:

```
install.packages('package name')
```

Once you have installed any package, you should load it into the workspace to use its functionalities, and for that, you should include the following command in your R code:

```
library('package name')
```

Momentum or directional trading

Momentum trading is trading when the instrument is trending up or down or, in other words, continuation in the trend as like historical winners are expected to be winners and historical losers are expected to lose. You bet on the direction of the instrument and you aim for buying at a low price and selling at a high price. I will not cover the pros and cons and what the different types of momentum trading strategies are. It is left to the trader to devise any idea. I will cover how to implement momentum trading rules and backtest using historical data in R. Stock return depends on various factors, and later in this chapter, I will show you how to use the multifactor model which explains stock return.

Let me start with simple technical indicators.

Technical indicators are implemented in the quantmod package so I will be using quantmod for this:

```
> library('quantmod')
>getSymbols("^DJI",src="yahoo")
[1] "DJI"
> head(DJI)
```

We have to start by loading the quantmod package into the R workspace and the first line explains how to do it. Next we extract the **Dow Jones Index** (**DJI**) data from the Yahoo repository. The data consists of many columns, such as DJI.Open, DJI.High, DJI.Low, DJI.Close, and so on. This can be seen using the head(dji) command. The next line shows how to extract only close prices and store in new variabledji:

```
>dji<- DJI[,"DJI.Close"]
> class(dji)
[1] "xts" "zoo"
```

The preceding line shows the dji class, which is xts, and zoo means dji is in time index format, so I used the following command to extract dji data between two specified dates:

```
>dji<- dji[(index(dji) >= "2010-01-01" & index(dji) <= "2015-12-31"),]
```

`Delt()` converts the raw closing prices to return and by default it is one period return:

```
>ret_dji<- Delt(dji,k=1)
```

You can use `Delt()` to calculate any period return using the parameter k. However, there is an option to calculate the normal return or logarithmic return of a stock price as well. In the following command, I used k=1:3, which means we are calculating the `dji` return for lag 1 to 3 incremented by 1:

```
>ret_dji<- Delt(dji,k=1:3)
```

You can see the output of the preceding command using `head()`. In the following result, `Delt.1`, `Delt.2`, and `Delt.3` are returned for lag 1, 2, and 3 respectively:

```
> head(ret_dji)
                   Delt.1          Delt.2          Delt.3
2010-01-04           NA              NA              NA
2010-01-05      -0.0011281628        NA              NA
2010-01-06       0.0001570331    -0.0009713069       NA
2010-01-07       0.0031380432     0.0032955691    0.002163688
2010-01-08       0.0010681840     0.0042095792    0.004367273
2010-01-11       0.0043133342     0.0053861256    0.008541071
```

The preceding output has a few NAs, which are because of data starting. For the first column, the first point does not have any reference value to calculate the return. So the first point will be NA and then from the second point onward, we get return values. In the second column, we have to calculate the return of current data points from two data points before it, which is not possible for the first two data points, leaving first two NAs, and on similar lines, three NAs in the third column.

The function `Delt()` has a few more parameters and each parameter has its type, which is specific to this function. Sometimes it is necessary to look into the output, what kind of return it generates, and in which format it generates output. If you would like to know more about the function, and its parameters along with examples, you can do so using the following command, which will open another window explaining all the details about this function:

```
> ? Delt
```

The Dow Jones Index closing price in *Figure 5.1* shows a clear trend. We have to define a set of indicators, rules which are able to generate signals at appropriate times, and have the potential to generate a positive return on investment. It is very important to understand the generalization capacity of the model and for that we should divide the dataset in two smaller datasets, one dataset consisting of 70-80% of the data and the second dataset consisting of the remaining 20-30% of the data. The first dataset is called the in-sample dataset and the second is called the out-sample dataset:

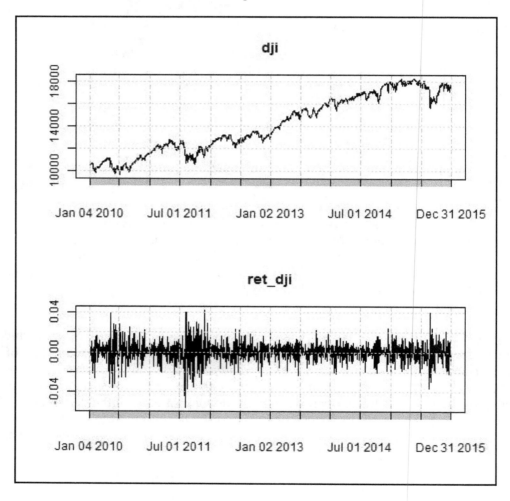

Figure 5.1: Dow Jones Index closing price and return series

To backtest our strategy idea and its generalization power, we have to divide the dataset into two smaller datasets called in-sample and out-sample datasets. Here I am going to define four dates. `in_sd` defines the date by which the in-sample data starts, and `in_ed` the in-sample end date. Similarly, `out_sd` and `out_ed` are defined for the out-sample start and end dates. The dates are defined in order as our data is in time series format and we are interested in building a model on historical data which would be used on real-time data, that is, a dataset which has dates later than historical data:

```
>in_sd<- "2010-01-01"
>in_ed<- "2014-12-31"
>out_sd<- "2015-01-01"
>out_ed<- "2015-12-31"
```

The variables `in_dji` and `in_ret_dji` contain the Dow Jones Index closing price and return respectively within the in-sample dates defined previously, and `out_dji` and `out_ret_dji` contain the Dow Jones Index closing price and return data respectively for the out-sample dates defined previously:

```
>in_dji<- dji[(index(dji) >= in_sd& index(dji) <= in_ed),]
>in_ret_dji<- ret_dji[(index(ret_dji) >= in_sd& index(ret_dji) <= in_ed),]
>out_dji<- dji[(index(dji) >= out_sd& index(dji) <= out_ed),]
>out_ret_dji<- ret_dji[(index(ret_dji) >= out_sd& index(ret_dji) <=
out_ed),]
```

The purpose of creating an in-sample and out-sample is logical and helps to control human bias towards parameter estimation. We should use in-sample data to backtest our strategy, estimate the optimal set of parameters, and evaluate its performance. The optimal set of parameters has to be applied on out-sample data to understand the generalization capacity of rules and parameters. If the performance on out-sample data is pretty similar to in-sample data, we assume the parameters and rule set have good generalization power and can be used for live trading.

I will use **moving average convergence divergence (MACD)** and **Bollinger** band indicators to generate automated trading signals. MACD and Bollinger band indicators are calculated using the following two lines of code. I used the same parameter values in both of these functions; however, you can use the parameters which you think are best for your dataset. The output variable `macd` contains the MACD indicator and its signal value; however, the output variable bb contains the lower band, average, upper band, and percentage Bollinger band:

```
>macd<- MACD(in_dji, nFast =12, nSlow = 26, nSig = 9,maType="SMA", percent
= FALSE)
> bb <- BBands(in_dji, n = 20, maType="SMA", sd = 2)
```

The first line creates the variable `signal` and initializes it with `NULL`. In the second line, I generated a buy signal (1) when `dji` is above the upper Bollinger band and the `macd` value is above its `macd-signal` value; a sell signal (-1) when `dji` is down the lower Bollinger band and `macd` is less than its `macd-signal` value; and out of market when the signal is 0:

```
> signal <- NULL
> signal <- ifelse(in_dji> bb[,'up'] &macd[,'macd']
>macd[,'signal'],1,ifelse(in_dji< bb[,'dn'] &macd[,'macd']
<macd[,'signal'],-1,0))
```

I had generated for both long and short; however, you can implement a long only or short only strategy as well. You can also modify this signal generation mechanism and use any other exit criterion you want. We haven't included any transaction cost and slippage cost to calculate its performance as none of the strategies are directly for trading. These strategies are used just to show the implementation mechanism:

```
>trade_return<- in_ret_dji*lag(signal)
```

Trade return is calculated using the return of the Dow Jones Index and the previous day signal. I will use the package `PerformanceAnalytics` to calculate various matrices of strategy performance.

First you should load this package into the R workspace:

```
> library(PerformanceAnalytics)
>cumm_ret<- Return.cumulative(trade_return)
>annual_ret<- Return.annualized(trade_return)
```

Cumulative and annualized return of the strategy can be calculated using the preceding two lines of code. `Chart.PerformanceSummary` plots cumulative and daily return along with drawdown at a given point of time, as can be seen in *Figure 5.2*:

```
>charts.PerformanceSummary(trade_return)
```

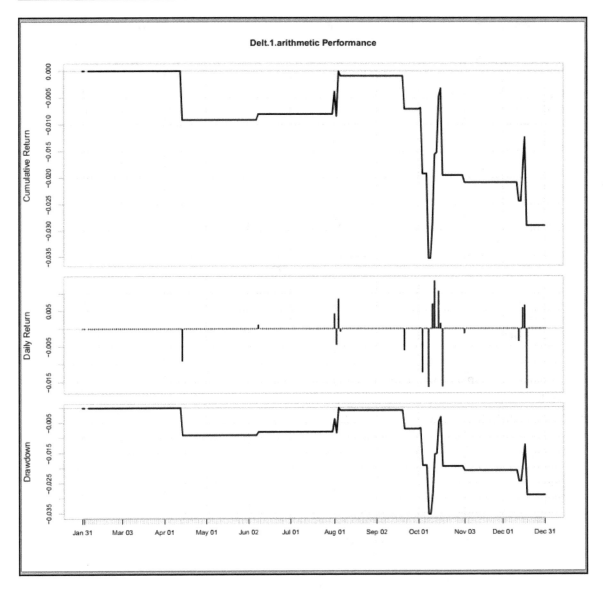

Figure 5.2: Cumulative return, daily return, and drawdown of strategy

To understand more about the performance of trade returns, you have to use the `summary()` command. `summary()` will give the minimum, first quartile, median, mean, third quartile, and maximum of all trade return on a daily basis. The variable `trade_return` has a few NAs as well and `summary()` shows the number of NAs as well. In the following line of code, we first convert `trade_return` to a time series object because it generates output in a specific format. The output shows minimum, first quartile, median, third quartile, maximum, and NA. NA has the value 20, which means `trade_return` has 20 NAs:

```
> summary(as.ts(trade_return))
     Min.    1st Qu.     Median      Mean    3rd Qu.      Max.       NA's
  -0.039770   0 0 0.000062   0 0.055460          20
```

The following are a few commands to calculate the performance of the strategy on in-sample trade return.

The first command is to calculate the maximum drawdown of trade return throughout the trading period and we can see that `0.1173028` means the maximum drawdown is 11.73%. The second and third commands are to calculate the daily and annualized standard deviation for trade returns. Next is the `VaR` calculation for strategy return and the last two commands are to calculate the Sharpe ratio of the strategy on a daily and annualized basis respectively.

The Sharpe ratio on a daily basis is `0.01621421` and annualized is `0.2289401`. The Sharpe ratio has two parameters: `Rf` and `FUN`. `Rf` is for risk-free rate of interest and `FUN` is for the denominator. In the Sharpe ratio calculation, I used `FUN=StdDev`; it could also be `VaR`:

```
>maxDrawdown(trade_return)
0.1173028
>StdDev(trade_return)
StdDev0.00379632
>StdDev.annualized(trade_return)
Annualized Standard Deviation        0.06026471
>VaR(trade_return, p = 0.95)
>SharpeRatio(as.ts(trade_return), Rf = 0, p = 0.95, FUN = "StdDev")
StdDev Sharpe (Rf=0%, p=95%): 0.01621421
>SharpeRatio.annualized(trade_return, Rf = 0)
Annualized Sharpe Ratio (Rf=0%)          0.2289401
```

Now, if we find the performance is good for the in-sample data then we can use this strategy on the out-sample data and calculate all the matrices for the out-sample data and check for the consistency in strategy performance. The next two lines are to calculate the moving average, and convergence divergence and Bollinger band for out of sample data:

```
>macd<- MACD(out_dji, nFast = 7, nSlow = 12, nSig = 15,maType="SMA",
percent = FALSE)
> bb <- BBands(out_dji, n = 20, maType="SMA", sd = 2)
```

Next I use these out-sample indicators and generate signals like we generated for the in-sample data:

```
>signal <- NULL
> signal <- ifelse(out_dji> bb[,'up'] &macd[,'macd']
>macd[,'signal'],1,ifelse(out_dji< bb[,'dn'] &macd[,'macd']
<macd[,'signal'],-1,0))
```

Trade return and all its relevant metrics for out-sample data are calculated using the following lines of code. These are like the in-sample data:

```
>trade_return<- out_ret_dji*lag(signal)
>cumm_ret<- Return.cumulative(trade_return)
>annual_ret<- Return.annualized(trade_return)
>charts.PerformanceSummary(trade_return)
>maxdd<- maxDrawdown(trade_return)
>sd<- StdDev(trade_return)
>sda<- StdDev.annualized(trade_return)
>VaR(trade_return, p = 0.95)
>SharpeRatio(as.ts(trade_return), Rf = 0, p = 0.95, FUN = "StdDev")
>SharpeRatio.annualized(trade_return, Rf = 0)
```

I implemented this strategy for one particular time series, that is, the **Dow Jones Index (DJI)**; however, you can test this same strategy on other stocks as well and understand strategy behavior across the universe of stocks. If you find the strategy performs better on most of the stocks, it shows consistency in the idea and it might work well on real-time trading as well. It's very important to note here that even if one particular strategy works well on a few stocks, we should not forget to check the variance of the portfolio. Let me show you an example. I calculate the variance of the DJI time series return:

```
>var(ret_dji,na.rm=T)
Delt.1.arithmetic       8.093402e-05
```

In the preceding code, I used `na.rm=T` to remove `Nan` in the time series. Now I import another symbol, which is S&P 500, into the workspace. The next line of code imports S&P 500 into the workspace:

```
>getSymbols("GSPC",src="yahoo")
```

Now I extract only the closing price of S&P 500 and refine it between two dates.

Next I calculate the return of S&P 500:

```
>snp<- GSPC[,"GSPC.Close"]
>snp<- snp[(index(snp) >= "2010-01-01" & index(snp) <= "2015-12-31"),]
>ret_snp<- Delt(snp)
```

I also calculate the variance of the S&P 500 series return:

```
>var(ret_snp,na.rm=T)
Delt.1.arithmetic    8.590805e-05
```

Now I combine both time series returns and calculated variance of sum of two returns:

```
>var(ret_dji + ret_snp,na.rm=T)
Delt.1.arithmetic    0.000218383
```

We find the following:

```
Variance(ret_dji + ret_snp) ≠ Variance(ret_dji) + Variance(ret_snp)
```

As we can see, $0.000218383 \neq 8.093402e-05 + 8.590805e-05$.

What causes this difference is very important to understand. If we go back to the basics of probability theory, we find the following:

```
Variance (X + Y) = Variance(X) + Variance(Y) + 2  Covariance(X,Y)
.......... (5.1)
Variance (X + Y) = Variance(X) + Variance(Y) + 2
ρσXσY................(5.2)
```

Here, ρ is the correlation between X and Y; σX is the standard deviation of X; and σY is standard deviation of Y.

We calculate the standard deviation of `ret_dji`, `ret_snp` and correlation between `ret_dji` and `ret_snp` using the following commands:

```
>sd(ret_dji,na.rm=T)
[1] 0.00926866
>sd(ret_snp,na.rm=T)
[1] 0.008996333
>cor(ret_dji[!is.na(ret_dji)],ret_snp[!is.na(ret_snp)])
                    Delt.1.arithmetic
Delt.1.arithmetic          0.3090576
```

The correlation between `ret_dji` and `ret_snp` is `0.3090576`. Now we put these values into the equation 5.2 and you will see both sides are equal. It means if two stocks are positively correlated, they cause an increase in the variance of the portfolio as compared to the sum of variance of two individual stocks. If we are able to pick two stocks which are uncorrelated, that is, *correlation = 0*, then the variance of the portfolio would be the linear sum of two individual securities; or if we manage to pick two stocks with negative correlation then the variance of the portfolio would be less than the sum of two individual stocks.

So we have to look at the correlation matrix of the stocks in the portfolio to figure out which stocks would help to minimize risk. As we have only two stocks in the portfolio, I created `port_ret` as a data frame which consists of NAs, number of rows same as the number of data points, and two columns:

```
>port_ret<- data.frame(matrix(NA,dim(ret_dji)[1],2))
```

The next two commands copy `ret_dji` into the first column and `ret_snp` into the second column of the data frame:

```
>port_ret[,1] <- ret_dji
>port_ret[,2] <- ret_snp
```

Now we can calculate the correlation matrix of stocks in the portfolio. The following code calculates the correlation of stock 1 with stock 2:

```
>cor(port_ret)
        X1          X2
X1      1           NA
X2      NA          1
```

The preceding correlation matrix has NAs and these are because the port_ret data frame has NA somewhere, so we have to remove NA from the data frame and is.na() helps us to get rid of this NA. The following code filters port_ret from NA and then calculates the correlation matrix:

```
>port_ret<- port_ret[!is.na(port_ret[,1]),]
>cor(port_ret)

            X1                      X2
X1      1.0000000               0.3090576
X2      0.3090576               1.0000000
```

As correlation between two stocks is order independent that is the reason that diagonal elements are same. It is rarely possible to find a pair of stocks which are uncorrelated or perfectly correlated. More negative correlation shows better diversification. As the correlation increases, diversification becomes less relevant, as the variance of the portfolio increases with the increase in the correlation. That is the reason correlation is one of the most important criteria to select stocks in a portfolio and to control the risk of the portfolio.

Pairs trading

You are familiar with the concept of diversification. For diversification, we have to choose negative correlated stocks; however, in pairs trading, we can choose stocks with positive correlation and enter opposite trades in both of the stocks. Enter a buy position for the stock which is undervalued and short the stock which is overvalued.

The variance of the X – Y portfolio is defined as follows:

```
Variance (X -Y) = Variance(X) + Variance(Y) - 2 ρ σXσY...............(5.3)
```

Pairs trading is a market-neutral strategy, as the difference in two stocks is uncorrelated or correlated close to zero with the overall market. I will show you how to start pairs trading using the distance approach. I will use same two time series, Dow Jones Index, and S&P 500 for pairs trading and explain how the distance-based approach can be implemented in R.

Distance-based pairs trading

Different time series might have different scaling and so you first normalize the series. I did it using an initial investment of 1 and then taking cumulative return of this investment:

```
>ret_dji[1] <- 1
>ret_snp[1] <- 1
```

The following commands calculate the cumulative return of the investment which was started at 1. This way, we can track the relative performance of series one against the second series and the last command is to calculate the difference between the two series:

```
>norm_dji<- apply(ret_dji,2,cumprod)
>norm_snp<- apply(ret_snp,2,cumprod)
```

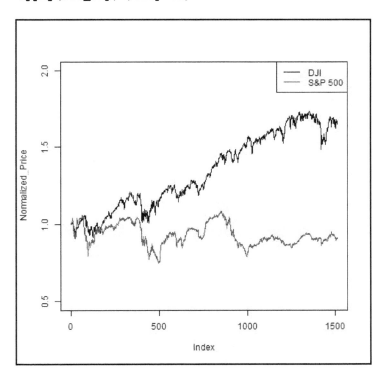

Figure 5.3: Normalized prices for Dow Jones Index and S&P 500

The formula to calculate cumulative return is defined here:

```
(Norm_dji)t =  (norm_dji)t-1 * (1 + rt)
```

Now I used the plot() command to plot normalized prices norm_dji and type="l", help to connect all points in the graph and generate a line graph. You will get dots if you do not use this and ylim=c(0.5,2) is used to scale the vertical axis. I also used lines() to plot another series on the same graph so that we can at least look at both series in the same figure. ylab is for labeling along the y axis:

```
>plot(norm_dji,type="l",ylim=c(0.5,2) ,ylab="Normalized_Price")
>lines(norm_snp,col="red")
>legend('topright',c("DJI","S&P 500") ,  lty=1, col=c('black','red'),
bty='o', cex=1)
```

The legend command helps to place the box at the top-right corner in the plot which mentioned DJI and S&P500 series are plotted. The parameter lty is used for the type of line in the plot; lty=1 means solid line. The next plot is used to plot the difference between normalized prices.

When you look at this plot, you will realize that the distance between both series is converging and diverging before index 500 and after that, diverging continuously. As this pair doesn't converge frequently, you should not consider using it for pairs trading. You have to find another pair which diverge and converge frequently on historical data, which implies some similarity in both series fundamentals on historical data.

I chose **Exxon Mobil (XOM)** and **Chevron corporation (CVX)** for this. *Figure 5.4* shows normalized price series and their difference along with the signals generated for trading.

Normalized prices are not going very far from each other for a long time, as can be seen in *Figure 5.4*. This pair seems to be a good member for distance based pairs trading.

We calculate norm_xom and norm_cvx like we calculated norm_dji and norm_snp and plot these using the following commands:

```
> class(norm_xom)
[1] "matrix"
> class(norm_cvx)
[1] "matrix"
```

You have to look into the class of these two variables. Both of these are matrices, as can be seen above, and this has to be an xts, zoo object. So the next thing you have to do is to convert these matrix objects into an xts, zoo object:

```
norm_xom<- xts(norm_xom,index(ret_xom))
norm_cvx<- xts(norm_cvx,index(ret_cvx))
```

`xts()` does this job and converts both of these into `xts` objects:

```
>par(mfrow=c(3,1))
> plot(norm_xom,type="l",ylim=c(0.5,2) ,ylab="Normalized_Price")
> lines(norm_cvx,col="red")
> legend('topright',c("XOM","CVX") ,  lty=1, col=c('black','red'), bty='o',
cex=1)
> diff = norm_xom - norm_cvx
> plot(diff,type="l",ylab="Normalized_Price_difference")
```

Mean, standard deviation of the normalized price difference is calculated as follows:

```
> me <- mean(diff)
>std<- sd(diff)
```

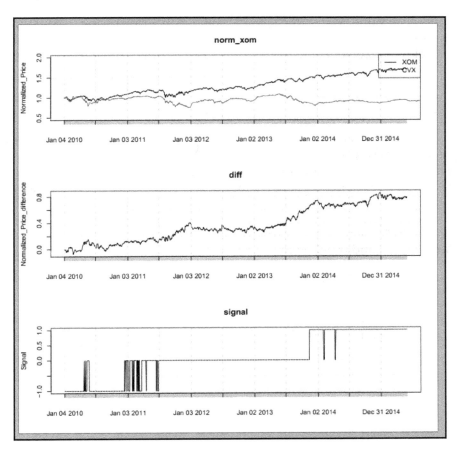

Figure 5.4: Normalized price series, difference, and trading signals

The upper (ub) and lower bounds (lb) of the difference series can be calculated by adding and subtracting *n* times standard deviation from the mean:

```
>ub<- me + n * std
>lb<- me  - n*std
```

Finding optimal parameter values for *n* is not straightforward. We either have to use the hit and trial method to come up with the optimal value of *n* or use a grid-based parameter optimizer to find the optimal value.

As an example, here I used n = 1 just for the sake of demonstration. A buy signal (1) is generated when the difference value is lower than the lower band, and a short signal (-1) is generated when the difference is above the upper band; otherwise the signal is hold (0).

When the difference value, that is, the spread, is above the upper band, we speculate it will return to its mean value as, historically, it has been there most of the time. Similarly, when the spread is below the lower band, even in this case, we speculate it will return to its mean value:

```
> n <- 1
> signal <- ifelse(diff > ub,1,ifelse(diff < lb,-1,0))
```

Here I used the full time series of difference values to calculate mean and standard deviation, as can be seen previously where I calculated me and std. You can also calculate mean and standard deviation dynamically on a rolling window. This dynamic mean and standard deviation will change signal generation, and entry and exit will be even more frequent.

Dynamic mean and standard deviations can be calculated using rollapply(). You should define dataset, length, and function in rollapply():

```
>me_dynamic<-  rollapply(diff,10,mean)
>std_dynamic<-  rollapply(diff,10,sd)
```

The plot() function plots the signal as presented in *Figure 5.4*. A non-zero signal value shows our participation in the market and zero means we are not participating in the market:

```
>plot(signal, type="l")
```

Difference in normalized prices is also called spread. As we are generating signals using spread, we will be trading spread instead of individual stock. So, we have to clearly understand what is meant by spread trading. When I say buy, it means I am buying spread, which implies long position on XOM and short position on CVX or short on XOM and long on CVX when we have short signal. The following two lines calculate the spread and trade return:

```
>spread_return<- ret_xom - ret_cvx
>trade_return<- spread_return*lag(signal) - cost
```

The variable named `spread_return` is the return spread, `trade_return` is the return of trade, and cost is the expenses to carry out trading activities; it includes transaction cost, brokerage cost, and slippage.

The purpose of this book is only to teach you R coding, not to generate profitable trading ideas. So, I considered the cost as 0, but you have to incorporate the appropriate cost while backtesting your ideas and putting money into a real account.

Now we apply performance measure commands to extract a performance summary:

```
> summary(trade_return)
      Min.     1st Qu.      Median       Mean     3rd Qu.        Max.
-0.0330000   0.0000000   0.0000000   0.0002135   0.0000000   0.0373400
```

All key performance indicators can be calculated using the following commands. All these commands have already been used in the Momentum trading section:

```
>cumm_ret<- Return.cumulative(trade_return)
>annual_ret<- Return.annualized(trade_return)
>charts.PerformanceSummary(trade_return)
>maxdd<- maxDrawdown(trade_return)
>sd<- StdDev(trade_return)
>sda<- StdDev.annualized(trade_return)
>VaR(trade_return, p = 0.95)
>SharpeRatio(as.ts(trade_return), Rf = 0, p = 0.95, FUN = "StdDev")
>SharpeRatio.annualized(trade_return, Rf = 0)
```

Figure 5.5 shows cumulative performance, daily return, and drawdown on a day-to-day basis for this distance-based pairs trading strategy:

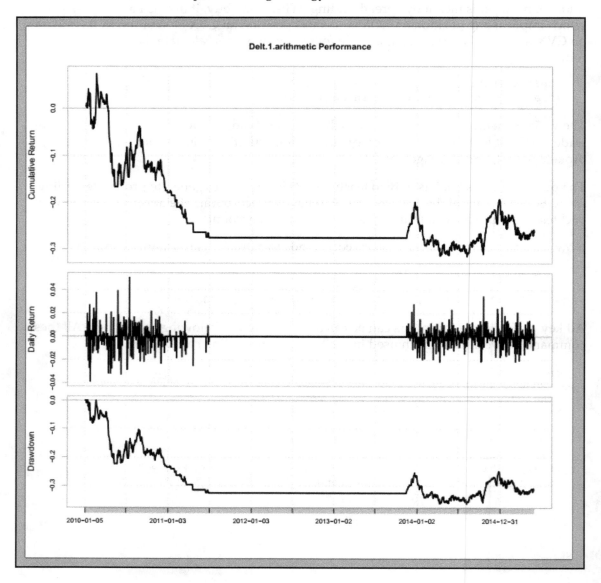

Figure 5.5: Cumulative return of strategy, return, and drawdown on a daily basis

Here I demonstrated an approach to implement the distance-based pairs trading model practically. You should segregate the data into in-sample and out-sample datasets. Optimization of parameters should be done using in-sample data and validate those parameters for out-sample data. I have already shown you this approach in the Momentum trading section.

Correlation based pairs trading

Another, traditional way to trade in pairs is correlation. You have to pick a pair which is highly correlated historically and the spread of the pair is least correlated with market benchmark. A trading opportunity occurs whenever you see correlation strength weakens. This is also on the premise of mean reversion and traders bet on correlation reversion to its mean whenever they see significant deviation in correlation from its mean at least by n times standard deviation.

A market-neutral strategy can be implemented in two different ways:

- Beta neutral
- Dollar neutral

Beta neutrality means the beta of the spread is close to zero; this can be reached by choosing two stocks or instruments whose betas are almost same. However, dollar neutral means you are only a little exposed to the market as investment in long stock is offset by the amount you receive on short trade.

Practically, even if we are little exposed to the market doesn't mean that we have no risk or little risk. Risk has to be managed properly to make a profitable trade. Here I am going to show you how to implement the correlation based pairs trading model.

First of all, you have to create a data frame which consist of returns of XOM and CVX as I am using XOM and CVX as my pair of stocks.

The first column is for XOM and the second is for CVX returns:

```
>data <- data.frame(matrix(NA,dim(ret_xom)[1],2))
>data[,1] <- ret_xom
>data[,2] <- ret_cvx
> class(data)
[1] "data.frame"
```

The type of this can be checked using `class()` and you see that the data is of `data.frame` type. You have to convert it to an `xts` object and this can be done using the following code:

```
> data <- xts(data,index(ret_xom))
> class(data)
[1] "xts" "zoo"
```

Now you can check the type of the data; it is of type `xts`, `zoo`. Next, I created a function named correlation, with one single parameter x, which calculates the correlation between the first and second columns of x and returns the correlation:

```
>correlation <- function(x)
{
        result <- cor(x[,1],x[,2])
        return (result)
}
```

I used `rollapply()` which does calculations on a rolling window basis as per the function rolling window length defined in this function. Here I supplied four parameters to this: the first parameter is the data which is used for calculation, the second for window length, the third for the function to be used for calculation, and the fourth to direct the function whether calculation should on done on each column separately.

I used data length as `252`, the function is correlation which has been defined above, and by.`column=FALSE`, which means this function is not applied on columns separately.

So this keeps on moving and using the last 10 data points to calculate correlation:

```
>corr<- rollapply(data,252,correlation ,by.column=FALSE)
```

The strategy continuously monitors the performance of two historically correlated securities. When the correlation between the two securities temporarily weakens, that is, one stock moves up while the other moves down, the pairs trade would be to short the outperforming stock and to long the underperforming one, betting that the spread between the two would eventually converge.

The divergence within a pair can be caused by temporary supply/demand changes, large buy/sell orders for one security, reaction for important news about one of the companies, and so on.

Figure 5.6 shows the correlation between XOM and CVX returns at rolling length 252. You can see that almost every time, correlation is over 0.6. It shows this pair's high correlation persists almost every day:

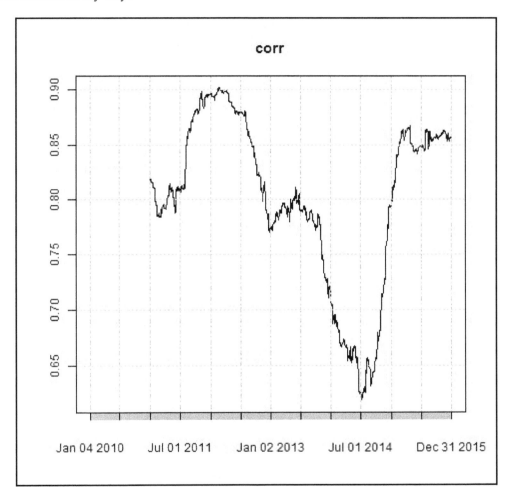

Figure 5.6: Correlation between returns of XOM and CVX

Normally, correlation greater than 0.8 is considered as strong correlation and less than 0.5 as weak correlation. You also need to calculate the hedge ratio of XOM and CVX, which can be calculated by dividing the XOM price and CVX price:

```
>hedge_ratio<-  xom  / cvx
```

Then you have to calculate the mean and standard deviation of the hedge ratio and upper and lower bounds. In the distance based model, I presented a technique to use static mean and standard deviation; however, in this section, I am presenting rolling-window-based mean and standard deviation for the calculation of bounds. As the mean and standard deviation will be function of time so the upper and lower bounds. I used `rollapply()` to calculate the rolling mean and standard deviation of spread for every 14 data points:

```
>roll_me<- rollapply(hedge_ratio,14,mean)
>roll_std<- rollapply(hedge_ratio,14,sd)
> n <- 1
>roll_ub<- roll_me + n * roll_std
>roll_lb<- roll_me - n * roll_std
```

If you look at preceding two commands, you will see the parameter n, which is arbitrary and should be optimized. Once you have bounds, you should go for signal generation and this can be done using the following code:

```
> signal <- NULL
> signal <- ifelse(hedge_ratio> roll_ub,-1,ifelse(hedge_ratio<
roll_lb,1,0))
>lagsignal<- Lag(signal,1)
> signal <- ifelse(lagsignal == -1 &hedge_ratio> roll_me,
-1,ifelse(lagsignal == 1 &hedge_ratio< roll_me,1,0))
```

It generates a short signal (-1) when the hedge ratio is over the upper band and generates a buy signal (1) when the hedge ratio is down the lower band. Then, calculate the signal at lag 1 and use it to generate an exit signal when the hedge ratio crosses the rolling mean. Short signal implies short 1 unit of XOM and long hedge ratio time CVX; however, buy signal implies long 1 unit on XOM and short hedge ratio time CVX. You should use the following commands to calculate spread return and trade return:

```
>spread_return<- ret_xom - ret_cvx
>trade_return<- spread_return*lag(signal) - cost
```

Once you have done that, you should analyze the quality of these signals, so you need to calculate all metrics of trade return, which can be calculated using the commands mentioned in earlier sections, particularly the Momentum trading and Distance based pairs trading sections. You also need to optimize parameters using in-sample data and use those optimized parameters for out-sample data to really get strategy performance on out-sample data.

Co-integration based pairs trading

Co-integration based pairs trading is the latest arsenal in pairs trading and its use is picking up very fast these days.

Co-integration considers the regression of one price series against another price series. As these series are non-stationary, the regression results will be spurious if these series are not co-integrated. Co-integration becomes crucial when we have to regress non-stationary series. You first check the time series you are using is non-stationary. You need to load the package tseries into your workspace and the data used in this section is from January 1, 2014 to December 31, 2014:

```
> library(tseries)
>adf.test(xom)
```

Augmented Dickey-Fuller test:

```
data:   xom
Dickey-Fuller = -1.4326, Lag order = 11, p-value = 0.8185
alternative hypothesis: stationary
```

You can see the Dicky-Fuller statistic is -1.4326, which is higher than -3.43. This implies the series is non-stationary and you can also check the first difference of the series:

```
> diff <- xom - Lag(xom,1)
>adf.test(diff[!is.na(diff)])
   Augmented Dickey-Fuller Test
data:   diff[!is.na(diff)]
Dickey-Fuller = -11.791, Lag order = 11, p-value = 0.01
alternative hypothesis: stationary
```

As diff contain NA, you should consider only non-NAs and use adf.test() to test it for unit roots. The Dickey-Fuller statistic using the first difference of time series is -11.97, which is less than -3.43, which shows the first difference is stationary and this suggests XOM is integrated of order 1, that is, O(1).

Now I am going to fit the model for XOM and CVX using `lm()`. `lm()` corresponds to the linear model and it regresses XOM against CVX original prices and 0 in `lm()` means regression without intercept:

```
> model <- lm(xom ~ cvx + 0)
> model
Call:
lm(formula = xom ~ cvx + 0)
Coefficients:
cvx
0.8008
```

A summary of the model can be looked into using the `summary()` command:

```
> summary(model)
Call:
lm(formula = xom ~ cvx + 0)
Residuals:
     Min        1Q    Median        3Q       Max
-12.7667   -2.2833    0.4533    2.9224   13.9694
Coefficients:
Estimate Std. Error t value Pr(>|t|)
cvx 0.800802    0.001123    713.4    <2e-16 ***
---
Signif. codes:  0 '***' 0.001 '**' 0.01 '*' 0.05 '.' 0.1 ' ' 1
Residual standard error: 4.587 on 1509 degrees of freedom
Multiple R-squared:  0.997,    Adjusted R-squared:  0.997
F-statistic: 5.09e+05 on 1 and 1509 DF,  p-value: < 2.2e-16>
```

The next thing is we have to extract residuals from the variable called `model` and test it for unit roots, which you have to do using the following command. You can see in the output that the `Dickey-Fuller` statistic is -2.6088, which is greater than -3.43, which implies that there is unit root. In probability theory, unit root has an important feature which needs to be verified. The presence of unit root causes inference problems as time series with unit root inflate which does not converge or keep on diverging. Non-stationary time series have unit root and they do not converge. Finding of unit root implies XOM and CVX are not co-integrated:

```
>adf.test(as.ts(model$residuals))
Augmented Dickey-Fuller Test
data:  as.ts(model$residuals)
Dickey-Fuller = -2.6088, Lag order = 11, p-value = 0.3206
alternative hypothesis: stationary
```

Mobil (XOM) and hedge ratio times BP Plc (BP) along
with its residuals. If you look at the prices series, you can see the closeYou have to find
another pair which is co-integrated, so let us try to find another pair. Let me show you co-
integration between **Exxon Mobil (XOM)** and BP Plc (BP).

Extract XOM and BP Price closing prices using GetSymbols() and use them to regress to
establish the relationship:

```
> model <- lm(xom ~ bp + 0)
>adf.test(as.ts(model$residuals))
Augmented Dickey-Fuller Test
data:  as.ts(model$residuals)
Dickey-Fuller = -3.9007, Lag order = 11, p-value = 0.01395
alternative hypothesis: stationary
```

Here, the Dickey-Fuller statistic is -3.9007, which is less than critical value at 95%
confidence value (-3.43) so this doesn't have unit root and this pair is stationary:

```
> par(mfrow=c(2,1))
> plot(dji,type="l")
> lines(snp*model$coefficients,col="red")
> plot(model$residuals,type="l")
```

Figure 5.7 shows the XOM and hedge ratio times for BP price series and its spread. plot()
and lines() are used to plot this figure. Now, as the residuals are mean reverting, so the
next target is to generate bounds and signal using the following commands:

```
>roll_me<- rollapply(model$residuals,14,mean)
>roll_std<- rollapply(model$residuals,14,sd)
> n <- 1
>roll_ub<- roll_me + n * roll_std
>roll_lb<- roll_me - n * roll_std
```

The preceding two commands have the parameter n, which is arbitrary and should be
optimized:

```
> signal <- NULL
> signal <- ifelse(model$residuals> roll_ub,-1,ifelse(model$residuals<
roll_lb,1,0))
>lagsignal<- Lag(signal,1)
>signal <- ifelse(lagsignal == -1 &model$residuals>
roll_me,-1,ifelse(lagsignal == 1 &model$residuals< roll_me,1,0))
```

Figure 5.7 shows the series **Exxon Mobil (XOM)** and hedge ratio times BP Plc (BP) along with its residuals. If you look at the prices series, you can see the close relation between both series and these two series do not deviate too much for so long. If these deviate at all, very soon they return close by:

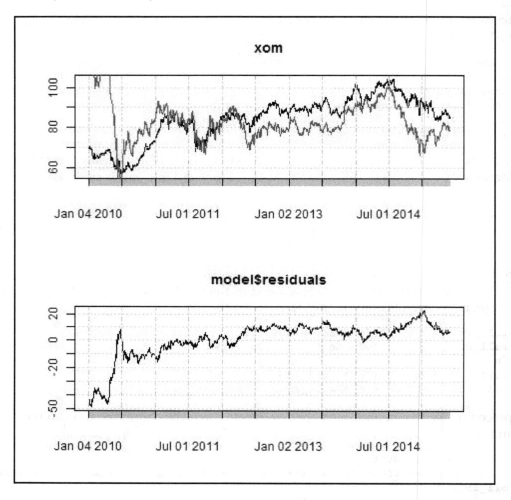

Figure 5.7: Series of XOM and hedge ratio times BP along with their spread series

As you have generated signals, you should calculate the performance of the strategy, as can be done using the commands I mentioned in the Momentum trading or Distance based pairs trading sections.

Capital asset pricing model

The **capital asset pricing model** (CAPM) model helps to gauge risk contributed by security or portfolio to its benchmark and is measured by beta (β). Using the CAPM model, we can estimate the expected excess return of an individual security or portfolio which is proportional to its beta:

$E(Ri) - Rf = \beta i*(E(Rm) - Rf)$ (5.4)

Here:

- *E(Ri)*: Expected return of security
- *E(Rm)*: Expected return of market
- *Ri*: Rate of return of security
- *Rf*: Risk Free rate of return
- *Rm*: Benchmark or market return
- βi: Beta of the security

CVX is regressed against DJI using linear model as per equation 5.4.

Here I used zero as risk-free return in the following command:

```
>rf<- rep(0,length(dji))
>model <- lm((ret_cvx  -rf) ~ (ret_dji -rf) )
> model
Call:
lm(formula = (ret_cvx - rf) ~ (ret_dji - rf))
Coefficients:
(Intercept)   ret_dji
-0.0002013     1.1034521
```

You can see the intercept term in the above result is alpha (-0.0002013) and coefficient for ret_dji is beta (1.1034521). However, you can also use the PerformanceAnalytics package to calculate CAPM alpha and beta using CAPM.alpha() and CAPM.beta().

The following command shows how to use this whose result are same as preceding one:

```
>CAPM.beta(ret_cvx,ret_dji)
[1] 1.103452
>CAPM.alpha(ret_cvx,ret_dji)
[1] -0.0002013222
```

The beta value from `CAPM.beta()` is the same as the coefficient, and `CAPM.alpha()` is the same as intercept in the above regression. You can also see a scatter plot of the returns and its fitted lines:

```
>plot(as.ts(ret_cvx),as.ts(ret_dji),xlab="CVX_ Return",ylab="DJI_Return")
>abline(model,col="red")
```

Figure 5.8 shows the fitted line has a positive slope, which implies positive correlation between the returns. We can check this statement using the following command:

```
>cor(ret_cvx,ret_dji)
 Delt.1.arithmetic
Delt.1.arithmetic          0.7881967
```

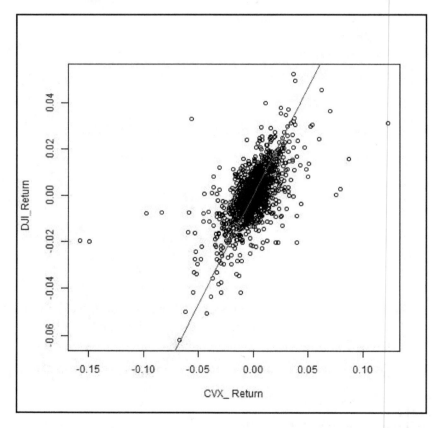

Figure 5.8: Scatter plot of DJI and CVS return and its fitted line

Multi factor model

The multi factor model can be used to decompose returns and calculate risk. The factors are constructed using pricing, fundamental, and analyst estimates data. I will use Systematic Investor Toolbox for this section.

The `gzcon()` function creates a connection and reads data in compressed format. Once we create a connection, we also have to close the connection.

The following commands explain this:

```
> con = gzcon(url('http://www.systematicportfolio.com/sit.gz', 'rb'))
>   source(con)
> close(con)
```

The following function is used to fetch Dow Jones components data from `http://money.cnn.com` and `join()` is taken from Systematic Investor Toolbox:

```
>dow.jones.components<- function(){
url = 'http://money.cnn.com/data/dow30/'
    txt = join(readLines(url))
    temp = gsub(pattern = '">', replacement = '<td>', txt, perl = TRUE)
    temp = gsub(pattern = '</a>', replacement = '</td>', temp, perl = TRUE)
    temp = extract.table.from.webpage(temp, 'Volume', has.header = T)
    trim(temp[,'Company']) }
```

The next single line of code is a call to the preceding function, which extracts the Dow Jones constituent list:

```
>tickers = dow.jones.components()
```

The following commands explain how to extract fundamental data for the last 80 months of all companies in the tickers list. These commands will take a few minutes to extract data so it is recommended to save the data once you extract it and later you should use the `load()` command to load it:

```
>data.fund<- new.env()
>   temp = paste(iif( nchar(tickers) <= 3, 'NYSE:', 'NASDAQ:'), tickers,
sep='')
>for(i in 1:len(tickers)) data.fund[[tickers[i]]] = fund.data(temp[i], 80)
>save(data.fund, file='data.fund.Rdata')
# load(file='data.fund.Rdata')
```

The next set of commands is the same as preceding code, but to extract price data:

```
# get pricing data
>data <- new.env()
>getSymbols(tickers, src = 'yahoo', from = '1970-01-01', env = data,
auto.assign = T)
>for(i in ls(data)) data[[i]] = adjustOHLC(data[[i]], use.Adjusted=T)
>save(data, file='data.Rdata')
#load(file='data.Rdata')
```

The subsequent function creates various date variables in date format:

```
>date.fund.data<- function(data){
quarter.end.date = as.Date(paste(data['quarter end date',], '/1', sep=''),
'%Y/%m/%d')
quarterly.indicator = data['quarterly indicator',]
date.preliminary.data.loaded = as.Date(data['date preliminary data
loaded',], '%Y-%m-%d') + 1
months = seq(quarter.end.date[1], tail(quarter.end.date,1)+365, by='1
month')
index = match(quarter.end.date, months)
quarter.end.date = months[ iif(quarterly.indicator == '4', index+3,
index+2) + 1 ] - 1
fund.date = date.preliminary.data.loaded
fund.date[is.na(fund.date)] = quarter.end.date[is.na(fund.date)]
return(fund.date) }
```

Now you have extracted price and fundamental data, you should use this data to construct various fundamental factors such as EPS, number of shares outstanding, market capitalization, market value to book value, and so on. This loop calculates fundamental factors for every ticker one by one and creates a list:

```
> library(quantmod)
>for(i in tickers) {
fund = data.fund[[i]]
fund.date = date.fund.data(fund)
# Earnings per Share
EPS = get.fund.data('Diluted EPS from Total Operations', fund, fund.date,
is.12m.rolling=T)
# Common Shares Outstanding
CSHO = get.fund.data('total common shares out', fund, fund.date)
# Common Equity
CEQ = get.fund.data('total equity', fund, fund.date)
# merge
data[[i]] = merge(data[[i]], EPS, CSHO, CEQ) }
```

Next, I filtered the preceding data for the period starting at 1995 and lasting at 2011:

```
>bt.prep(data, align='keep.all', dates='1995::2011')
```

Prices for all tickers can be extracted and NAN can be replaced with previous values using the following commands:

```
>       prices = data$prices
>       prices = bt.apply.matrix(prices, function(x) ifna.prev(x))
```

Now you have to construct fundamental ratios using fundamental factors and prices. I created three ratios; however, you can create any number of ratios that you would like to consider. I created market capitalization, EPS to price ratio, and book value to price:

```
# Financial Ratios
>factors$TV = list()
# Market Value - capitalization
> CSHO =  bt.apply(data, function(x) ifna.prev(x[, 'CSHO']))
> MKVAL = prices * CSHO
 #  Earnings / Price
> EPS = bt.apply(data, function(x) ifna.prev(x[, 'EPS']))
>factors$TV$EP = EPS / prices
#  Book Value / Price
> CEQ = bt.apply(data, function(x) ifna.prev(x[, 'CEQ']))
>factors$TV$BP = CEQ / MKVAL
```

As scaling for all of these ratios might be different, before moving on, we shouldn't forget to standardize it. I calculated the Z score to standardize this data:

```
# normalize (convert to z scores) cross sectional all Traditional Value
factors
>for(i in names(factors$TV)) {
factors$TV[[i]] = (factors$TV[[i]] -
cap.weighted.mean(factors$TV[[i]], MKVAL)) /
                      apply(factors$TV[[i]], 1, sd, na.rm=T)
}
This is how we bind different data in multidimensional case
# compute the overall Traditional Value factor
>load.packages('abind')
> temp = abind(factors$TV, along = 3)
```

Calculate the average of all the normalized factors:

```
>factors$TV$AVG = factors$TV[[1]]
>factors$TV$AVG[] = apply(temp, c(1,2), mean, na.rm=T)
```

As of now, we have daily data and created financial ratios on a daily basis. You can convert it to any frequency you desire. I converted it to monthly frequency and extracted data for the last day of the month:

```
# find month ends
>month.ends = endpoints(prices, 'months')
> prices = prices[month.ends,]
>       n = ncol(prices)
>nperiods = nrow(prices)
```

This is how you should calculate monthly return and its `lag`:

```
> ret = prices / mlag(prices) - 1
>next.month.ret = mlag(ret, -1)
```

Marker capitalization at the end of every month can be calculated using the following:

```
> MKVAL = MKVAL[month.ends,]
```

Extract all ratios for the last day of the month:

```
>for(j in 1:len(factors)) {
for(i in 1:len(factors[[j]])) {
        factors[[j]][[i]] = factors[[j]][[i]][month.ends,]
    }}
```

Next you should calculate quantiles, which can be calculated using the following commands. I created five quantiles, and the average next month return of each quantile is calculated using the earning price factor. Quantiles are created month by ranging stocks based on EP factor:

```
> out = compute.quantiles(factors$TV$AVG, next.month.ret, plot=F)
> models = list()
>for(i in 1:5) {
data$weight[] = NA
data$weight[month.ends,] = iif(out$quantiles == i, out$weights, 0)
        capital = 100000
data$weight[] = (capital / prices) * (data$weight)
    models[[paste('Q',i,sep='')]] = bt.run(data, type='share',
capital=capital) }
```

The top and bottom are very extreme and should be used to create a spread (Q5 – Q1). The dynamics of this spread helps to design and develop an investing strategy, that is, momentum or mean reverting:

```
# spread
>data$weight[] = NA
>data$weight[month.ends,] = iif(out$quantiles == 5, out$weights,
```

```
iif(out$quantiles == 1, -out$weights, 0))
>     capital = 100000
>data$weight[] = (capital / prices) * (data$weight)
> models$Q5_Q1 = bt.run(data, type='share', capital=capital)
```

Now you should run cross-sectional regression to estimate alpha and portfolio loadings and these can be calculated using the following commands:

```
>factors.avg = list()
>for(j in names(factors)) factors.avg[[j]] = factors[[j]]$AVG
>factors.avg = add.avg.factor(factors.avg)
>nperiods = nrow(next.month.ret)
> n =ncol(next.month.ret)
# create matrix for each factor
>factors.matrix = abind(factors.avg, along = 3)
>all.data = factors.matrix
> # betas
> beta = all.data[,1,] * NA
# append next.month.ret to all.data
>all.data = abind(next.month.ret, all.data, along = 3)
>dimnames(all.data)[[3]][1] = 'Ret'
# estimate betas (factor returns)
>for(t in 30:(nperiods-1)) {
    temp = all.data[t:t,,]
    x = temp[,-1]
    y = temp[,1]
    beta[(t+1),] = lm(y~x-1)$coefficients
 }
 # create Alpha return forecasts
> alpha = next.month.ret * NA
>for(t in 40:(nperiods-1)) {
    # average betas over the last 6 months
coef = colMeans(beta[(t-5):t,],na.rm=T)
    alpha[t,] = rowSums(all.data[t,,-1] * t(repmat(coef, 1,n)), na.rm=T)
}
```

We can also use these alpha and beta to estimate future portfolio return as well.

Portfolio construction

Investors are interested in reducing risk and maximizing return of their investment and creating a portfolio does this job provided we have constructed it by keeping in mind the investor risk-return profile. I will guide you through creating an efficient frontier that can help you to measure risk with respect to your return expectation. For that, I will start extracting data for four securities. The first line of code creates a new environment to store data; the next few lines are for symbols list, data starting date, and extracting data using `getSymbols()`:

```
>stockData<- new.env()
> symbols <- c("MSFT","FB","GOOG","AAPL")
>start_date<- as.Date("2014-01-01")
>getSymbols(symbols, src="yahoo", env=stockData, from=start_date)
> x <- list()
```

The next for loop stores individual stock data in a list, and calculates the day's gain and a data frame consisting of closing prices of all stocks in portfolio:

```
>for (i in 1:length(symbols)) {
  x[[i]] <- get(symbols[i], pos=stockData)  # get data from stockData
environment
  x[[i]]$gl<-((Cl(x[[i]])-Op(x[[i]]))/Op(x[[i]]))*100 #Daily gain loss
percentage
  if(i==1)
     data <- Cl(x[[i]])
 else
 data <- cbind(data,Cl(x[[i]])) }
```

The return, average return for each stocks, and covariance matrix can be calculated using the following commands:

```
>data_ret<- apply(data,2,Delt)
>napos<- which(apply(data_ret,2,is.na))# Remove Na's
>avg_ret<- apply(data_ret[-napos,],2,mean)
>covariance_mat<- cov(data_ret,use='na')
```

I will be using the following weights to assign to portfolio:

```
> weights <- c(0.2,0.3,0.35,0.15)
```

Now you have to browse link
`http://faculty.washington.edu/ezivot/econ424/portfolio.r` and save this R code in
the file `portfolio.R`. You should use the following command to access the function
developed under `portoflio.R`:

```
> source("portfolio.R")
```

To calculate portfolio expected return and standard deviations, we require return, weights,
and covariance matrix. Now we have all the data and can use the following commands to
generate portfolio expected return and risk:

```
>weightedport = getPortfolio(avg_ret,covariance_mat,weights)
>weightedport
Call:
getPortfolio(er = avg_ret, cov.mat = covariance_mat, weights = weights)
Portfolio expected return:      0.0004109398
Portfolio standard deviation:   0.01525882
Portfolio weights:
MSFT.CloseFB.CloseGOOG.CloseAAPL.Close
      0.20        0.30        0.35        0.15
```

The global minimum variance portfolio is obtained using the following command. You can
see here that portfolio weights are different compared to weights in the previous command
and this set of weights helps to generate a portfolio which has lower standard deviation:

```
>minvar_port<- globalMin.portfolio(avg_ret, covariance_mat)
>minvar_port
Call:
globalMin.portfolio(er = avg_ret, cov.mat = covariance_mat)
Portfolio expected return:      0.0007211767
Portfolio standard deviation:   0.01349528
Portfolio weights:
MSFT.CloseFB.CloseGOOG.CloseAAPL.Close
0.5889      0.2415      0.1001      0.0696
```

Now suppose you want to generate a portfolio which has 0.0002 as the expected return.
The following command will help generate portfolio weights and standard deviation for the
portfolio of expected return 0.0002:

```
>rf<- 0.0002
>effcient_port<- efficient.portfolio(avg_ret, covariance_mat,rf)
>effcient_port
Call:
efficient.portfolio(er = avg_ret, cov.mat = covariance_mat, target.return =
2e-04)
Portfolio expected return:      2e-04
Portfolio standard deviation:   0.0169678
```

```
Portfolio weights:
MSFT.CloseFB.CloseGOOG.CloseAAPL.Close
0.4626    -0.1292    0.4184    0.2482
```

A tangency portfolio is a portfolio of risky assets which has the highest Sharpe's slope. To compute this, I used the `tangency.portfolio()` function:

```
>tangency_port<- tangency.portfolio(avg_ret,covariance_mat , rf)
>tangency_port
Call:
tangency.portfolio(er = avg_ret, cov.mat = covariance_mat, risk.free =
2e-04)
Portfolio expected return:       0.4942792
Portfolio standard deviation:    0.02226374
Portfolio weights:
MSFT.CloseFB.CloseGOOG.CloseAAPL.Close
0.8062     0.8797    -0.4480    -0.2378
```

We have already calculated the global minimum variance portfolio, and the other portfolio with maximum expected return can be considered as the second portfolio. Call these portfolios *P1* and *P2* respectively. Now, for any α, another portfolio can be constructed as follows:

$$P = \alpha * P_1 + (1-\alpha) * P_2 \ (5.5)$$

The efficient frontier can be calculated using the following command. This generates 50 portfolios using α in the range -2 to 2:

```
>efficient_frontier<- efficient.frontier(avg_ret, covariance_mat,
alpha.min=-2,alpha.max=2, nport=50)
```

Next, in *Figure 5.9*, I plotted the efficient frontier, red and blue points for minimum variance and tangency portfolio, and tangent to the frontier:

```
>plot(efficient_frontier, plot.assets=T)
>points(minvar_port$sd, minvar_port$er, col="blue")
>points(tangency_port$sd,tangency_port$er, col="red")
>tangenet_sharpe_ratio = (tangency_port$er - rf)/tangency_port$sd
>abline(a=rf, b=tangenet_sharpe_ratio)
```

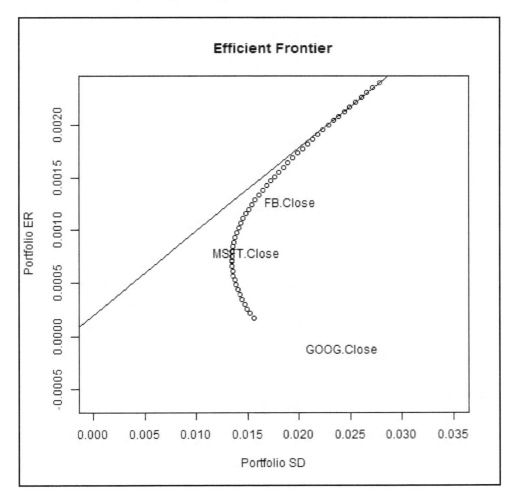

Figure 5.9: Efficient frontier for portfolio and tangent line

Questions

1. How do you import stock data into the R workspace from Yahoo Finance?
2. How do you generate a momentum strategy using moving average crossover?
3. Which package helps to calculate the performance metrics of a strategy?
4. How do you calculate the covariance matrix for a portfolio consisting of five stocks?
5. Extract MSFT data from Yahoo and test that the closing price series is non-stationary.
6. Use the distance method to generate trading signals which exit when the spread reverts to mean.
7. How do you test a pair of stocks for co-integration and write code to test it?
8. How do you calculate hedge ratio and how does it helps in trading?
9. How do you calculate portfolio beta? Show it using an example.
10. How do you use the fundamental factor to create quantiles and quantile spread?
11. Write code to calculate portfolio expected _return and standard deviation.
12. How do you calculate the efficient frontier and plot it using the R command?

Summary

In this chapter, I presented different concepts of trading using R. I started with trend following strategy and explained in depth how the trading signals are generated and how various parameters related to its performance are captured. Momentum strategies was followed by pairs trading using three different methods. The first method covered was distance based pairs trading, the second was correlation based, and the third and final method was co-integration based pairs trading. Sometimes, trading in a portfolio is important to control the risk and reward ratio and for that I have covered capital asset pricing, the multi factor model, and portfolio construction. I used Systematic Investor Toolbox for implementing portfolio ideas.

In the next chapter, I will explain trading strategies using machine learning algorithms, which are gaining in popularity. Machine learning algorithms learn automatically from historical market behavior and try to mimic this behavior.

6

Trading Using Machine Learning

In the capital market, machine learning-based algorithmic trading is quite popular these days and many companies are putting a lot of effort into machine learning-based algorithms which are either proprietary or for clients. Machine learning algorithms are programmed in such a way that they learn continuously and change their behavior automatically. This helps to identify new patterns when they emerge in the market. Sometimes patterns in the capital market are so complex they cannot be captured by humans. Even if humans somehow managed to find one pattern, humans do not have the tendency to find it efficiently. Complexity in patterns forces people to look for alternative mechanisms which identify such complex patterns accurately and efficiently.

In the previous chapter, you got the feel of momentum, pairs-trading-based algorithmic trading, and portfolio construction. In this chapter, I will explain step by step a few supervised and unsupervised machine learning algorithms which are being used in algorithm trading:

- Logistic regression neural network
- Neural network
- Deep neural network
- K means algorithm
- K nearest neighborhood
- Support vector machine
- Decision tree
- Random forest

A few of the packages used in this chapter are `quantmod`, `nnet`, `genalg`, `caret`, `PerformanceAnalytics`, `deepnet`, `h2o`, `clue`, `e1071`, `randomForest`, **and** `party`.

Logistic regression neural network

Market direction is very important for investors or traders. Predicting market direction is quite a challenging task as market data involves lots of noise. The market moves either upward or downward and the nature of market movement is binary. A logistic regression model help us to fit a model using binary behavior and forecast market direction. Logistic regression is one of the probabilistic models which assigns probability to each event. I am assuming you are well versed with extracting data from Yahoo as you have studied this in previous chapters. Here again, I am going to use the `quantmod` package. The next three commands are used for loading the package into the workspace, importing data into R from the `yahoo` repository and extracting only the closing price from the data:

```
>library("quantmod")
>getSymbols("^DJI",src="yahoo")
>dji<- DJI[,"DJI.Close"]
```

The input data to the logistic regression is constructed using different indicators, such as moving average, standard deviation, RSI, MACD, Bollinger Bands, and so on, which has some predictive power in market direction, that is, `Up` or `Down`. These indicators can be constructed using the following commands:

```
>avg10<- rollapply(dji,10,mean)
>avg20<- rollapply(dji,20,mean)
>std10<- rollapply(dji,10,sd)
>std20<- rollapply(dji,20,sd)
>rsi5<- RSI(dji,5,"SMA")
>rsi14<- RSI(dji,14,"SMA")
>macd12269<- MACD(dji,12,26,9,"SMA")
>macd7205<- MACD(dji,7,20,5,"SMA")
>bbands<- BBands(dji,20,"SMA",2)
```

The following commands are to create variable direction with either `Up` direction (1) or `Down` direction (0). `Up` direction is created when the current price is greater than the 20 days previous price and `Down` direction is created when the current price is less than the 20 days previous price:

```
>direction<- NULL
>direction[dji> Lag(dji,20)] <- 1
>direction[dji< Lag(dji,20)] <- 0
```

Now we have to bind all columns consisting of price and indicators, which is shown in the following command:

```
>dji<-
cbind(dji,avg10,avg20,std10,std20,rsi5,rsi14,macd12269,macd7205,bbands,dire
ction)
```

The dimension of the `dji` object can be calculated using `dim()`. I used `dim()` over `dji` and saved the output in `dm()`. `dm()` has two values stored: the first value is the number of rows and the second value is the number of columns in `dji`. Column names can be extracted using `colnames()`. The third command is used to extract the name for the last column. Next I replaced the column name with a particular name, `Direction`:

```
>dm<- dim(dji)
>dm
[1] 2493    16
>colnames(dji)[dm[2]]
[1] "..11"
>colnames(dji)[dm[2]] <- "Direction"
>colnames(dji)[dm[2]]
[1] "Direction"
```

We have extracted the **Dow Jones Index (DJI)** data into the R workspace. Now, to implement logistic regression, we should divide the data into two parts. The first part is in-sample data and the second part is out-sample data.

In-sample data is used for the model building process and out-sample data is used for evaluation purposes. This process also helps to control the variance and bias in the model. The next four lines are for in-sample start, in-sample end, out-sample start, and out-sample end dates:

```
>issd<- "2010-01-01"
>ised<- "2014-12-31"
>ossd<- "2015-01-01"
>osed<- "2015-12-31"
```

The following two commands are to get the row number for the dates, that is, the variable isrow extracts row numbers for the in-sample date range and osrow extracts the row numbers for the out-sample date range:

```
>isrow<- which(index(dji) >= issd& index(dji) <= ised)
>osrow<- which(index(dji) >= ossd& index(dji) <= osed)
```

The variables isdji and osdji are the in-sample and out-sample datasets respectively:

```
>isdji<- dji[isrow,]
>osdji<- dji[osrow,]
```

If you look at the in-sample data, that is, isdji, you will realize that the scaling of each column is different: a few columns are in the scale of 100, a few others are in the scale of 10,000, and a few others are in the scale of 1. Difference in scaling can put your results in trouble as higher weights are being assigned to higher scaled variables. So before moving ahead, you should consider standardizing the dataset. I will use the following formula:

$$\text{standardized data} = \frac{X - Mean(X)}{Std(X)} \quad \ldots\ldots\ldots\ldots\ldots\ldots\ldots(6.1)$$

The mean and standard deviation of each column using apply() can be seen here:

```
>isme<- apply(isdji,2,mean)
>isstd<- apply(isdji,2,sd)
```

An identity matrix of dimension equal to the in-sample data is generated using the following command, which is going to be used for normalization:

```
>isidn<- matrix(1,dim(isdji)[1],dim(isdji)[2])
```

Use formula 6.1 to standardize the data:

```
>norm_isdji<-   (isdji - t(isme*t(isidn))) / t(isstd*t(isidn))
```

The preceding line also standardizes the direction column, that is, the last column. We don't want direction to be standardized so I replace the last column again with variable direction for the in-sample data range:

```
>dm<- dim(isdji)
>norm_isdji[,dm[2]] <- direction[isrow]
```

Now we have created all the data required for model building. You should build a logistic regression model and it will help you to predict market direction based on in-sample data. First, in this step, I created a formula which has direction as dependent and all other columns as independent variables. Then I used a generalized linear model, that is, `glm()`, to fit a model which has formula, family, and dataset:

```
>formula<- paste("Direction ~ .",sep="")
>model<- glm(formula,family="binomial",norm_isdji)
```

A summary of the model can be viewed using the following command:

```
>summary(model)
```

Next use `predict()` to fit values on the same dataset to estimate the best fitted value:

```
>pred<- predict(model,norm_isdji)
```

Once you have fitted the values, you should try to convert it to probability using the following command. This will convert the output into probabilistic form and the output will be in the range [0,1]:

```
>prob<- 1 / (1+exp(-(pred)))
```

Figure 6.1 is plotted using the following commands. The first line of the code shows that we divide the figure into two rows and one column, where the first figure is for prediction of the model and the second figure is for probability:

```
>par(mfrow=c(2,1))
>plot(pred,type="l")
>plot(prob,type="l")
```

`head()` can be used to look at the first few values of the variable:

```
>head(prob)
2010-01-042010-01-05 2010-01-06 2010-01-07
0.8019197  0.4610468  0.7397603  0.9821293
```

The following figure shows the above-defined variable `pred`, which is a real number, and its conversion between 0 and 1, which represents probability, that is, `prob`, using the preceding transformation:

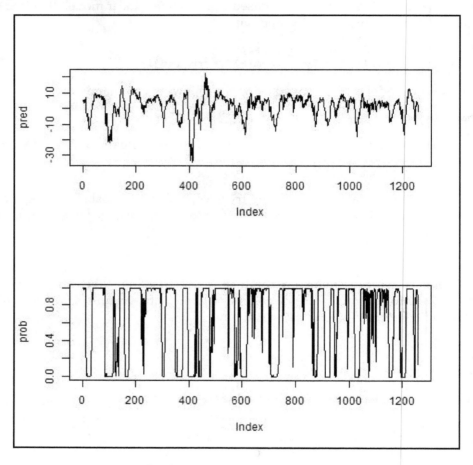

Figure 6.1: Prediction and probability distribution of DJI

As probabilities are in the range of (0,1) so is our vector `prob`. Now, to classify them as one of the two classes, I considered `Up` direction (1) when `prob` is greater than `0.5` and `Down` direction (0) when `prob` is less than `0.5`. This assignment can be done using the following commands. `prob> 0.5` generate true for points where it is greater and `pred_direction[prob> 0.5]` assigns 1 to all such points. Similarly, the next statement shows assignment 0 when probability is less than or equal to `0.5`:

```
>pred_direction<- NULL
>pred_direction[prob> 0.5] <- 1
>pred_direction[prob<= 0.5] <- 0
```

Once we have figured out the predicted direction, we should check model accuracy: how much our model has predicted `Up` direction as `Up` direction and `Down` as `Down`. There might be some scenarios where it predicted the opposite of what it is, such as predicting down when it is actually `Up` and vice versa. We can use the `caret` package to calculate `confusionMatrix()`, which gives a matrix as an output. All diagonal elements are correctly predicted and off-diagonal elements are errors or wrongly predicted. One should aim to reduce the off-diagonal elements in a confusion matrix:

```
>install.packages('caret')
>library(caret)
>matrix<- confusionMatrix(pred_direction,norm_isdji$Direction)
>matrix
Confusion Matrix and Statistics
                       Reference
Prediction             0                      1
        0             362                     35
        1              42                    819
Accuracy : 0.9388        95% CI : (0.9241, 0.9514)
    No Information Rate : 0.6789    P-Value [Acc>NIR] : <2e-16
Kappa : 0.859            Mcnemar's Test P-Value : 0.4941
Sensitivity : 0.8960     Specificity : 0.9590
PosPredValue : 0.9118    NegPred Value : 0.9512
Prevalence : 0.3211        Detection Rate : 0.2878
Detection Prevalence : 0.3156    Balanced Accuracy : 0.9275
```

The preceding table shows we have got 94% correct prediction, as 362+819 = 1181 are correct predictions out of 1258 (sum of all four values). Prediction above 80% over in-sample data is generally assumed good prediction; however, 80% is not fixed, one has to figure out this value based on the dataset and industry. Now you have implemented the logistic regression model, which has predicted 94% correctly, and need to test it for generalization power. One should test this model using out-sample data and test its accuracy. The first step is to standardize the out-sample data using formula (6.1). Here mean and standard deviations should be the same as those used for in-sample normalization:

```
>osidn<- matrix(1,dim(osdji)[1],dim(osdji)[2])
>norm_osdji<-  (osdji - t(isme*t(osidn))) / t(isstd*t(osidn))
>norm_osdji[,dm[2]] <- direction[osrow]
```

Next we use `predict()` on the out-sample data and use this value to calculate probability:

```
>ospred<- predict(model,norm_osdji)
>osprob<- 1 / (1+exp(-(ospred)))
```

Once probabilities are determined for the out-sample data, you should put it into either Up or Down classes using the following commands. `ConfusionMatrix()` here will generate a matrix for the out-sample data:

```
>ospred_direction<- NULL
>ospred_direction[osprob> 0.5] <- 1
>ospred_direction[osprob<= 0.5] <- 0
>osmatrix<- confusionMatrix(ospred_direction,norm_osdji$Direction)
>osmatrix
Confusion Matrix and Statistics
                      Reference
Prediction            0                          1
        0             115                        26
        1             12                         99
Accuracy : 0.8492          95% CI : (0.7989, 0.891)
```

This shows 85% accuracy on the out-sample data. Quality of accuracy is beyond the scope of the book so I am not going to cover whether out-sample accuracy is good or bad and what the techniques are to improve this performance. A realistic trading model also accounts for trading cost and market slippage, which decrease the winning odds significantly. The next thing to be done is to devise a trading strategy using predicted directions. I will explain how to implement an automated trading strategy using predicted signals in the next section.

Neural network

In the previous section, I implemented a model using two classes. In reality, it might be possible that traders do not want to enter trade when the market is range-bound. That is to say, we have to add one more class, Nowhere, to the existing two classes. Now we have three classes: Up, Down, and Nowhere. I will be using an artificial neural network to predict Up, Down, or Nowhere direction. Traders buy (sell) when they anticipate a bullish (bearish) trend in some time and no investment when the market is moving Nowhere. An artificial neural network with feedforward backpropagation will be implemented in this section. A neural network requires input and output data to the neural network. Closing prices and indicators derived from closing prices are input layer nodes and three classes (Up, Down, and Nowhere) are output layer nodes. However, there is no limit on the number of nodes in the input layer. I will use a dataset consisting of prices and indicators used in the logistic regression. However, it is not mandatory to use same dataset. If you would like to use different indicators, you can do so. You can also increase or decrease the number of indicators in the dataset; it is left to the reader to construct a dataset of their choice. I will continue this section using the same the dataset that is used in logistic regression except direction. In this section, we have Nowhere as the third dimension in the direction so I have to calculate the direction parameter again to train the neural network:

```
>getSymbols("^DJI",src="yahoo")
>dji<- DJI[,"DJI.Close"]
> ret <- Delt(dji)
>avg10<- rollapply(dji,10,mean)
>avg20<- rollapply(dji,20,mean)
>std10<- rollapply(dji,10,sd)
>std20<- rollapply(dji,20,sd)
>rsi5<- RSI(dji,5,"SMA")
>rsi14<- RSI(dji,14,"SMA")
>macd12269<- MACD(dji,12,26,9,"SMA")
>macd7205<- MACD(dji,7,20,5,"SMA")
>bbands<- BBands(dji,20,"SMA",2)
```

I will generate Up (Down) direction when the return over the last 20 days is greater (less) than 2% (-2%), and Nowhere when the return over the last 20 days is between -2% and 2%.

The first line generates a data frame named direction which consists of NA and a number of rows the same as the number of rows in `dji` and one column. The second command is the return over the last 20 days. The parameter value 20 is sacrosanct; however, you can choose any value you wish to. The third, fourth, and fifth commands are basically the assignment of Up, `Down` and `NoWhere` direction as per the condition:

```
>direction<- data.frame(matrix(NA,dim(dji)[1],1))
>lagret<- (dji - Lag(dji,20)) / Lag(dji,20)
>direction[lagret> 0.02] <- "Up"
>direction[lagret< -0.02] <- "Down"
>direction[lagret< 0.02 &lagret> -0.02] <- "NoWhere"
```

Closing price and indicators are clubbed into one variable called `dji` using the following command line:

```
>dji<-
cbind(dji,avg10,avg20,std10,std20,rsi5,rsi14,macd12269,macd7205,bbands)
```

Data for the neural network is divided into three parts, that is, training dataset, validating dataset, and testing dataset. Training data should be used for training the neural network; however, validating data should be used for validating estimated parameters and testing dataset to measure the accuracy of the prediction. I have used the following `date` variables to define the date range and extract data as per the date range:

```
>train_sdate<- "2010-01-01"
>train_edate<- "2013-12-31"
>vali_sdate<- "2014-01-01"
>vali_edate<- "2014-12-31"
>test_sdate<- "2015-01-01"
>test_edate<- "2015-12-31"
```

Date ranges for the three datasets can be constructed using the following commands, where `train_sdate` and `train_edate` define training period start and end dates respectively. Similarly, validating and testing period dates are also used.

The function `which()` is used to generate row numbers where the date is greater than and equal to the start date and less than and equal to the end date:

```
>trainrow<- which(index(dji) >= train_sdate& index(dji) <= train_edate)
>valirow<- which(index(dji) >= vali_sdate& index(dji) <= vali_edate)
>testrow<- which(index(dji) >= test_sdate& index(dji) <= test_edate)
```

Now, using the preceding row numbers, you should extract data for training, validating, and testing periods:

```
>traindji<- dji[trainrow,]
>validji<- dji[valirow,]
>testdji<- dji[testrow,]
```

The following commands are used to calculate the mean and standard deviations of training data column wise. The function `apply()` uses data as the first parameter, direction as the second parameter, in which we would like to apply a certain function, and function is provided as the third parameter:

```
>trainme<- apply(traindji,2,mean)
>trainstd<- apply(traindji,2,sd)
```

To normalize the three datasets, we have to create three identity matrices of dimensions equal to the training, validating, and testing data dimensions.

The following commands do this nicely:

```
>trainidn<- (matrix(1,dim(traindji)[1],dim(traindji)[2]))
>valiidn<- (matrix(1,dim(validji)[1],dim(validji)[2]))
>testidn<- (matrix(1,dim(testdji)[1],dim(testdji)[2]))
```

Training, validating, and testing data is normalized using the following commands. `t()` is used for transposing of the data frame, matrix, or vector:

```
>norm_traindji<-  (traindji - t(trainme*t(trainidn))) /
t(trainstd*t(trainidn))
>norm_validji<-  (validji - t(trainme*t(valiidn))) / t(trainstd*t(valiidn))
>norm_testdji<-  (testdji - t(trainme*t(testidn))) / t(trainstd*t(testidn))
```

The previously defined normalized data consists of price and indicator values. We should also define training, validating, and testing period direction using the following commands:

```
>traindir<- direction[trainrow,1]
>validir<- direction[valirow,1]
>testdir<- direction[testrow,1]
```

Now, I assume the package `nnet()` is installed on your machine. If not, you should `install.package()` to install it. Once installed, you should use the following line to load this into the workspace:

```
>library(nnet)
```

The following line sets the seed for the neural network, otherwise every time the neural network will start with some random weights and output will differ. We should use `set.seed()` to get the same output every time you run this command. The next line explains neural network fitting, where the first parameter is the set of all normalized columns, the second parameter is the target vector for training period dates which consist of directions, the third parameter is the number of neurons in the hidden layer, and the fourth parameter is the trace, which prints output at the end of execution. I used hidden layer neurons as `4`; however, you should optimize this parameter. I do not want output to get printed at the end of the execution unless I explicitly want it so I use `trade=F`:

```
>set.seed(1)
>model<- nnet(norm_traindji,class.ind(traindir),size=4,trace=F)
```

In the second parameter, you must have observed the use of the `class.ind()` function. This function converts three classes to three columns where every column corresponds to each class and each column has `1` at the place where it has the same class, otherwise `0`.

You can see the model output using the following:

```
>model
a 15-4-3 network with 79 weights
```

There are a few more parameters in `nnet()` which you can set as per your requirement. For more information on `nnet()`, you should type the following command on the command prompt:

```
> ? nnet
```

This explains the neural network architecture, which is 15-4-3. This shows three layers; the first layer (input layer), second layer (hidden layer), and third layer (output layer) have 15, 4, and 3 neurons respectively, and 79 generated weight parameters. You can see that the number of neurons in the first layer is equal to the number of columns in norm_traindji:

```
>dim(norm_traindji)
[1] 1006    15
```

You can see that output has 15 columns, which is the same as the number of input data features. That number of columns are 15 so does the number of neuron in input layer. The second parameter is the number of neurons in the hidden layer, which is provided as input in nnet() (in our case, this is 4), and the final parameter is the number of neurons in the output layer, which is 3, the same as the number of directions (Up, Down and NoWhere). You must use predict() using the trained neural network over the validating dataset:

```
>vali_pred<- predict(model,norm_validji)
>head(vali_pred)
Down            NoWhere             Up
2014-01-02      01.336572e-01       1
2014-01-03      0 1.336572e-01      1
2014-01-06      0 1.336572e-01      1
2014-01-07      0 1.336572e-01      1
2014-01-08      0 8.666505e-02      1
2014-01-09      0 5.337864e-07      1
```

Now, we have to figure out the predicted direction using the above information. I define 0.5 as the threshold and pick directions which have a value greater than 0.5. The first line creates a data frame of length equal to the vali_pred length. The next commands are used for each class one by one; it checks condition and writes the name of class where vali_pred is greater than 0.5:

```
>vali_pred_class<- data.frame(matrix(NA,dim(vali_pred)[1],1))
>vali_pred_class[vali_pred[,"Down"] > 0.5,1] <- "Down"
>vali_pred_class[vali_pred[,"NoWhere"] > 0.5,1] <- "NoWhere"
>vali_pred_class[vali_pred[,"Up"] > 0.5,1] <- "Up"
```

Now we are going to create a confusion matrix to check for its accuracy. First of all, load the caret package into the workspace and use `confusionMatrix()` over the predicted class and original class for the validating dataset:

```
>library(caret)
>matrix<- confusionMatrix(vali_pred_class[,1],validir)
>matrix
Confusion Matrix and Statistics
          Reference
Prediction  Down NoWhere Up
  Down        33       3  0
NoWhere        6     125  8
  Up           0      15 62
Overall Statistic
Accuracy : 0.873                   95% CI : (0.8255, 0.9115)
    No Information Rate : 0.5675        P-Value [Acc>NIR] : <2.2e-16
Kappa : 0.7811              Mcnemar'sTest P-Value : NA
Statistics by Class:
                     Class: Down Class: NoWhereClass: Up
Sensitivity             0.8462        0.8741     0.8857
Specificity             0.9859        0.8716     0.9176
PosPred Value           0.9167        0.8993     0.8052
NegPred Value           0.9722        0.8407     0.9543
Prevalence              0.1548        0.5675     0.2778
Detection Rate          0.1310        0.4960     0.2460
Detection Prevalence    0.1429        0.5516     0.3056
Balanced Accuracy       0.9160        0.8728     0.9016
```

If you look at the accuracy level in the result output, you can see accuracy is 87% and this level of accuracy is quite good. This 87% accuracy for a model trained on training data and accuracy is tested on validating data. Now we should also check accuracy on testing data and check its generalization power. Normalization of the testing dataset is already above so I go to the `predict()` command right away:

```
>test_pred<- predict(model,norm_testdji)
```

Classes for the testing data are defined as the same as the validating data:

```
>test_pred_class<- data.frame(matrix(NA,dim(test_pred)[1],1))
>test_pred_class[test_pred[,"Down"] > 0.5,1] <- "Down"
>test_pred_class[test_pred[,"NoWhere"] > 0.5,1] <- "NoWhere"
>test_pred_class[test_pred[,"Up"] > 0.5,1] <- "Up"
```

`ConfusionMatrix()` is generated for testing data using the following command and accuracy on testing dataset is 82% as can be seen here; this prediction accuracy is very similar to the prediction accuracy on the validating dataset. We found results are consistently good as compared to the validating data:

```
>test_matrix<- confusionMatrix(test_pred_class[,1],testdir)
>test_matrix
Confusion Matrix and Statistics
                      Reference
Prediction      Down            NoWhere           Up
    Down          31               4               0
Nowhere           26              138              8
    Up             0               6               38
Overall Statistics
Accuracy : 0.8247            95% CI :  (0.7719, 0.8696)
```

Consistency in accuracy across validating and testing datasets shows its generalization power and this model got good generalization power. Now, as we have got classes, the next thing is we should use these classes for signal generation. People buy when they anticipate Up direction and sell when they anticipate Down direction. So I generate signals using the same human psychology and the following command does that for you:

```
>signal<- ifelse(test_pred_class =="Up",1,ifelse(test_pred_class
=="Down",-1,0))
Return  ofdji closing price is calculated below
> ret<- ret[testrow]
```

Trade return is calculated as defined here. `Lag()` is used over signal as the signal generated in the previous session contributes to trade return. I am assuming cost as `0`:

```
>cost<-  0
>trade_ret<- ret * Lag(signal)- cost
```

To evaluate the performance of the strategy, we have to load the package and use all relevant commands defined in the following section:

```
>library(PerformanceAnalytics)
>cumm_ret<- Return.cumulative(trade_ret)
>annual_ret<- Return.annualized(trade_ret)
```

The following commands generate *Figure 6.2*, which shows cumulative return, daily return, and drawdown. We can see the cumulative return of the strategy is negative. Generating profitable strategy is beyond the scope of this book. This book only explains how one should go about implementing strategy using R:

```
>charts.PerformanceSummary(trade_ret)
```

The output is as follows:

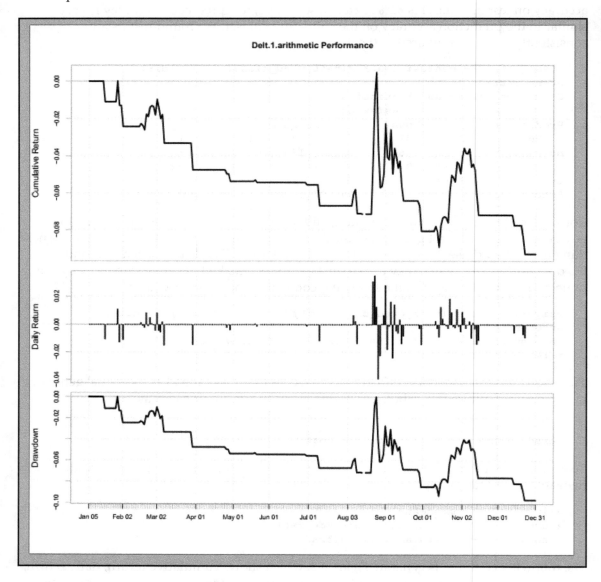

Figure 6.2: Cumulative return, daily return, and drawdown for DJI

Deep neural network

Deep neural networks are under the broad category of deep learning. In contrast to neural networks, deep neural networks contain multiple hidden layers. The number of hidden layers can vary from problem to problem and needs to be optimized. R has many packages, such as `darch`, `deepnet`, `deeplearning`, and `h20`, which can create deep networks. However, I will use the `deepnet` package in particular and apply a deep neural network on **DJI** data. The package `deepnet` can be installed and loaded to the workspace using the following commands:

```
>install.packages('deepnet')
>library(deepnet)
```

I will use `set.seed()` to generate uniform output and `dbn.dnn.train()` is used for training deep neural networks. The parameter `hidden` is used for the number of hidden layers and the number of neurons in each layer.

In the below example, I have used a three hidden layer structure and 3, 4, and 6 neurons in the first, second, and third hidden layers respectively. `class.ind()` is again used to convert three directions into column vector, where each column represents one direction:

```
>set.seed(1)
>model<- dbn.dnn.train(norm_traindji,class.ind(traindir),hidden=c(3,4,6))
```

The following command is to generate the output of three classes using the normalization validation dataset:

```
>nn.predict(model,norm_validji)
```

To obtain the accuracy of the model over the validation dataset, you can also use following command. I chose `t=0.4` just for the purpose of showing results. You should use a value as per your requirement. It will create each column of output to certain direction if its value is greater than `0.4`:

```
>nn.test(model,norm_validji,class.ind(validir),t=0.4)
[1] 0.7222222
```

H2o is another package which can be used for deep neural network learning. It is implemented in Java and can use multithreads and multinodes of the CPU; however, deepnet is implemented in R itself and uses only a single thread and doesn't have the flexibility to use multithreads and multinodes of the CPU. The following commands install and load it into the workspace:

```
>install.packages(h2o)
>library(h2o)
```

Next I combined the normalized training data and direction into one variable. I converted the normalized data into a data frame as the original data in xts, zoo format. As the normalized training data is numeric, if I had not converted it into a data frame then adding traindir, which is character, would have converted traindir to NAs. To avoid this, I used a data frame in the following commands and the class of the input variables can be verified using the next two commands:

```
>data<- cbind(as.data.frame(norm_traindji),traindir)
>class(norm_traindji)
[1] "xts" "zoo"
>class(traindir)
[1] "character"
```

Once I am done with creating a variable then I convert it into an h2o object because model fitting requires input data to be in h2o format. In the following command, the first parameter is the variable which I would like to be converted and the second parameter is the name of the class in which we would like the first parameter to be converted.

In the following command, I would like to convert data into h2o type. This can also be verified using the second command:

```
>datah2o<- as.h2o(data, "h2o")
>class(datah2o)
[1] "H2OFrame"
```

We looked into the dimension of the h2o class object which I just created, where the last column is the direction vector and the remaining columns are normalized data columns:

```
>dim(datah2o)
[1] 1006    16
```

Below, h2o.deeplearning() trains a deep neural network with a four hidden layer architecture and the number of neurons is 4,5,2, and 7 respectively in each hidden layer. The first parameter is the vector of column number 1 to 15 assumed as input data and the second parameter 16 implies the 16th column as output supplied to the deep neural network for training. The third parameter is datah2o, which is supplied for deep neural network fitting, and the fourth parameter is hidden. The parameter hidden has important significance here, which shows the total number of hidden layers, and the following example shows four hidden layers: the first hidden layer has 4 neurons, the second has 5 hidden neurons, and the third and fourth layers have 2 and 7 neurons:

```
> model    <-
h2o.deeplearning(1:15,16,training_frame=datah2o,hidden=c(4,5,2,7))
>vali_pred<- predict(model,as.h2o(norm_validji,"h2o"))
       predict      Down            NoWhere          Up
1        Up        8.774719e-06    0.05996300       0.9400282
2        Up        4.715592e-06    0.04561811       0.9543772
3        Up        8.522070e-06    0.06120060       0.9387909
4        Up        1.384947e-06    0.02668458       0.9733140
5        Up        3.698133e-06    0.04144544       0.9585509
6        Up        2.016126e-06    0.03151435       0.9684836
[252 rows x 4 columns]
```

As vali_pred is of H2OFrame, we should convert it to a data frame to apply the following operations:

```
>vali_pred<- as.data.frame(vali_pred)
>vali_pred_class<- data.frame(matrix(NA,dim(vali_pred)[1],1))
>vali_pred_class[vali_pred[,"Down"] > 0.5,1] <- "Down"
>vali_pred_class[vali_pred[,"NoWhere"] > 0.5,1] <- "NoWhere"
>vali_pred_class[vali_pred[,"Up"] > 0.5,1] <- "Up"
```

I used the caret package and confusionMatrix() to create a misclassification matrix:

```
>library(caret)
>vali_matrix<- confusionMatrix(vali_pred_class[,1],validir)
```

As we have done this for validation dataset, if accuracy percentage is within desired limit. We should go ahead and predict directions using the testing data and use those predicted directions to generate trading signals as generated in the *Neural network* section. To generate signal and performance of strategy, you should use the command mentioned in the *Neural network* section.

K means algorithm

The K means algorithm is an unsupervised machine learning algorithm. Unsupervised learning is another way of classifying the data as it does not require labeling of the data. In reality, there are many instances where labeling of the data is not possible, so we require them to classify data based on unsupervised learning. Unsupervised learning uses the similarity between data elements and assigns each data point to its relevant cluster. Each cluster has a set of data points which are similar in nature. The K means algorithm is the most basic unsupervised learning algorithm and it just requires data to plug into the algorithm along with the number of clusters we would like it to cluster returning the vector of cluster labeling for each data point. I used normalized data along with the number of clusters. I used the in-sample data which was used during logistic regression, to be divided into three clusters.

`set.seed()` is used to have the same output in every iteration; without using `set.seed()`, the output changes every time:

```
>clusters<- 3
>set.seed(1)
```

Normalized in-sample and out-sample data has direction (labels) as the last column, which is not required for unsupervised learning. So I removed the last column in both of these datasets using the following command:

```
>norm_isdji<- norm_isdji[,-dm[2]]
>norm_osdji<- norm_osdji[,-dm[2]]
```

Now I do not have any labeling for this data and run `kmeans()`:

```
>model<- kmeans(norm_isdji,clusters)
```

`model$cluser` returns the relevant cluster number corresponding to each data point and `head()` is used to print out the first few:

```
>head(model$cluster)
2010-01-04  2010-01-05   2010-01-06   2010-01-07   2010-01-08
    3           3            3            3            3
```

The preceding command shows the first few data points belong to cluster number 3. Similarly, centers of final clusters can be extracted using the following command:

```
>model$center
```

The number of data points in each cluster can be extracted using the following line of command:

```
>model$size
      260           434              564
```

As we are using k means to cluster, which is unsupervised learning, performance or accuracy can be calculated using the ratio of the sum of squares to the total sum of squares. The sum of squares between clusters and the total sum of squares can be extracted using the following commands:

```
>model$tot.withinss
9703.398
>model$totss
19129.26
```

The ratio of these values indicates the sum of squares within clusters with respect to the total sum of squares. In our case, it is around 50.7%, as is shown below, which shows the sum of squares within cluster is almost half of the total sum of squares. The model which minimizes this ratio is chosen over a range of models. This is a minimization problem:

```
>model$tot.withinss / model$totss
0.5072543
```

If we are satisfied with the accuracy of the algorithm, we will go ahead and use this fitted model to predict clusters for the out-sample dataset, which can be done using the predict() command:

```
>ospredict<- cl_predict(model,norm_osdji)
```

The next line extracts the first few predicted cluster numbers for the out-sample data using head():

```
>head(ospredict)
2      2         2          2          2          2
```

This algorithm assigns each data point from the out-sample dataset into any one of the clusters, where each cluster belongs to one of the market directions, that is, Up, Down, and Nowhere. It is very important to figure out upfront which cluster represents Up and which ones represent Down and Nowhere. Once you recognize each cluster as either Up, Down, or Nowhere, we can enter a relevant trade when a data point falls in the relevant cluster. For example, in the preceding case, the output is two for the first six data points, which implies that these data points lie in the same cluster, but we do not know whether this is the Up cluster, Down cluster, or Nowhere cluster. You can figure out this using the average price of data points in one cluster and if the average is greater than a certain threshold from the first data point then you can consider it as the Up cluster; if the average price is less than a certain threshold from the first data point then this is the Down cluster; and it is the Nowhere cluster if the average price is within a certain threshold above and below the first data point. There are other techniques as well to figure out the class of the cluster; you can use any technique, whichever you would like to use. When a data point falls in the Up cluster, we enter long trade; it happens for the other two clusters as well. We should design a trading strategy by looking into each cluster. Behavior recognition is critical as this will help us design a trading strategy. We should know which cluster represents the Up, Down, or Nowhere direction. We should generate a trading signal and return using the example mentioned in the *Neural network* section.

K nearest neighborhood

K nearest neighborhood is another supervised learning algorithm which helps us to figure out the class of the out-sample data among k classes. K has to be chosen appropriately, otherwise it might increase variance or bias, which reduces the generalization capacity of the algorithm. I am considering Up, Down, and Nowhere as three classes which have to be recognized on the out-sample data. This is based on Euclidian distance. For each data point in the out-sample data, we calculate its distance from all data points in the in-sample data. Each data point has a vector of distances and the K distance which is close enough will be selected and the final decision about the class of the data point is based on a weighted combination of all k neighborhoods:

```
>library(class)
```

The K nearest neighborhood function in R does not need labeled values in the training data. So I am going to use the normalized in-sample and normalized out-sample data created in the *Logistic regression* section and remove the last column in the normalized in-sample and normalized out-sample data:

```
>norm_isdji<- norm_isdji[,-dm[2]]
>norm_osdji<- norm_osdji[,-dm[2]]
```

Labeling of the training data is a vector of three directions, that is, Up, Down, and Nowhere, which is constructed using the following command:

```
>lagret<- (dji - Lag(dji,20)) / Lag(dji,20)
```

lagret is the return over the last 20 data points and is used to generate three directions as in the *Neural network* section:

```
>direction[lagret> 0.02] <- "Up"
>direction[lagret< -0.02] <- "Down"
>direction[lagret< 0.02 &lagret> -0.02] <- "NoWhere"
>isdir<- direction[isrow]
>osdir<- direction[osrow]
```

I choose three neighborhoods and fix the set.seed() value to generate the same output every time:

```
>neighborhood<- 3
>set.seed(1)
>model<- knn(norm_isdji,norm_osdji,isdir,neighborhood)
```

The knn() model has the first three mandatory parameters which are the normalized in-sample data, the normalized out-sample data, and the training labeled data in our case. The fourth parameter is optional; I supplied 3 as input here. If this is not supplied by the user, R will consider the default value, which is 1. However, 3 is not fixed; it needs to be optimized using multiple values of neighborhood. The knn() function returns classes over the out-sample data which can be checked using the following command:

```
>head(model)
[1]NoWhere       Nowhere        Nowhere         Nowhere         NoWhere
```

Summary() over the model generates the total number of data points in each class, as you can see in the following command. It has generated 44, 172, and 36 data points into the Down, Nowhere, and Up classes respectively:

```
>summary(model)
  Down  NoWhere   Up
   44    172    36
```

We are not sure about the accuracy. We have to test it for accuracy using the following commands. `confusionMatrix()` generates a matrix of counts for correct and wrong predictions:

```
>library(caret)
>matrix<- confusionMatrix(model,osdir)
>matrix
Confusion Matrix and Statistics
          Reference
Prediction Down NoWhere  Up
Down         32     12    0
NoWhere      26    133   13
Up            0      3    3
Overall Statistics
Accuracy : 0.7857            95% CI : (0.7298, 0.8347)
No Information Rate : 0.5873            P-Value [Acc>NIR] : 2.173e-11
```

We also have to minimize off-diagonal elements as these are wrong classified classes. Diagonal elements can be extracted using the following command:

```
>diag(matrix$table)
Down NoWhere   Up
32      133    33
```

We can use a `for` loop over the neighborhood varying from 1 to 30 and find the accuracy at each value. We can pick the optimal value of k, which has the highest and consistent accuracy in its neighborhood.

The following few lines of codes explain this. The `For` loop is used for values from 1 to 30. Inside the `for` loop, I fit model for every value of, that is, `confusionMatrix()` calculate matrix for every i followed by calculation of elements as diagonal and total number of elements in out-sample data. The sum of all elements of `matrix$table` is equal to the number of data points in the out-sample data. The misclassification number is calculated by subtracting `diag` from the total number of points and accuracy is calculated by dividing it by the total number of data points:

```
>  accuracy<- NULL
>for(i in c(1:30))
{
model<- knn(isdji,osdji,isdir,i)
matrix<- confusionMatrix(model,osdir)
diag<- sum(diag(matrix$table))
total<- sum(matrix$table)
accuracy[i] <- (total - diag) / total
}
```

We can check the variable `accuracy` output using `head()`:

```
>head(accuracy)
0.4404762 0.4087302 0.3452381 0.4563492 0.4801587 0.4642857
```

The following command `plot()` generates *Figure 6.3*, which explain accuracy variation across the value of neighborhood. *Figure 6.3* clearly explains the importance of neighborhood, as error is minimum for **k=14** which is assumed to be the optimal value. However, **k=15** spike the error which means **k=14** is not stable in its neighborhood. The value **k=12** is considered stable in its neighborhood as well, so it is left to the reader, how you would like to pick the optimal value:

```
>plot(accuracy, type="l")
```

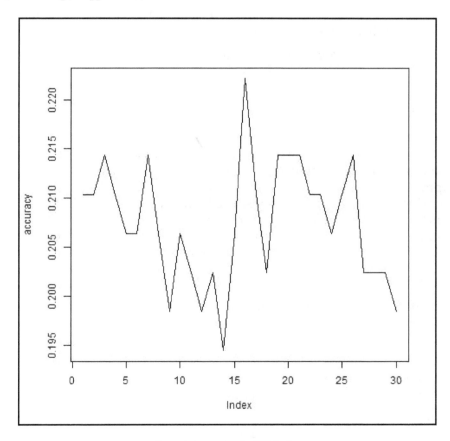

Figure 6.3: Accuracy level for KNN classifier

Support vector machine

Support vector machine is another supervised learning algorithm that can be used for classification and regression. It is able to classify data linearly and nonlinearly using kernel methods. Each data point in the training dataset is labeled, as it is supervised learning, and mapped to the input feature space, and the aim is to classify every point of new data to one of the classes. A data point is an *N* dimension number, as *N* is the number of features, and the problem is to separate this data using *N-1* dimensional hyperplane and this is considered to be a linear classifier. There might be many classifiers which segregate the data; however, the optimal classifier is one which has the maximum margin between classes. The maximum margin hyperplane is one which has the maximum distance from the closest point in each size and the corresponding classifier is called the maximum margin classifier. Package e1071 has all functionalities related to the support vector machine so I am going to install it first using the following command:

```
>install.packages("e1071",dependencies=TRUE)
```

Once it is installed, I am going to load it into the workspace using the following command:

```
>library(e1071)
```

I am going to use the same normalized in-sample and out-sample data that was used in the previous section. The svm() function takes a few more parameters, such as type of support vector machine, kernel type, and a few more. The type parameter has the option to train the support vector machine with respect to a classification or regression problem; by default, it considers classification problems. The kernel type has many options to choose from, such as linear, polynomial, radial, and sigmoid, and the linear kernel type is set as the default parameter. The following command explains the use of support vector machine using only the first two parameters and the remaining default parameters:

```
>model<- svm(norm_isdji,as.factor(isdir))
```

The output of the svm() function is saved in the variable model and can be seen by typing the variable name model on the command prompt:

```
>model
Call:
svm.default(x = norm_isdji, y = as.factor(isdir))
Parameters:
SVM-Type:  C-classification
SVM-Kernel:  radial
cost:  1              gamma:  0.06666667
Number of Support Vectors:  505
```

The preceding results show the type of fitted support vector machine, and the kernel type which is used to fit the model. `predict()` helps to predict direction for the out-sample data:

```
>pred<- predict(model,norm_osdji)
```

The first few predicted directions can be seen using the following line of command:

```
>head(pred)
    1       2       3       4       5
NoWhere NoWhere NoWhere NoWhere NoWhere
```

The `table()` command generates a misclassification matrix and clearly shows 45 misclassified data points in total:

```
>table(pred, osdir)
  osdir
  pred        Down        NoWhere        Up
   Down        32           6             0
 NoWhere       26          139           10
    Up          0            3            36
```

If you would like to see the vectors generated by support vector machine, you can do so using the following command:

```
>model$SV
```

You can also see the corresponding index values using the following command:

```
>model$index
```

The first few index values can be seen using the following command:

```
>head(model$index)
[1]   1   4   5  11  12  34
```

The corresponding coefficients can be accessed using the following command:

```
>model$coefs
```

Decision tree

Tree-based learning algorithms are one of the best supervised learning methods. They generally have stability over results, and great accuracy and generalization capacity to the out-sample dataset. They can map linear and nonlinear relationships quite well. It is generally represented in the form of a tree of variables and its results. The nodes in a tree are variables and end values are decision rules. I am going to use the package `party` to implement a decision tree. This package first need to be installed and loaded into the workspace using the following commands:

```
>install.packages("party")
>library(party)
```

The `ctree()` function is the function to fit the decision tree and it requires a formula and data as mandatory parameters and it has a few more optional variables. The normalized in-sample and normalized out-sample data does not have labels in the data so we have to merge labels in the data.

The following commands bind labels into the normalized in-sample and normalized out-sample data and add a column name to the last column for both datasets:

```
>norm_isdji<- cbind(norm_isdji,isdir)
>norm_osdji<- cbind(norm_osdji,osdir)
>colnames(norm_isdji)[dim(norm_isdji)[2]] <- "Direction"
>colnames(norm_osdji)[dim(norm_osdji)[2]] <- "Direction"
```

Now both datasets have labeled data in the dataset and we now choose to fit the decision tree using `ctree()`.

The first parameter is the formula which has `Direction`, that is, labels as dependent variable and dot (`.`) on the other side of the formula, which means we are considering all other variables as independent variables.

The second parameter is the normalized in-sample data:

```
>model<- ctree(Direction ~ .,norm_isdji)
```

You can use `print()` to see the fitted model output. The variable model is the output of the model so use the following command to see what it contains:

```
>print(model)
```

If you would like to plot the model, this can be done using `plot()`:

```
>plot(model)
```

You can also use `summary()` to get the output in summarized form:

```
>summary(model)
```

`predict()` can be used to estimate the labels using the fitted model and out-sample data. I calculated the dimension of the normalized out-sample data and plugged this data, except the last column, into `predict()`:

```
>dm<- dim(norm_osdji)
>pred<- predict(model,norm_osdji[,1:(dm[2]-1)])
```

The first few values of `pred` can be seen using `head()` as shown here:

```
>head(pred)
      Direction
[1,]  2.040816
[2,]  2.040816
[3,]  2.040816
[4,]  2.040816
```

The command `plot()` generates a graph for the predicted variable `pred`, which is shown in the figure which follows:

```
>plot(pred)
```

The following figure clearly shows three classes: one class is between **1.0** and **1.5**, the second class around **2.0,** and the third class around **3.0**. Data points are clearly distinguished based on the clustered and separation criteria:

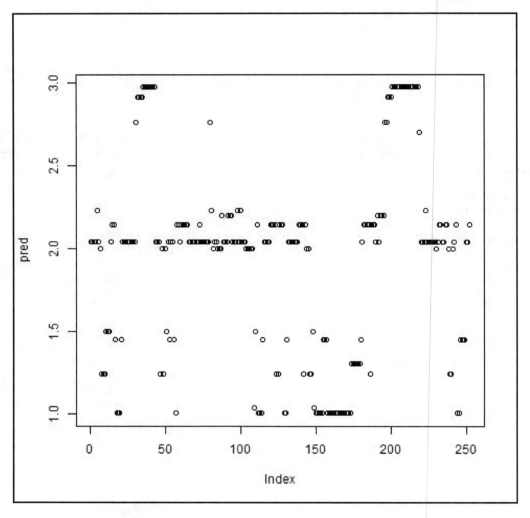

Figure 6.4: Predicted values for normalized out-sample data

Random forest

Random forest is one of the best tree-based methods. Random forest is an ensemble of decision trees and each decision tree has certain weights associated with it. A decision of the random forest is decided like voting, as the majority of decision tree outcomes decide the outcome of the random forest. So we start using the `randomForest` package and this can be installed and loaded using the following commands:

```
>install.packages("randomForest")
>library(randomForest)
```

We can also use the following command to know more about this `randomForest` package, including version, date of release, URL, set of functions implemented in this package, and much more:

```
>library(help=randomForest)
```

Random forest works best for any type of problem and handles classification, regression, and unsupervised problems quite well. Depending upon the type of labeled variable, it will implement relevant decision trees; for example, it uses classification for factor target variables, regression for numeric or integer type target variables, and unsupervised decision tree when the target vector is not defined or completely unknown. I will use the labeled data which I have used throughout this chapter: the normalized in-sample data for model building and normalized out-sample data for model validation. You can see the column names of the input data using the following commands:

```
>names(norm_isdji)
[1] "DJI.Close"   "DJI.Close.1" "DJI.Close.2" "DJI.Close.3" "DJI.Close.4"
"SMA"         "SMA.1"       "macd"        "signal"      "macd.1"
"signal.1"    "dn"          "mavg"        "up"          "pctB"
```

The following command helps you to know the number of independent variables in the input data. It shows our input dataset is going to have 15 independent variables which can be seen previously:

```
>length(names(norm_isdji))
[1] 15
```

As the labeled data has three classes, Up, Down, and Nowhere, we should build a classification random forest. For classification, the `randomForest()` function accepts labeled data as a factor so the first thing is we should check the labeled data type, which can be done using the following command and it shows the labeled data is character:

```
>class(isdir)
[1] "character"
```

The next thing is we should convert the labeled data into factors as `randomForest()` accepts factor labeled data for classification problems. The following two lines convert character data into factors:

```
>isdir<- as.factor(isdir)
>osdir<- as.factor(osdir)
```

Now, if we check the class of the labeled data, we can use the `class()` function again and the following command shows we have converted character data type to factor:

```
>class(as.factor(isdir))
[1] "factor"
```

Now we are set with the in-sample and out-sample datasets and plug these datasets into `randomForest()` using the following command. The first parameter in the function is the normalized in-sample independent variables data frame, the second parameter is in-sample labels, the third parameter is the out-sample independent variables data frame, the fourth parameter is out-sample labels, and the fifth parameter is the number of trees to be used for random forest model building and I used this equal to `500`:

```
>model<- randomForest(norm_isdji, y=as.factor(isdir),
xtest=norm_osdji, ytest=as.factor(osdir), ntree=500)
```

However, there many more parameters which one can use if required. If you want to know more about the other parameters, the following single line of code will open a new window which explains everything for the `randomForest` function, including input variables, input variables type, output variables, examples, and so on:

```
>help(randomForest)
```

You can look at the model output using the following command. First it shows the command which is used to fit the model, then the type of forest, which is classification in our case as the labeled data was factor or consisted of three classes, and next the number of trees, as we provided `500` as parameter in the previous command. It also calculates a confusion matrix for the in-sample as well as for out-sample data. The error rate for the in-sample data is `11.76%` and `21.03%` for the out-sample data, which is assumed to be quite good. If you look deep into the in-sample and out-sample confusion matrix, you can also find the error rate for each class separately. In the case of the in-sample confusion matrix, the fourth column contains errors which are `11.34%`. `14.40%`, and `9.55%` for Down, NoWhere, and Up classes respectively. Similarly, you can also interpret the out-sample confusion matrix:

```
>print(model)
Call:
randomForest(x = norm_isdji, y = as.factor(isdir),
```

```
xtest = norm_osdji,        ytest = as.factor(osdir), ntree = 500)
Type of random forest: classification
Number of trees: 500
No. of variables tried at each split: 3
OOB estimate of  error rate: 11.76%
Confusion matrix:
          Down NoWhere Up class.error
Down       211      27  0  0.11344538
NoWhere     19     416 51  0.14403292
Up           0      51 483  0.09550562
Test set error rate: 21.03%
Confusion matrix:
          Down NoWhere Up class.error
Down        26      32  0  0.55172414
NoWhere      6     138  4  0.06756757
Up           0      11 35  0.23913043
```

The fitted model generates errors in matrix form and if you would like to dive deep into error matrices, you can look into the matrix format using `head()`. The following matrix shows the error rate for the in-sample data and the next three columns for each class separately across 500 decision trees:

```
>head(model$err.rate)
OOBDown    NoWhere    Up
[1,] 0.2159329 0.08791209 0.2967033 0.2009804
[2,] 0.1855263 0.16438356 0.2430556 0.1441718
[3,] 0.1911765 0.15508021 0.2320442 0.1712159
[4,] 0.1854991 0.16097561 0.2369077 0.1513158
[5,] 0.1901408 0.17129630 0.2534884 0.1428571
```

The following commands plot the overall in-sample and three classes errors for all 500 decision trees and you can see in *Figure 6.5* that after 100 decision trees, there is no significant decrease in the error:

```
>plot(model$err.rate[,1],type="l",ylim=c(0.05,0.3),ylab="Error")
>lines(model$err.rate[,2],col="red")
>lines(model$err.rate[,3],col="green")
>lines(model$err.rate[,4],col="blue")
```

The plot looks as follows:

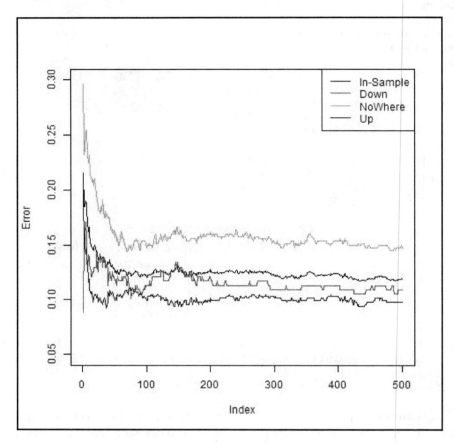

Figure 6.5: Error rate for 500 decision trees

If you want to extract variables which help to control error, you can choose those variables depending upon MeanDecreaseGinni. MeanDecreaseGinni can be accessed using the following lines of code:

```
>value<- importance(model,type = 2)
>head(value)
MeanDecreaseGini
DJI.Close          22.09961
DJI.Close.1        18.55651
DJI.Close.2        16.87061
DJI.Close.3        27.23347
```

Questions

1. What is machine learning and how it being used in the capital market? Explain in brief.
2. What is logistic regression and in which form does it generate its output?
3. Write a small piece of code to use a neural network for any stock time series.
4. How does a confusion matrix explain the accuracy of a model?
5. How do you standardize data and why is it important in the model building process?
6. How is support vector machine different from logistic regression?
7. Explain supervised and unsupervised learning and how to use these techniques in algorithmic trading.
8. Write a small piece of code for the k means algorithm using any one stock closing price.
9. Apart from `confusionMatrix()`, what is the other function to calculate classification and misclassification matrices?
10. What is the difference between decision tree and random forest and how are features selected from random forest?

Summary

This chapter presents advanced techniques which are implemented for capital markets. I have presented various supervised and unsupervised learning in detail along with examples. This chapter particularly used Dow Jones Index closing price as dataset, which was divided into in-sample and out-sample data. The in-sample data was used for model building and the out-sample data for validation of the model. Overfitting and underfitting generally questions the generalization capacity of the model which can be understand using confusion matrix. The accuracy of the model was defined using `confusionMatrix()` or `table()`.

There are various types of risks that exists in the market and in the next chapter, I will explain how to calculate risk associated with various investments, in particular market risk, portfolio risk, and so on. I will also explain Monte Carlo simulation for risk, hedging techniques, and credit risk, along with Basel regulations.

7
Risk Management

In this chapter, we are going to discuss the various types of risk associated with the banking and financial domains. Banks and financial institutions are all exposed to risk, and they need to develop risk identification and risk mitigation mechanisms with the implementation of regulatory norms to stay competitive and profitable. In this chapter, we are going to discuss various techniques to measure different types of risk using R. It also includes risk pertaining to banking operations such as credit risk, fraud detection, and Basel regulations.

The chapter covers the following topics:

- Market risk
- Portfolio risk
- VaR
- Monte Carlo simulations
- Hedging
- Basel regulation
- Credit risk
- Fraud detection

Market risk

The risk for an investor to encounter losses due to changes in overall performance of the market in which he has invested, is known as market risk. Market risk is a kind of systematic risk which cannot be tackled with diversification. It may be hedged. The risks happening due to recessions, political instability, interest rate changes, natural disasters, and terrorist attacks are examples of market risks. Market risks are measured differently for banks, individual stocks, portfolios, and so on.

Let us consider how market risks are measured for individual securities. The market risk of a stock which is a part of a portfolio is measured as the contribution of a security in the overall risk of the portfolio. The individual stock risk is measured by the beta coefficient, which is the volatility of stock with respect to the market.

Let us run regression analysis on stock IBM as dependent variable and GPSC index as the independent variable and try to estimate the beta. It can be done by executing the following code, which uses monthly data of GPSC and IBM both between 2010 to 2016:

```
> GPSCMonthlyUrl<-
'http://ichart.yahoo.com/table.csv?s=%5EGSPC&a=00&b=1&c=2010&d=00&e=1&f=201
7&g=m'
> GPSCMonthlyData <- read.csv(GPSCMonthlyUrl)
> IBMMonthlyUrl<-
'http://ichart.yahoo.com/table.csv?s=IBM&a=00&b=1&c=2010&d=00&e=1&f=2017&g=
m'
> IBMMonthlyData <- read.csv(IBMMonthlyUrl)
> DateRange <- GPSCMonthlyData$Date == IBMMonthlyData$Date
> GPSCPrice<-GPSCMonthlyData$Close[DateRange]
> IBMPrice<-IBMMonthlyData$Close[DateRange]
> GPSCReturns <- ( GPSCPrice[1:(length(GPSCPrice) - 1)] -
GPSCPrice[2:length(GPSCPrice)] ) / GPSCPrice[2:length(GPSCPrice)]
> IBMReturns <- ( IBMPrice[1:(length(IBMPrice) - 1)] -
IBMPrice[2:length(IBMPrice)] ) / IBMPrice[2:length(IBMPrice)]
> betafit <- lm(IBMReturns ~ GPSCReturns)
> result <- summary(betafit)
> beta <- result$coefficients[2,1]
> print(beta)
```

It gives an estimate of beta, as shown here:

```
[1] 0.72390819
```

Another technique used by investors and analysts is value at risk. It is a very common method of measuring risk in financial markets. The value at risk method is a well-known and established risk management method, but it comes with some assumptions that limit its correctness. For instance, one of the assumptions is that the content of the portfolio being measured is unchanged over a provided period. So, this may generate good results for short-term horizons but will not be such an accurate measurement for long-term horizons of investments, because it is more exposed to changes in interest rates and monetary policies. We will be discussing calculating VaR and CVAR/ES in R later on.

Portfolio risk

With the use of R language, we can manage portfolios better by mitigating the risk and portfolio optimization. To avoid the risk associated with portfolio analysis, diversification of the portfolio is required, with the selection of optimum weights for the portfolio's constituents.

Let us try to find the optimal weight of the portfolio whose stocks are IBM and FB, and using the CAPM. First, let us get the relevant data by executing the following code:

```
>GPSCMonthlyUrl<-
'http://ichart.yahoo.com/table.csv?s=%5EGSPC&a=00&b=1&c=2015&d=00&e=1&f=201
7&g=m'
>GPSCMonthlyData <- read.csv(GPSCMonthlyUrl)
>IBMMonthlyUrl<-
'http://ichart.yahoo.com/table.csv?s=IBM&a=00&b=1&c=2015&d=00&e=1&f=2017&g=
m'
>IBMMonthlyData <- read.csv(IBMMonthlyUrl)
>FBMonthlyUrl<-
'http://ichart.yahoo.com/table.csv?s=FB&a=00&b=1&c=2015&d=00&e=1&f=2017&g=m
'
>FBMonthlyData <- read.csv(FBMonthlyUrl)
>VMonthlyUrl<-
'http://ichart.yahoo.com/table.csv?s=V&a=00&b=1&c=2015&d=00&e=1&f=2017&g=m'
VMonthlyData <- read.csv(VMonthlyUrl)
```

It is monthly-level data between 2015 and 2016.

Now, let us try to find the returns for the preceding data for close prices by executing the following code:

```
> DateRange <- GPSCMonthlyData$Date
> GPSCPrice<-GPSCMonthlyData$Close[DateRange]
> IBMPrice<-IBMMonthlyData$Close[DateRange]
> FBPrice<-FBMonthlyData$Close[DateRange]
> VPrice<-VMonthlyData$Close[DateRange]
> GPSCReturns <- ( GPSCPrice[1:(length(GPSCPrice) - 1)] -
GPSCPrice[2:length(GPSCPrice)] ) / GPSCPrice[2:length(GPSCPrice)]
> IBMReturns <- ( IBMPrice[1:(length(IBMPrice) - 1)] -
IBMPrice[2:length(IBMPrice)] ) / IBMPrice[2:length(IBMPrice)]
> FBReturns <- ( FBPrice[1:(length(FBPrice) - 1)] -
FBPrice[2:length(FBPrice)] ) / FBPrice[2:length(FBPrice)]
> VReturns <- ( VPrice[1:(length(VPrice) - 1)] - VPrice[2:length(VPrice)] )
/ VPrice[2:length(VPrice)]
```

It generates the returns for all the series.

Now, let us try to find the excess return for all the series. The excess return is given by monthly return minus monthly T-Bills interest rate (let it be .0015). This can be done by executing the following code:

```
> EGPSCReturns<- GPSCReturns-.0015
> EIBMReturns<- IBMReturns-.0015
> EFBReturns<- FBReturns-.0015
> EVReturns<- VReturns-.0015
```

Next, find the mean and SD for the excess returns of all the series. It is given by executing the following code:

```
> MeanSD<-
rbind(cbind("GPSC",mean(EGPSCReturns),sd(EGPSCReturns)),cbind("FB",mean(EFB
Returns),sd(EFBReturns)),cbind("IBM",mean(EIBMReturns),sd(EIBMReturns)),cbi
nd("V",mean(EVReturns),sd(EVReturns)))
> MeanSD
```

It generates the following output:

```
       [,1]    [,2]                      [,3]
[1,]  "GPSC"  "-0.00595542418976726"    "0.0336391046748448"
[2,]  "FB"    "-0.0180513406031643"     "0.0531419708900752"
[3,]  "IBM"   "-0.00357192217566396"    "0.0532556216736508"
[4,]  "V"     "0.12613583240944"        "0.660078019072646"
```

Figure 7.1: Mean and standard deviation of all the stocks considered

Now, let us find out the beta of all the excess returns of stocks by regressing them individually against the excess return of the S&P index.

This can be done by executing the following code:

```
> lmIBM<- lm(IBMReturns ~ EGPSCReturns)
> summary(lmIBM)
```

It gives the following output:

```
Call:
lm(formula = IBMReturns ~ EGPSCReturns)

Residuals:
      Min        1Q     Median        3Q        Max
-0.069358 -0.016185   0.001289   0.017361   0.116624

Coefficients:
               Estimate Std. Error t value  Pr(>|t|)
(Intercept)   0.0045003  0.0082818   0.5434 0.5925797
EGPSCReturns  1.1035670  0.2477030   4.4552 0.0002188 ***
---
Signif. codes:  0 '***' 0.001 '**' 0.01 '*' 0.05 '.' 0.1 ' ' 1

Residual standard error: 0.039083 on 21 degrees of freedom
Multiple R-squared:  0.48591,    Adjusted R-squared:  0.46143
F-statistic: 19.849 on 1 and 21 DF,  p-value: 0.00021882
```

Figure 7.2: Output summary of regression

This shows that the beta for IBM is 1.1035670.

Similarly, we can find the beta for FB and V.

So using the CAPM, the excess expected return for IBM is given as follows:

```
Beta of IBM*expected excess return of GPSC
=1.1035670*(-.005955424) =  -0.0065722094
```

According to the single-factor model, the variance of IBM is given by this formula:

$$\sigma_{IBM^2} = \beta_{IBM^2} {}^* \sigma_{GPSC^2} + \sigma^2(e)$$

Figure 7.3: Variance given by single-factor model

Here, e is the residual error coming from regression.

So by running regression for all the independent variables and calculating excess returns and variance, we have the following:

	IBM	FB	V
Variance	0.002906	0.002949	0.455695
Beta	1.103567	0.423458	3.74228
Expected excess return	-0.00657	-0.00252	-0.02229

The covariance matrix can be calculated using the following formula:

$$\sigma_{IBMFB} = \beta_{IBMB}\beta_{FB}\sigma_{GPSC^2}$$

Figure 7.4: Covariance formula

It generates the following matrix:

	IBM	FB	V
IBM	0.001378	0.000529	0.004673
FB	0.000529	0.000203	0.001793
V	0.004673	0.001793	0.015848

Now, let us find the optimal weight for the portfolio by executing the following code:

```
> returns_avg<-
matrix(c(-0.0180513406031643,-0.00357192217566396,0.12613583240944),nrow
=1)
> covariance<-
matrix(c(0.001378118,0.000528808,0.004673302,0.000528808,0.000202913,0.0017
93228,0.004673302,0.001793228,0.015847524),nrow=3)
> library(tseries)
> sol<-portfolio.optim(x=returns_avg,covmat=covariance, shorts=F)
> sol$pw
```

It generates the optimal weight as given in the following table:

IBM	FB	V
0	0.70387703	0.29612297

VaR

Value at risk is a measure in risk management to measure the potential risk which can occur to the portfolio of an investor. VaR imputed at 5% confidence means that the loss will not be less than predicted value 95% of the time or, in other words, loss will be greater in 5% of times than predicted value.

There are three common ways of computing value at risk:

- Parametric VaR
- Historical VaR
- Monte Carlo VaR

In this section, we will be capturing the first two, and the third one will be captured in the next section.

Parametric VaR

Parametric VaR is also known as the variance-covariance method and is used to find VaR using mean and standard deviation as parameters.

`qnorm` is used for value at risk calculation using parametric methods. It uses the parameters mean and standard deviation. The general syntax is as follows:

```
qnorm(p,mean,sd)
```

Here, `p` is the desired percentile; `mean` is the given mean of the sample; and `sd` is the standard deviation of the sample.

Let us assume that the average return of a stock is 2% and standard deviation is 4%, then the value at risk for a one day horizon at 95% confidence level using the parametric approach is given by executing the following approach:

```
>mean = 2
>sigma = 4
>Alpha = .05
>Var_parametric = qnorm(alpha, mean, sigma)
>Var_parametric
```

It generates the following output upon execution:

```
[1] -4.579
```

Alternatively, we can find the VaR by the parametric method using the following code:

```
> Var_parametric = mean + sigma*qnorm(alpha,0,1)
> Var_parametric
```

It generates the output as shown here:

```
[1] -4.579
```

Let us assume we have VaR for a one day horizon and, if we want to convert it at a different horizon, say a month, then it can be converted using the formula given here:

$$VAR_{monthly} = VAR_{daily} * (T)^{\wedge(.5)}$$

Here, T is the number of days in a month.

Expected shortfall (ES) is also known as conditional value of risk and it is an alternative to VaR. ES is a weighted average between the value at risk and the losses greater than value at risk. By means of ES, we try to quantify VaR.

The ES/CVAR for the above example can be computed using the following example:

```
alpha_z=qnorm(alpha)
ES_parametric = mean + sigma*(dnorm(alpha_z)/(1-alpha))
ES_parametric
```

It generates the following output:

```
[1] 2.434
```

Historical VaR

The main assumption is that the past repeats itself. It does not assume any particular type of distribution. Historical VaR is estimated by simulating or constructing the **cumulative distribution function** (**CDF**) of asset returns over time. Generally, we find the returns on the regular time interval basis and sort them, and then find the relevant percentile.

Now let us try to find individual, as well as portfolio, VaR on a dataset. The dataset is generated by executing the following code:

```
>library(quantmod)
> symbollist = c("FB", "V","JNJ")
> getSymbols(symbollist, from ="2016-01-01", to = "2017-01-01")
> FB = FB[, "FB.Adjusted", drop=F]
> V = V[, "V.Adjusted", drop=F]
> JNJ = JNJ[, "JNJ.Adjusted", drop=F]
> FB_return = CalculateReturns(FB, method="log")
> V_return = CalculateReturns(V, method="log")
> JNJ_return = CalculateReturns(JNJ, method="log")
> FB_return = FB_return[-1,]
> V_return = V_return[-1,]
> JNJ_return = JNJ_return[-1,]
> FB_V_JNJ_return<-cbind(FB_return,V_return,JNJ_return)
> head(FB_V_JNJ_return)
```

It prepares the dataset required for historical VaR and displays a sample of the data as shown here:

	FB.Adjusted	V.Adjusted	JNJ.Adjusted
2016-01-05	0.004977	0.007502	0.004171
2016-01-06	0.002333	-0.013198	-0.005067
2016-01-07	-0.050287	-0.019858	-0.011723
2016-01-08	-0.006044	-0.012409	-0.010741
2016-01-11	0.001848	0.014169	-0.006029
2016-01-12	0.018895	0.011300	0.006843

Figure 7.5: Return calculation output

Now, let us try to estimate individual `historical` VaR of stocks by running the following code:

```
> HVAR<-VaR(FB_V_JNJ_return, p=0.95, method="historical")
> HVAR
```

It generates the following output:

```
       FB.Adjusted V.Adjusted JNJ.Adjusted
VaR      -0.02607   -0.02248     -0.01211
```

Figure 7.6: Historical individual output

Similarly, let us try to estimate CVAR/ES, which can be computed using the following code:

```
> HCVAR<-ES(FB_V_JNJ_return, p=0.95, method="historical")
> HCVAR
```

Upon executing, it generates the output as shown:

```
      FB.Adjusted V.Adjusted JNJ.Adjusted
ES      -0.03773   -0.03056      -0.0183
```

Figure 7.7: Historical CVAR individual output

We can find a lot of options in the VaR() function. The most important ones are given here:

- R: Matrix, xts vector, or DataFrame
- p: Confidence level
- method: It uses four methods – modified, Gaussian, historical, and kernel
- portfolio_method: It has options – single, component, and marginal – defining whether to do univariate, component, or marginal calculation

Now let us try to find the component VaR of the portfolio. If the weights are not specified then it takes equal weights. It can be obtained by running the following code:

```
> VaR(FB_V_JNJ_return, p=0.95,portfolio_method="component")
```

It generates the following output:

```
$MVaR
         [,1]
[1,] 0.0161

$contribution
 FB.Adjusted    V.Adjusted JNJ.Adjusted
    0.006437      0.006798     0.002861

$pct_contrib_MVaR
 FB.Adjusted    V.Adjusted JNJ.Adjusted
      0.3999        0.4224       0.1778
```

Figure 7.8: Historical VaR output by component method

Similarly, we can find the `marginal` VaR by executing the following code:

```
> VaR(FB_V_JNJ_return, p=0.95,portfolio_method="marginal")
```

It generates the following result:

	PortfolioVaR	FB.Adjusted	V.Adjusted	JNJ.Adjusted
1	-0.01606	0.002398	0.003049	-0.004629

Figure 7.9: Historical VaR output by marginal output

Monte Carlo simulation

Monte Carlo simulation plays a very important role in risk management. Even if we have access to all the relevant information pertaining to risk associated with a firm, it is still not possible to predict the associated risk and quantify it. By the means of Monte Carlo simulation, we can generate all the possible scenarios of risk and using it, we can evaluate the impact of risk and build a better risk mitigation strategy.

Monte Carlo simulation is a computational mathematical approach which gives the user the option of creating a range of possible outcome scenarios, including extreme ones, with the probability associated with each outcome. The possible outcomes are also drawn on the expected line of distribution, which may be closer to real outcomes. The range of possible outcomes can be used in risk analysis for building the models and drawing the inferences. Analysis is repeated again and again using a different set of random values from the probability function to test the model in order to build a robust model. Probability distributions are a much more realistic way of describing uncertainty in variables of a risk analysis. Monte Carlo simulation uses the concept of Brownian motion dynamics. Now we will demonstrate how to build a sample with a given distribution using Monte Carlo simulation, and will try to estimate VaR.

Let us assume we are trying to generate a sample of returns for 2000 months for a stock using normal distribution of mean .20, sigma .25 and deltat = .08333 for month. This can be done using the following code:

```
> Sample_Size<-2000
> set.seed(2345)
> Z<-rnorm(Sample_Size)
> mean<-.20
> sigma<-.25
> deltat<-.08333
> returns<-mean*deltat+sigma*Z*sqrt(deltat)
> hist(returns, breaks = 50)
```

It generates the following displayed histogram:

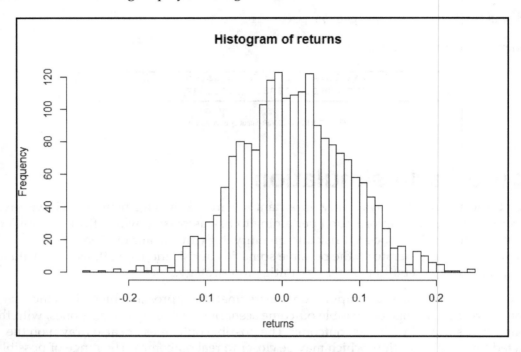

Figure 7.10: Histogram of returns generated by MCM

Now let us try to find the mean and standard deviation of newly constructed sample, which is given by executing the following code:

```
> Mean_new<-mean(returns)*12
> Mean_new
> std_new<-sd(returns)*(12)^(.5)
> std_new
```

It generates the mean as 0.1821 and standard deviation as 0.2439, which is close to the mean and standard deviation taken for constructing the sample. Thus, clearly, the new sample is a normal distribution.

The value at risk of the above series can be computed using the following code:

```
VaR(returns, p = 0.95, method="historical")
```

It generates the following output:

```
VaR -0.09665
```

Hedging

Hedging is basically taking a position in the market to reduce the risk. It is a strategy built to reduce the risk in investment using call/put options/futures short selling. The idea of hedging is to reduce the volatility of a portfolio by reducing the potential risk to loss. Hedging especially protects small businesses against catastrophic or extreme risk by protecting the cost at the time of distress. The tax laws also benefit those who do hedging. For firms who do hedging, it works like insurance and they have more independence to make their financial decisions without thinking about the risks.

Now, let us consider some scenarios of hedging:

- **Currency risk**: Also known as exchange-rate risk, it happens due to fluctuations in the prices of one currency with respect to another. Investors or companies who operate across the world are exposed to currency risk, which may lead to profit and losses. This risk can be reduced by hedging, which can prevent losses happening due to price fluctuation.
- **Short hedge**: Let us suppose a farmer is planning to plant 200,000 bushels of corn and will be ready for harvesting in the next 2 months and for delivery in the consecutive month. The farmer knows from his experience that the cost of planting and harvesting is $5.30 per bushel. Delivery month corn futures are traded at $5.70 per bushel. The farmer wants to lock his selling price so he enters a short hedge by selling some delivery month futures. Each corn future contract consists of 5,000 bushels. He will need to sell 40 future contracts. For his crop protection in the delivery month, he realizes that the price of corn has gone down and is priced at $5.20 per bushel and the price of a delivery month future contract has also reduced to **$5.40 per bushel**.

Selling the corn in the cash market generates him a sum of **$5.20*200,000 = $1,040,000**.

Total cost incurred is $1,060,000 so he may suffer a loss of **$20,000**.

But, since he has hedged some value of corn futures sold in planting month = **$5.70*200,000=$1,140,000**.

Value of corn futures bought in delivery month = **$5.40*200,000=1,080,000**.

So gain in future market is **1,140,000-1,080,000=$60,000**.

So overall profit is **$60,000-$20,000=$40,000**.

Similarly, according to requirement, the investor can do long hedging.

The most common instruments used for hedging are forward contracts, future contracts, and option contracts.

Basel regulation

The main goal for the Basel Committee on Banking Supervision is to improve understanding of key supervisory issues to set a healthy banking supervision worldwide. Its main objective is to develop regulatory frameworks in order to improve banking systems. Currently, Basel III has been developed to meet the deficiencies in financial regulations exposed during the financial crisis of 2007-2008. Basel III is a global voluntary regulatory framework on bank capital adequacy, stress testing, and market liquidity risk. It is assumed to strengthen bank capital requirements by decreasing bank leverage and increasing bank liquidity. The objective of implementing Basel III is to make the banking sector more robust so that it can absorb shocks arising from financial and economic stress, improve risk management and governance, and strengthen banks' transparency and disclosures.

The R community has developed a library, SACCR, keeping in mind the regulations of Basel III. This library has many methods which are based upon the standardized norms of Basel III. It has implemented all the examples appearing in the regulatory framework. For example, it computes exposure at default according to Basel norms.

It uses the function `CalcEAD(RC,PFE)` to calculate the exposure of default.

Here, `RC` is replacement cost and `PFE` is projected future exposure.

So, if the `RC` component is `50` and `PFE` is `400` then executing the following code finds exposure at default:

```
> CalcEAD(50,400)
```

It generates the output `630`.

Similarly, there are other functions in this library on the basis of implementation of Basel III.

Credit risk

Credit risk is the risk associated with an investment where the borrower is not able to repay the amount to the lender. This can happen on account of poor financial conditions of the borrower, and it represents a risk for the lender. The risk is for the lender to incur loss due to non-payment and hence disruption of cash flows and increased collection costs. The loss may be complete or partial. There are multiple scenarios in which a lender can suffer loss. Some of the scenarios are given here:

- A customer not making a payment on a mortgage loan, credit card, line of credit, or other type of loan
- Business/consumer not paying due trade invoice
- A business not paying an employee's due earned wages
- A business/government bond issuer not making payment on a due coupon or principal
- An insurance company not obliging its policy obligation due
- A bank not returning funds of depositors

It is a practice of mitigating losses by understanding the adequacy of a bank's capital and loan loss reserves at any given time. In order to reduce the credit risk, the lender needs to develop a mechanism to perform a credit check on the prospective borrower. Generally, banks quantify the credit risk using two metrics – expected loss and economic capital. Expected loss is the value of a possible loss times the probability of that loss occurring. Economic capital is the amount of capital necessary to cover unexpected losses. There are three risk parameters that are essential in the process of calculating the EL and EC measurements: the **probability of default (PD)**, **loss given default (LGD)**, and **exposure at default (EAD)**. Calculation of PD is more important, so we will be discussing it.

For building the PD model, let us use the subset of German Credit Data available in R. Data used for the analysis is given by executing the following code:

```
> data(GermanCredit)
> LRData<-GermanCredit[,1:10]
```

Before starting the modeling, we need to understand the data, which can be done by executing the following code:

```
> str(LRData)
```

It gives us the column types and kind of values it has, as shown here:

```
'data.frame':    1000 obs. of  10 variables:
 $ Duration               : int  6 48 12 42 24 36 24 36 12 30 ...
 $ Amount                 : int  1169 5951 2096 7882 4870 9055 2835 6948 3059 5234 ...
 $ InstallmentRatePercentage: int  4 2 2 2 3 2 3 2 2 4 ...
 $ ResidenceDuration      : int  4 2 3 4 4 4 4 2 4 2 ...
 $ Age                    : int  67 22 49 45 53 35 53 35 61 28 ...
 $ NumberExistingCredits  : int  2 1 1 1 2 1 1 1 1 2 ...
 $ NumberPeopleMaintenance : int  1 1 2 2 2 2 1 1 1 1 ...
 $ Telephone              : num  0 1 1 1 1 0 1 0 1 0 ...
 $ ForeignWorker          : num  1 1 1 1 1 1 1 1 1 1 ...
 $ Class                  : Factor w/ 2 levels "Bad","Good": 2 1 2 2 1 2 2 2 2 1 ...
```

Figure 7.11: Column description of the dataset

In this example, our target variable is `Class`. `Class = Good` means non-defaulter and `Class = bad` means defaulter. Now, to understand the distribution of all the numeric variables, we can compute all the basic statistics related to the numeric attributes. This can be done by executing the following code:

```
> summary(LRData)
```

A sample of the output generated by the preceding code is displayed here:

Duration	Amount	InstallmentRatePercentage
Min. : 4.000	Min. : 250.0	Min. :1.000
1st Qu.:12.000	1st Qu.: 1365.5	1st Qu.:2.000
Median :18.000	Median : 2319.5	Median :3.000
Mean :20.903	Mean : 3271.3	Mean :2.973
3rd Qu.:24.000	3rd Qu.: 3972.2	3rd Qu.:4.000
Max. :72.000	Max. :18424.0	Max. :4.000

Figure 7.12 Basic statistics of numeric variables

Now let us prepare our data for modeling by executing the following code:

```
> set.seed(100)
> library(caTools)
> res = sample.split(LRData$Class, 0.6)
> Train_data = subset(LRData, res == TRUE)
> Test_data=subset(LRData, res==FALSE)
```

The preceding code generates `Train` and `Test` data for modeling.

The proportion of selecting the `Train` and `Test` data is quite subjective. Now we can do basic statistics for imputation of missing/outlier values and exploratory analysis (such as information value analysis and correlation matrix) of the independent variables with respect to dependent variables for understanding the relationship.

Now let us try to fit the model on the `Train` data, which can be done by executing the following code:

```
> lgfit = glm(Class ~. , data=Train_data, family="binomial")
> summary(lgfit)
```

It generates the summary of the model as displayed here:

```
Call:
glm(formula = Class ~ ., family = "binomial", data = Train_data)

Deviance Residuals:
    Min       1Q    Median       3Q       Max
-2.30253  -1.09597   0.65063   0.83278   1.72219

Coefficients:
                           Estimate  Std. Error z value  Pr(>|z|)
(Intercept)               3.0424e+00  8.7864e-01  3.4627 0.0005349 ***
Duration                 -3.4100e-02  9.9148e-03 -3.4393 0.0005832 ***
Amount                   -8.2553e-05  4.5772e-05 -1.8036 0.0712979 .
InstallmentRatePercentage -2.4899e-01 9.8090e-02 -2.5384 0.0111364 *
ResidenceDuration        -1.3645e-01  9.0829e-02 -1.5023 0.1330280
Age                       2.6855e-02  9.6083e-03  2.7950 0.0051907 **
NumberExistingCredits     1.9129e-01  1.7016e-01  1.1242 0.2609318
NumberPeopleMaintenance  -2.3006e-01  2.5637e-01 -0.8974 0.3695030
Telephone                -2.9688e-01  2.0601e-01 -1.4411 0.1495483
ForeignWorker            -7.8564e-01  6.5254e-01 -1.2040 0.2285969
---
Signif. codes:  0 '***' 0.001 '**' 0.01 '*' 0.05 '.' 0.1 ' ' 1

(Dispersion parameter for binomial family taken to be 1)

    Null deviance: 733.037  on 599  degrees of freedom
Residual deviance: 672.018  on 590  degrees of freedom
AIC: 692.018

Number of Fisher Scoring iterations: 4
```

Figure 7.13: Output summary of logistic regression

As we can see in the summary, by means of Pvalues, there are significant as well as insignificant attributes in the model. Keeping in mind the significance of attributes and multicollinearity, we can iterate the model to find the best model. In our case, let us rerun the model with only significant attributes.

This can be done by executing the following code:

```
> lgfit = glm(Class ~Duration+InstallmentRatePercentage+Age ,
data=Train_data, family="binomial")
> summary(lgfit)
```

It generates the summary output as follows:

```
Call:
glm(formula = Class ~ Duration + InstallmentRatePercentage +
    Age, family = "binomial", data = Train_data)

Deviance Residuals:
    Min       1Q    Median        3Q       Max
-2.35494  -1.11680   0.66043   0.84251   1.64937

Coefficients:
                            Estimate Std. Error z value  Pr(>|z|)
(Intercept)                1.5958692  0.4339572  3.6775  0.0002355 ***
Duration                  -0.0456070  0.0074508 -6.1211  9.292e-10 ***
InstallmentRatePercentage -0.1760523  0.0859589 -2.0481  0.0405503 *
Age                        0.0229733  0.0090310  2.5438  0.0109644 *
---
Signif. codes:  0 '***' 0.001 '**' 0.01 '*' 0.05 '.' 0.1 ' ' 1

(Dispersion parameter for binomial family taken to be 1)

    Null deviance: 733.037  on 599  degrees of freedom
Residual deviance: 682.062  on 596  degrees of freedom
AIC: 690.062

Number of Fisher Scoring iterations: 4
```

Figure 7.14: Output summary of logistic regression having only significant attributes

The output summary shows that all the attributes considered in the model are significant.

There are a lot of statistics in logistic regression for checks of model accuracy and in this case, we will be showing the ROC curve and the confusion matrix for accuracy checks.

We can compute the threshold for classification by KS statistics but here let us assume the threshold value is 0.5 and try to score our Train sample by executing the following code:

```
> Train_data$predicted.risk = predict(lgfit, newdata=Train_data,
type="response")
> table(Train_data$Class, as.numeric(Train_data$predicted.risk >= 0.5))
```

It generates the confusion matrix as displayed here:

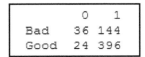

Figure 7.15: Confusion matrix for logistic regression

Now, let us compute the auc by executing the following code:

```
> library(ROCR)
> pred = prediction(Train_data$predicted.risk, Train_data$Class)
> as.numeric(performance(pred, "auc")@y.values)
```

It gives the value of auc as shown here:

```
0.67925265
```

Now, let us plot the ROC curve by executing the following code:

```
> predict_Train = predict(lgfit, type="response")
> ROCpred = prediction(predict_Train, Train_data$Class)
> ROCperf = performance(ROCpred, "tpr", "fpr")
> plot(ROCperf)
```

It plots the ROC curve as shown here:

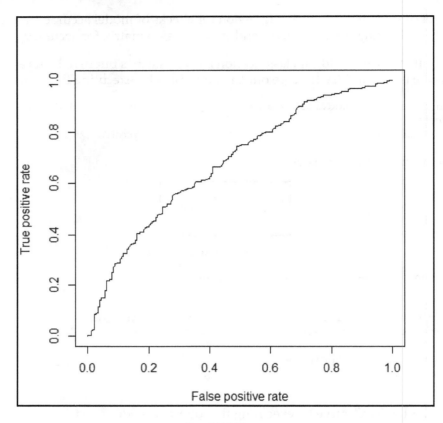

Figure 7.16: ROC curve

We can use the same model fit created on `Train_data` and score `Test_data` and check whether the accuracy measures are in the same range or not to validate the model.

Fraud detection

Identifying fraudulent transactions is one of the most important components of risk management. R has many functions and packages that can be used to find fraudulent transactions, including binary classification techniques such as logistic regression, decision tree, random forest, and so on. We will be again using a subset of the German Credit data available in R library. In this section, we are going to use random forest for fraud detection. Just like logistic regression, we can do basic exploratory analysis to understand the attributes. Here we are not going to do the basic exploratory analysis but will be using the labeled data to train the model using random forest, and then will try to do the prediction of fraud on validation data.

So the dataset used for the analysis will be given by executing the following code:

```
>data(GermanCredit)
>FraudData<-GermanCredit[,1:10]
> head(FraudData)
```

It generates a few lines of the sample data:

	Duration	Amount	InstallmentRatePercentage	ResidenceDuration	Age	NumberExistingCredits	NumberPeopleMaintenance	Telephone	ForeignWorker	Class
1	6	1169	4	4	67	2	1	0	1	Good
2	48	5951	2	2	22	1	1	1	1	Bad
3	12	2096	2	3	49	1	2	1	1	Good
4	42	7882	2	4	45	1	2	1	1	Good
5	24	4870	3	4	53	2	2	1	1	Bad
6	36	9055	2	4	35	1	2	0	1	Good

Figure 7.17: Sample data used for fraud analysis

The class will be our target variable in the dataset and a class with level bad means fraud has been committed by the customer. Now let us divide the preceding data into `train` and `test` samples by executing the following code:

```
> len<-dim(FraudData)[1]
> train<- sample(1:len , 0.8*len)
> TrainData<-FraudData[train,]
> TestData<-FraudData[-train,]
```

It generates the `Train` and `Test` data.

Now, let us try to build the classification model on the train sample with the random forest technique. This can be done by executing the following code:

```
> fraud_model <-
randomForest(Class~.,data=TrainData,ntree=50,proximity=TRUE)
> print(fraud_model)
```

It generates the following output:

```
Call:
 randomForest(formula = Class ~ ., data = TrainData, ntree = 50,        proximity = TRUE)
                Type of random forest: classification
                      Number of trees: 50
No. of variables tried at each split: 3

        OOB estimate of  error rate: 31.5%
Confusion matrix:
     Bad Good class.error
Bad   74  172  0.69918699
Good  80  474  0.14440433
```

Figure 7.18: Output summary of logistic random forest

The error for the trees can also be plotted by executing the following code:

```
> plot(fraud_model)
```

Here is the output generated:

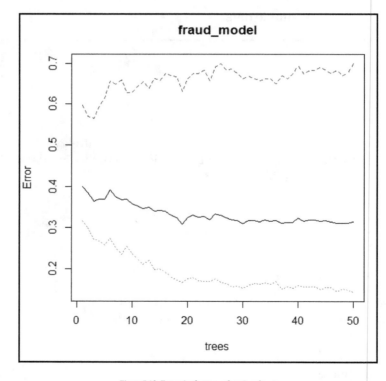

Figure 7.19: Error plot for trees of random forest

The comparative importance of the attributes can be given by executing the following code:

```
> importance(fraud_model)
```

It generates the following output:

```
                            MeanDecreaseGini
Duration                          58.9144389
Amount                            96.8189841
InstallmentRatePercentage         23.5223809
ResidenceDuration                 24.6044557
Age                               69.6605790
NumberExistingCredits             14.1947544
NumberPeopleMaintenance            9.1159574
Telephone                         13.4499048
ForeignWorker                      1.9841100
```

Figure 7.20: Variable comparison summary by random forest

Now, let us do classification on the test data by executing the following code:

```
> TestPred<-predict(fraud_model,newdata=TestData)
> table(TestPred, TestData$Class)
```

It generates the following classification table:

```
TestPred Bad  Good
    Bad   22    18
    Good  32   128
```

Figure 7.21: Classification summary of random forest

Liability management

Liability management is the process of keeping appropriate liquidity reserves and allocating assets by financial institutions to balance outstanding liabilities such as deposits, CDs, and so on to obtain best performance by simultaneously meeting liabilities and growing net assets. Banks have several risks – asset management risk, interest rate risk, and currency exchange risks – and by using liability management, banks and financial institutions try to minimize the risk.

In this chapter, we have discussed several topics, such as market risk, portfolio risk, credit risk, fraud detection, diversification of portfolios, optimization of portfolios, and rebalancing of the portfolio, which can help financial in situation with liability management.

Questions

1. What is market risk and how can R help in measuring market risk? Please give an example.
2. What are the ways of measuring risk associated with the portfolio?
3. What are the most common ways of measuring VaR? Please construct a portfolio and find VaR using all the methods.
4. How do you compute ES/CVAR in R?
5. Construct a sample using normal and lognormal distribution using the Monte Carlo method and find the historical VaR for each of them.
6. How do you find component and marginal VaR for a portfolio in R?
7. What is credit scoring and how do you execute it in R? Construct an example and build a scoring example along with validation.
8. What are the ways to identify fraud? How do you execute them in R?

Summary

In this chapter, we have covered the types of risks associated with financial institutions, such as market risk, portfolio risk, VaR, Monte Carlo simulation, hedging, Basel regulations, credit risk, and fraud detection. Also, we have discussed how the strengths of R can be leveraged for measuring different types of risk. In this chapter, we have demonstrated examples of measuring risks such as market, portfolio, and credit using R, and also how to use techniques such as random forest classification for fraud detection.

In the next chapter, we will be covering various optimization techniques used in trading algorithms and parameter estimation. Optimization techniques such as dynamic rebalancing, walk forward testing, grid testing, and genetic algorithm will be covered.

8
Optimization

Optimization is a way of selecting the best solution out of all feasible solutions. So, the first part of optimization is to formulate the problem according to given constraints, and to apply an advanced analytical method to get the best solution and help in making better decisions.

Optimization models play a pivotal role in quant and computational finance by solving complex problems more efficiently and accurately. Problems associated with asset allocation, risk management, option pricing, volatility estimation, portfolio optimization, and construction of index funds can be solved using optimization techniques such as nonlinear optimization models, quadratic programming formulations, and integer programming models. There is a variety of commercial and open source software available in the analytical space to solve these problems, and R is one of the preferred choices as it is open source and efficient.

In this chapter, we will be discussing some of the optimization techniques and how to solve them using R.

The chapter covers the following topics:

- Dynamic rebalancing
- Walk forward testing
- Grid testing
- Genetic algorithm

Dynamic rebalancing

Dynamic rebalancing is a process of keeping one's portfolio closer to your allocated target using the natural cash inflows and outflows to your portfolio. Rebalancing involves periodically buying or selling assets in a portfolio to maintain an original desired level of asset allocation, realigning the weightings of a portfolio of assets.

Let us consider an example. In a portfolio, the target asset allocation was 40% stocks and 60% bonds. If the bonds performed well during the period, the weights of bonds in the portfolio could result to 70%. Then, the investor will decide to sell some bonds and buy some stocks to get the portfolio back to the original target allocation of 40% stock and 60% bonds.

Now, let us see how to do rebalancing of the portfolio in R.

Periodic rebalancing

Let us consider data sourced from R:

```
>library(PerformanceAnalytics)
>data(edhec)
> data<-edhec["1999", 3:5]
> colnames(data) = c("DS","EM","EMN")
> data
```

It gives the following dataset:

```
                  DS       EM      EMN
1999-01-31   0.0181  -0.0120   0.0101
1999-02-28  -0.0021   0.0102   0.0023
1999-03-31   0.0159   0.0585   0.0033
1999-04-30   0.0418   0.0630   0.0107
1999-05-31   0.0207   0.0061   0.0089
1999-06-30   0.0273   0.0654   0.0168
1999-07-31   0.0084  -0.0061   0.0135
1999-08-31   0.0020  -0.0147   0.0095
1999-09-30  -0.0041  -0.0069   0.0095
1999-10-31   0.0027   0.0288   0.0066
1999-11-30   0.0220   0.0692   0.0133
1999-12-31   0.0300   0.1230   0.0198
```

Figure 8.1: Dataset used for rebalancing analysis

Now let us assume that on `1998-12-31`, the weights of the portfolio consisting of the above instruments are given as the following:

```
> wts <- xts(matrix(c(.3,.3,.4),nrow=1,ncol=3), as.Date("1998-12-31"))
> colnames(wts)<-colnames(data)
> wts
```

It gives the weights as follows at the end of the year 1998:

```
              DS  EM EMN
1998-12-31  0.3  0.3  0.4
```

Figure 8.2: Initial weights assigned

Now, if we want to balance the weights on a monthly basis then it can be done by executing the following code:

```
> Return.portfolio(data,weights =wts, rebalance_on="months",verbose=TRUE)
```

Here, `data` is the input data; `weights` is the defined weights for the components of the portfolio; `rebalance_on = True` means weighted rebalanced monthly portfolio returns; and `verbose = True` returns additional information.

When we execute the preceding code, it generates an output list which includes portfolio returns after adjustment for each interval, monthly contribution by each asset, before and after weights of assets after each interval, and before and after portfolio values for each interval. Thus it gives a complete picture of how rebalancing happens during a given time span.

The monthly rebalanced portfolio returns are given as follows:

```
              portfolio.returns
1999-01-31     0.00587000000
1999-02-28     0.00329184586
1999-03-31     0.02348319604
1999-04-30     0.03607136853
1999-05-31     0.01157542782
1999-06-30     0.03521133320
1999-07-31     0.00564451114
1999-08-31    -0.00047737110
1999-09-30     0.00022475853
1999-10-31     0.01234203539
1999-11-30     0.03361169256
1999-12-31     0.05663598375
```

Figure 8.3: Portfolio returns at different time periods

Monthly contribution by each asset is given as follows:

	DS	EM	EMN
1999-01-31	0.00543000000	-0.0036000000	0.00404000000
1999-02-28	-0.00063765994	0.0030056369	0.00092386889
1999-03-31	0.00480205026	0.0173569052	0.00132424059
1999-04-30	0.01253072220	0.0193315697	0.00420907659
1999-05-31	0.00623971634	0.0019204367	0.00341527477
1999-06-30	0.00830341973	0.0204781533	0.00642976020
1999-07-31	0.00253537323	-0.0019657422	0.00507488006
1999-08-31	0.00060531434	-0.0046817935	0.00359910805
1999-09-30	-0.00124397001	-0.0021663063	0.00363503484
1999-10-31	0.00081565772	0.0089775667	0.00254881099
1999-11-30	0.00658279927	0.0219217859	0.00510710741
1999-12-31	0.00887570110	0.0403066297	0.00745365299

Figure 8.4: Monthly contribution by each asset

Beginning-of-period weights are given as follows:

	DS	EM	EMN
1999-01-31	0.30000000	0.30000000	0.40000000
1999-02-28	0.30364759	0.29467029	0.40168213
1999-03-31	0.30201574	0.29669923	0.40128503
1999-04-30	0.29977804	0.30685031	0.39337164
1999-05-31	0.30143557	0.31482569	0.38373874
1999-06-30	0.30415457	0.31312161	0.38272382
1999-07-31	0.30183015	0.32225281	0.37591704
1999-08-31	0.30265717	0.31848935	0.37885348
1999-09-30	0.30340732	0.31395743	0.38263525
1999-10-31	0.30209545	0.31172107	0.38618348
1999-11-30	0.29921815	0.31678881	0.38399304
1999-12-31	0.29585670	0.32769618	0.37644712

Figure 8.5: Summary of weights at the beginning of each period

End-of-period weights are given as follows:

	DS	EM	EMN
1999-01-31	0.30364759	0.29467029	0.40168213
1999-02-28	0.30201574	0.29669923	0.40128503
1999-03-31	0.29977804	0.30685031	0.39337164
1999-04-30	0.30143557	0.31482569	0.38373874
1999-05-31	0.30415457	0.31312161	0.38272382
1999-06-30	0.30183015	0.32225281	0.37591704
1999-07-31	0.30265717	0.31848935	0.37885348
1999-08-31	0.30340732	0.31395743	0.38263525
1999-09-30	0.30209545	0.31172107	0.38618348
1999-10-31	0.29921815	0.31678881	0.38399304
1999-11-30	0.29585670	0.32769618	0.37644712
1999-12-31	0.28839866	0.34827775	0.36332358

Figure 8.6: Summary of weights at the end of each period

Beginning-of-period portfolio value is given as follows:

	DS	EM	EMN
1999-01-31	0.30000000	0.30000000	0.40000000
1999-02-28	0.30543000	0.29640000	0.40404000
1999-03-31	0.30478860	0.29942328	0.40496929
1999-04-30	0.30963474	0.31693954	0.40630569
1999-05-31	0.32257747	0.33690673	0.41065316
1999-06-30	0.32925482	0.33896186	0.41430797
1999-07-31	0.33824348	0.36112997	0.42126835
1999-08-31	0.34108472	0.35892708	0.42695547
1999-09-30	0.34176689	0.35365085	0.43101155
1999-10-31	0.34036565	0.35121066	0.43510616
1999-11-30	0.34128464	0.36132553	0.43797786
1999-12-31	0.34879290	0.38632925	0.44380296

Figure 8.7: Portfolio value at the beginning of each period

End-of-period portfolio value is given as follows:

	DS	EM	EMN
1999-01-31	0.30543000	0.29640000	0.40404000
1999-02-28	0.30478860	0.29942328	0.40496929
1999-03-31	0.30963474	0.31693954	0.40630569
1999-04-30	0.32257747	0.33690673	0.41065316
1999-05-31	0.32925482	0.33896186	0.41430797
1999-06-30	0.33824348	0.36112997	0.42126835
1999-07-31	0.34108472	0.35892708	0.42695547
1999-08-31	0.34176689	0.35365085	0.43101155
1999-09-30	0.34036565	0.35121066	0.43510616
1999-10-31	0.34128464	0.36132553	0.43797786
1999-11-30	0.34879290	0.38632925	0.44380296
1999-12-31	0.35925668	0.43384775	0.45259026

Figure 8.8: Portfolio value at the end of each period

Walk forward testing

Walk forward testing is used in quant finance for identifying the best parameters to be used in a trading strategy. The trading strategy is optimized on a subset of sample data for a specific time window. The rest of the unused data is kept separate for testing purposes. The testing is done on a small window of unused data with the recorded results. Now, the training window is shifted forward to include the testing window and the process is repeated again and again till the testing window is not available.

Walk forward optimization is a method used in finance for determining the best parameters to use in a trading strategy. The trading strategy is optimized with in-sample data for a time window in a data series. The remainder of the data is reserved for out-of-sample testing. A small portion of the reserved data following the in-sample data is tested with the results recorded. The in-sample time window is shifted forward by the period covered by the out-of-sample test, and the process repeated. At the end, all of the recorded results are used to assess the trading strategy.

Grid testing

Let us consider a typical classification problem. Assume you have a dataset and you divide it into training (T) and validating (V) datasets. Here you are trying to solve an optimization problem, let's say P, in which one is trying to reduce the training error in addition to regularization terms, where the optimization problem is a function of model parameter m, training sample T, and some hyperparameters α and β. Solving for given α and β gives you the value of parameter m. Now one can apply the estimated parameters on the validation sample to get the validation error function, and optimize it to get the set of α and β to minimize the error function. But this optimization problem will be very expensive as, for each set of α and β, you need to optimize the objective function, which might not be a convex, concave, or smooth function.

So we subset the set of α and β and, for each pair of selected α and β, we solve the optimization problem. This looks like a grid in space so we call it a grid search. So, a grid search is mostly used to tune the model.

Let us consider a classification example using the random forest technique. Now, construct first a base line model by executing the following code:

```
>library(randomForest)
>library(mlbench)
>library(caret)
>data(Shuttle)
>Analysis_Data<-head(Shuttle,10000)
>X <- Analysis_Data[,1:9]
>Y<- Analysis_Data[,10]
>control <- trainControl(method="repeatedcv", number=5, repeats=3)
>seed <- 4
>metric <- "Accuracy"
>set.seed(seed)
>Count_var <- sqrt(ncol(X))
>tunegrid <- expand.grid(.mtry=Count_var)
>rf_baseline <- train(Class~., data=Analysis_Data, method="rf",
metric=metric, tuneGrid=tunegrid, trControl=control)
>print(rf_baseline)
```

It generates the summary output of the random forest model:

```
Random Forest

10000 samples
    9 predictor
    7 classes: 'Rad.Flow', 'Fpv.Close', 'Fpv.Open', 'High', 'Bypass', 'Bpv.Close', 'Bpv.Open'

No pre-processing
Resampling: Cross-Validated (5 fold, repeated 3 times)
Summary of sample sizes: 8000, 8000, 7999, 7999, 8002, 8000, ...
Resampling results:

  Accuracy     Kappa
  0.99870012   0.99636874

Tuning parameter 'mtry' was held constant at a value of 3
```

Figure 8.9: Summary output for random forest

A grid search means you have given a pool of models which are different from each other in their parameter values, which lie on grids. Train each of the models and evaluate them using cross-validation to select the best model.

Now, let us try to apply the grid search method and check the accuracy. This can be done by executing the following code:

```
> control <- trainControl(method="repeatedcv", number=5, repeats=3,
search="grid")
> set.seed(seed)
> tunegrid <- expand.grid(.mtry=c(1:8))
> rf_gridsearch_method <- train(Class~., data=Analysis_Data, method="rf",
metric=metric, tuneGrid=tunegrid, trControl=control)
> print(rf_gridsearch_method)
```

It gives the following output with better estimates:

```
Random Forest

10000 samples
    9 predictor
    7 classes: 'Rad.Flow', 'Fpv.Close', 'Fpv.Open', 'High', 'Bypass', 'Bpv.Close', 'Bpv.Open'

No pre-processing
Resampling: Cross-Validated (5 fold, repeated 3 times)
Summary of sample sizes: 8000, 8000, 7999, 7999, 8002, 8000, ...
Resampling results across tuning parameters:

  mtry  Accuracy    Kappa
  1     0.99776668  0.99374580
  2     0.99853342  0.99590143
  3     0.99880015  0.99664946
  4     0.99886685  0.99683583
  5     0.99883357  0.99674691
  6     0.99880025  0.99665462
  7     0.99886685  0.99684045
  8     0.99886682  0.99683975

Accuracy was used to select the optimal model using  the largest value.
The final value used for the model was mtry = 4.
```

Figure 8.10: Grid search output for random forest

Now, let us plot the accuracy for different random forest models for different sets of attributes, which can be done by executing the following code:

```
> plot(rf_gridsearch_method)
```

This gives tuned random forest parameters in R using grid search:

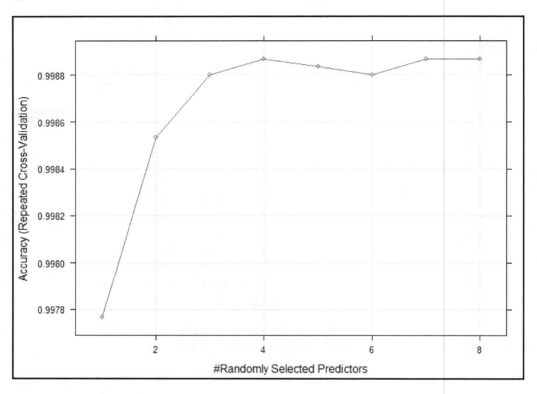

Figure 8.11: Accuracy plot for different random forest models

It compares the pool of models in terms of accuracy.

Genetic algorithm

Genetic algorithm (**GA**) is a search-based optimization technique whose fundamentals come from the theory of genetics and natural selection. It is used to solve optimization problems in research and machine learning areas which are very difficult and time-consuming solutions by alternative methods.

Optimization is the process of finding a solution which is better when compared to all other alternative solutions. It takes the space of all the possible solutions as search space, and then finds a solution which is most suited to the problem.

In GA, possible candidate solutions constitute the population and they recombine and mutate to produce new children, and this process is repeated over various generations. Each possible candidate solution is given a fitness value based upon the objective function. The fitter probable candidates are given preference for recombination and mutation to yield fitter candidate solutions.

Some of the most important terminology associated with GA is as follows:

- **Population**: It is a subset of all the possible candidate solutions of the existing problem
- **Chromosomes**: A chromosome is one solution to the given problem
- **Gene**: A gene is one element position of a chromosome

For example, let us assume that the last year of the portfolio with the following stocks, contributes with the returns mentioned if invested with the same proportion as mentioned here. Then we need to please maximize the performance of the portfolio by limiting the total weight to one:

Stocks	Returns	Weights
Stock1	10	.1
Stock2	11	.2
Stock3	15	.1
Stock4	20	.2
Stock5	12	.2
Stock6	13	.3

Let us try to solve it using GA in R.

First let us define the input data requirement, which can be done by executing the following code:

```
>install.packages("genalg")
>library(genalg)
>library(ggplot2)
>InputDataset <- data.frame(Stocks = c("Stock1", "Stock2", "Stock3",
"Stock4", "Stock5", "Stock6"), returns = c(10, 11, 15, 20, 12, 13), weight
= c(.1, .2, .1, .2, .2, .3))
>WTlimit <- 1
>InputDataset
```

This gives the following output:

```
  Stocks returns weight
1 Stock1      10    0.1
2 Stock2      11    0.2
3 Stock3      15    0.1
4 Stock4      20    0.2
5 Stock5      12    0.2
6 Stock6      13    0.3
```

Figure 8.12: Input dataset for GA

Now let us set the evaluation function as shown in the following code:

```
>evaluationFunc <- function(x) {
    current_solution_returns <- x %*% InputDataset$returns
    current_solution_weight <- x %*% InputDataset$weight

    if (current_solution_weight > WTlimit)
        return(0) else return(-current_solution_returns)
}
```

Then, let us design the model and execute it. This can be done by executing the following code:

```
> GAmodel <- rbga.bin(size = 6, popSize = 100, iters = 50, mutationChance =
0.01,
+     elitism = T, evalFunc = evaluationFunc)
> cat(summary(GAmodel))
```

Here:

- `size` is the number of genes in the chromosome
- `popsize` is the population size
- `iters` is the number of iterations
- `mutationChance` is the chance that the chromosome mutates
- `elitism` is the number of chromosomes that are kept for the next generation; by default, it is 20%
- `evalFunc` is the user-supplied evaluation function for given chromosomes

This, upon execution, gives the following output:

```
GA Settings
  Type                 = binary chromosome
  Population size      = 100
  Number of Generations = 50
  Elitism              = TRUE
  Mutation Chance      = 0.01

Search Domain
  Var 1 = [,]
  Var 0 = [,]

GA Results
  Best Solution : 1 0 1 1 1 1
```

Figure 8.13: Summary output for GA model

It says to retain all the stocks apart from `Stock2` to obtain the optimal portfolio.

Let us consider another example of genetic algorithm. Here, we will try to estimate the coefficients by genetic algorithm and the traditional OLS method.

First, let us consider a dataset using the following code:

```
>library(GA)
> data(economics)
> Data_Analysis<-data.frame(economics[,2:4])
>head(Data_Analysis)
```

This gives the following dataset:

```
    pce      pop psavert
1 507.4 198712    12.5
2 510.5 198911    12.5
3 516.3 199113    11.7
4 512.9 199311    12.5
5 518.1 199498    12.5
6 525.8 199657    12.1
```

Figure 8.14: Input sample for parameter estimates by GA

Now, let us try to estimate `pce` in terms of `pop` and `psavert` by GA. Let us now create a function to evaluate linear regression, which is given by the following code:

```
>OLS_GA <- function(Data_Analysis, a0, a1, a2){
  attach(Data_Analysis, warn.conflicts=F)
  Y_hat <- a0  + a1*pop + a2*psavert
  SSE = t(pce-Y_hat) %*% (pce-Y_hat)
  detach(Data_Analysis)
  return(SSE)
}
```

Then, let us try to estimate the coefficients by GA, which can be done by executing the following code:

```
>ga.OLS_GA <- ga(type='real-valued', min=c(-100,-100,-100),
          max=c(100, 100, 100), popSize=500, maxiter=500,
names=c('intercept', 'pop', 'psavert'),
          keepBest=T, fitness = function(a) -OLS(Data_Analysis,
a[1],a[2], a[3]))
        > summary(ga.OLS_GA)
```

This gives the following output:

```
+-----------------------------------+
|            Genetic Algorithm      |
+-----------------------------------+

GA settings:
Type                  =   real-valued
Population size       =   500
Number of generations =   500
Elitism               =   25
Crossover probability =   0.8
Mutation probability  =   0.1
Search domain =
     intercept  pop psavert
Min      -100 -100    -100
Max       100  100     100

GA results:
Iterations            = 500
Fitness function value = -50993.402
Solution =
       intercept        pop   psavert
[1,] -65.148507 -3.3523091 1.8071988
```

Figure 8.15: Summary output parameter estimates by GA

Questions

1. What is the significance of optimization in quant finance?
2. What is the dynamic rebalancing optimization method? Give an example of how to execute it in R.
3. How can a grid search be used to fine-tune a classification model? Please provide an example in R.
4. How can genetic algorithm be used in R for optimizing a trading algorithm?
5. How can genetic algorithm be used in R for estimating a model coefficient in R? Provide an example.

Summary

In this chapter, we have discussed various optimization techniques used in trading algorithms and parameter estimation. The covered optimization techniques were dynamic rebalancing, walk forward testing, grid testing, and genetic algorithm.

In the next chapter, the topics covered are using `foptions`, `termstrc`, `CreditMetrics`, `credule`, `GUIDE`, and `fExoticOptions` to price options, bond, credit spreads, credit default swaps, interest rate derivatives, and different types of exotic options.

9
Derivative Pricing

Algorithmic trading and financial engineering are the two most computationally intensive parts of finance. People in these areas are not only experts in finance, mathematics, and statistics, but they are also well versed in computationally intensive software. In the earlier chapters, we have learnt about algorithmic trading. In this chapter, we will study the different types of derivative pricing techniques in R, as pricing of derivatives is the most crucial part of financial engineering.

Derivative price depends upon the value of its underlying. We will start with a few basic option pricing models and move to other asset classes:

- Option pricing
- Implied volatility
- Bond pricing
- Credit spread
- Credit default swaps
- Interest rate derivatives
- Exotic options

Option pricing

The binomial model works with the continuous process, while the Cox-Ross-Rubinstein model works with the discrete process. Option price depends upon stock price, strike price, interest rates, volatility, and time to expiry. We will use the package fOption for the Black-Scholes model. The following commands install and load this into the workspace:

```
> install.packages("fOptions")
> library(fOptions)
```

Black-Scholes model

Let us consider an example of `call` and `put` options using hypothetical data in June 2015 with a maturity of September 2015, that is, 3 months to time to maturity. Assume that the current price of the underlying stock is USD 900, the strike price is USD 950, the volatility is 22%, and the risk-free rate is 2%. We also have to set the cost of carry (`b`); in the original Black-Scholes model (with underlying paying no dividends), it equals the risk-free rate.

The following command `GBSOption()` calculates the `call` option price using all other parameters. The first parameter is type of option, that is, `call` or `put`, the second is current stock price, the third is strike price, the fourth, fifth, sixth, and seventh are time to expiry, risk-free rate of interest, volatility, and cost of carry:

```
>model <- GBSOption(TypeFlag = "c", S = 900, X =950, Time   = 1/4, r =
0.02,sigma = 0.22, b = 0.02)
```

The output of the model can be seen by typing `model` on the R console and it consists of the title, which is Black-Scholes option, methodology, function syntax, parameters used and, toward the end, it has option price:

```
> model
Title:
Black Scholes Option Valuation
Call:
GBSOption(TypeFlag = "c", S = 900, X = 950, Time = 1/4, r = 0.02,   b =
0.02, sigma = 0.22)
Parameters:
Value:
 TypeFlag c
 S        900
 X        950
 Time     0.25
 r        0.02
b         0.02
sigma               0.22
Option Price:
               21.79275
Description:
 Sat Dec 31 11:53:06 2016
```

If you would like to find the option price, you can do so using the following line of code:

```
> model@price
[1] 21.79275
```

You can change the first parameter to p if you would like to calculate the put option price.

The following command will calculate the put option price and extract only price. It does not show other items in output as we used @price:

```
> GBSOption(TypeFlag = "p", S = 900, X =950, Time = 1/4, r = 0.02, sigma = 0.22, b = 0.02)@price
[1] 67.05461
```

Cox-Ross-Rubinstein model

The Cox-Ross-Rubinstein model assumes that the underlying asset price follows a discrete binomial process. The price either goes up or down in each period. The important feature of the CRR model is that the magnitude of the up movement is inversely proportional to the down movement, that is, *u=1/d*. The price after two periods will be the same if it first goes up and then goes down or vice versa, as shown in *Figure 9.1*.

The following two commands compute the call and put option prices using the binomial model and keeps all other parameters the same as in the continuous case except the last parameter. The last parameter is the number of steps time is to be divided to model the option. I used n=3, which means only three steps are used to price option:

```
> CRRBinomialTreeOption(TypeFlag = "ce", S = 900, X = 950, Time = 1/4, r = 0.02, b = 0.02, sigma = 0.22, n = 3)@price
[1] 20.33618
> CRRBinomialTreeOption(TypeFlag = "pe", S = 900, X = 950, Time = 1/4, r = 0.02, b = 0.02, sigma = 0.22, n = 3)@price
[1] 65.59803
```

However, all the values supplied to the Black-Scholes and binominal models are the same but the output is not exactly the same, it is a little bit different for both call and put options. If we are interested in the path or trajectory of the price movement then we should use the following command, which calculates the binomial tree of the call option price, and save the result in variable named model.

The second command uses the variable model to plot the binomial tree, which is done using BonimialTreePlot(); it also helps in placing the option value in tree. Third and fourth are x-axis and y-axis labels, and the fifth is x-axis limit.

The third command is used to place the title of the figure:

```
>model<- BinomialTreeOption(TypeFlag = "ce", S = 900, X = 950,Time = 1/4, r
= 0.02, b = 0.02, sigma = 0.22, n = 3)
> BinomialTreePlot(model, dy = 1, xlab = "Time steps",ylab = "Options
Value", xlim = c(0,4) ,ylim=c(-3,4))
> title(main = "Call Option Tree")
```

Now, if you are interested in calculating the put option value then you should use the first parameter, that is, `TypeFlag="pe"`, in `BinomialTreeOption()`. As the number of steps increases, the binomial tree results converge to continuous case. This can be verified using a `for` loop with 100 iterations. For this, we can define the `func` function with one parameter.

Here is the definition of the function:

```
> func <- function(n) {
       pr  <-  CRRBinomialTreeOption(TypeFlag = "ce", S = 900, X = 950, Time
= 1/4, r = 0.02, b = 0.02, sigma = 0.22, n = n)@price
    return(pr) }
```

In the following figure, you can see the option price, which shows the price at each node:

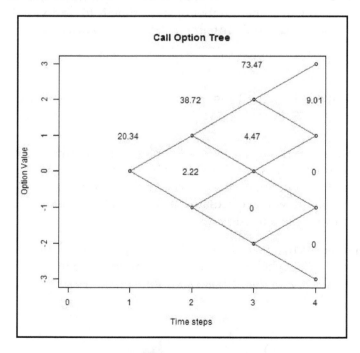

Figure 9.1: Call option value at each node

The rightmost layer has four nodes and the prices are **0, 0, 9.01**, and **138.9** from down. The third layer has three nodes and the prices are **0, 4.47** and **73.47**, and so on.

Figure 9.1 is for three time steps. However, we can increase the number of steps and the option price starts converging to fair price as the number of steps increases. We have to put the `func` function into the loop from 1 to 100. Next, we can plug this into `sapply()` along with iterations 1 to 100 and `func`, which results in a sequence of 100 option prices with an increasing number of steps.

The following code shows the use of `sapply()`, and *Figure 9.2* shows the binomial prices and CRR prices with 100 step sizes:

```
price <- sapply(1:100,func)
```

As the number of steps increases, we can see in the following figure that CRR price converges to Black-Scholes price:

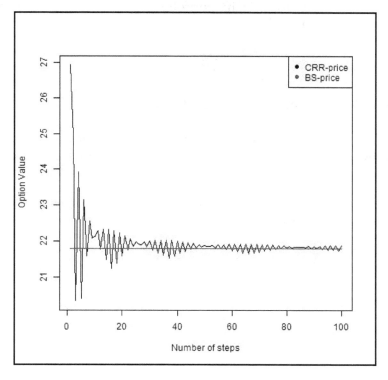

Figure 9.2: Black-Scholes and CRR prices

Greeks

Greeks are also very important in option pricing. It helps to understand the movement of option price against different factors such as underlying price, time to expiry, risk-free rate of return, and volatility. The GBSGreeks() function calculates Greeks, where the first parameter is for what Greek we are interested in, the second is for option type, the third is for underlying price, the fourth for exercise price, the fifth for time to maturity, the sixth for risk-free rate of interest, and the seventh and eighth for annualized cost of carry and annualized volatility. Using the following code, we can calculate delta of the call option:

```
> GBSGreeks(Selection = "delta", TypeFlag = "c", S = 900, X = 950,Time =
1/4, r = 0.02, b = 0.02, sigma = 0.22)
[1] 0.3478744
```

Similarly, you can change the second parameter to p, which will give you delta for the put options. Understanding of Greeks is important as this shows how Greeks change with other market parameters. This helps to diversify portfolios and control risk. Gamma can be calculated using the following code:

```
> GBSGreeks(Selection = 'gamma', TypeFlag = "c", S = 900, X = 950,Time =
1/4, r = 0.02, b = 0.02, sigma = 0.22)
[1] 0.003733069
```

Similarly, you can calculate Vega, Rho, and Theta for call and put options controlling the first and second parameters. Now, suppose you want to calculate delta of a straddle portfolio, that is, a portfolio of call and put options for the same underlying, striking price, and expiration date, you should calculate delta separately for call and put options and add them.

The following code calculates the delta for call and put options for prices ranging from 500 to 1500 with increment of 1:

```
>portfolio<- sapply(c('c', 'p'), function(otype)
sapply(500:1500, function(price) GBSGreeks(Selection = 'delta', TypeFlag =
otype, S = price,X = 950, Time = 1/4, r = 0.02, b = 0.02, sigma = 0.22)))
```

This command shows the first few values of the `call` and `put` option delta separately. The first column is for `call` and the second column is for `put` option delta:

```
> head(portfolio)
                  c           p
[1,] 4.902164e-09          -1
[2,] 5.455563e-09          -1
[3,] 6.068198e-09          -1
[4,] 6.746050e-09          -1
[5,] 7.495664e-09          -1
```

We plot the straddle portfolio's `delta` using `plot()` using the following code:

```
> plot(500:1500, rowSums(portfolio), type='l',xlab='underlying Price', ylab
= 'Straddle Delta')
```

The first parameter is the x axis, which is underlying price; in our case, it is ranging from 500 to 1500. The second parameter is the y axis, which is the sum of `call` and `put delta`, keeping all other parameters constant. The following figure shows the `delta` for the straddle portfolio which lies between -1 to 1 and is S-shaped:

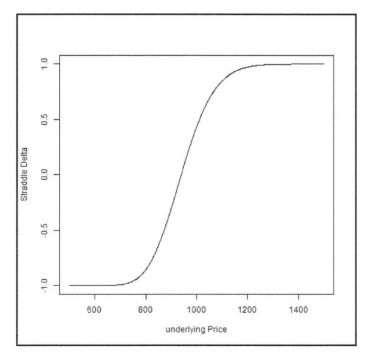

Figure 9.3: Delta of straddle portfolio

Implied volatility

In option trading, we calculated volatility as historical volatility and implied volatility. Historical volatility is the price deviation in the past one year while implied volatility, on the other hand, is calculated using option price and implies stock volatility in the future. Implied volatility is crucial in option trading as it gives the future estimate of stock volatility. European `call` option implied volatility can be calculated using `EuropeanOptionImpliedVolatility()`, as shown in the following code. The first parameter is type of option, the second is `call` or `put` price, the third and fourth are current price of underlying and strike price of option, the fifth is dividend yield, and the sixth, seventh, and eighth parameters are risk-free rate of return, time to maturity in years, and initial guess for volatility:

```
>iv  <-EuropeanOptionImpliedVolatility("call", 11.10, 100, 100, 0.01, 0.03,
0.5,0.4)
> iv
[1] 0.3805953
```

Similarly, implied volatility for the American option can be calculated using `AmericanOptionImpliedVolatility()`.

Bond pricing

Bonds are very important financial instruments as they provide cash flow at a certain time at the predetermined rate or current market rate. Bonds help investors to create well-diversified portfolios. One must calculate bond price, yield, and maturity precisely to get a better idea of the instrument. We are going to use package `termstrc` for this. We have to install and load it into the R workspace using the following code:

```
> install.packages('termstrc')
> library('termstrc')
```

We will use the data `govtbonds` in the package, which can be loaded and viewed using the following code:

```
> data(govbonds)
> govbonds
This is a data set of coupon bonds for:
GERMANY AUSTRIA FRANCE ,
observed at 2008-01-30.
```

The variable govbonds has bond data for three countries – Germany, Austria, and France. We will be using the Germany data to calculate bond prices, which can be accessed using govbonds[[1]]. The following two lines of code generate cashflow and maturity matrix:

```
> cashflow <- create_cashflows_matrix(govbonds[[1]])
> maturity <- create_maturities_matrix(govbonds[[1]])
```

Next, we will look at the usage of bond_prices(), which calculates the bond prices. beta is another parameter to be supplied to the function bond_prices(). Next we can create the beta variable and defined bond_prices(). The first parameter in this function is method, which supports three methods:

- ns for Nelson/Siegel
- dl for Diebold/Li
- sv for the Svensson approach

We will choose the ns method for the following code:

```
> beta <- c(0.0323,-0.023,-0.0403,3.234)
> bp <-  bond_prices(method="ns",beta,maturity,cashflow)
```

The variable bp has spot rates, discount factors, and bond prices. Any information can be accessed using $. For example, you can bond prices using the following code:

```
> bp$bond_prices
```

Bond yield is investor return which is realized on bond investment, and it can be calculated using bond_yields(). The following two lines of code generate cashflow and maturity matrices, which include dirty prices as well:

```
> cashflow <- create_cashflows_matrix(govbonds[[1]],include_price=T)
> maturity <- create_maturities_matrix(govbonds[[1]],include_price=T)
```

The following code calculates the bond yield and maturities in matrix form:

```
>by <- bond_yields(cashflow,maturity)
```

The output of the preceding code can be seen by typing the following command `head()` and the output has two columns, where the first column of the output matrix is maturity in years and the second column is the corresponding bond yield for the corresponding bonds. Bond names are given as an index of output:

```
> head(by)
                    Maturity                   Yield
DE0001141414        0.04383562                 0.03525805
DE0001137131        0.12054795                 0.03424302
DE0001141422        0.19726027                 0.03798065
DE0001137149        0.36986301                 0.03773425
```

The following figure shows yield curve or term structure against various maturities. Yields fluctuate initially for a very small maturity period and continuously increase as the maturity increases:

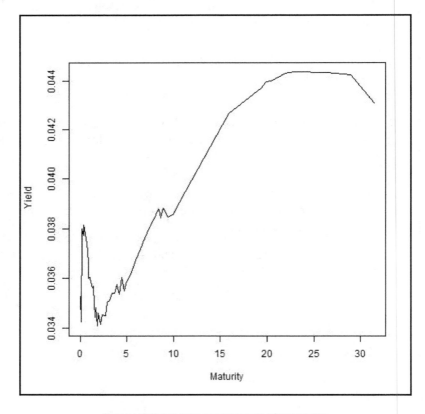

Figure 9.4: Yield curve, that is, term structure with different maturities

Duration measures the length of time it takes for the price of the bond to be repaid by its internal `cashflow`. It is a very important factor for investors to consider, as bonds with higher duration carry more risk and higher price volatility than bonds with lower duration. Duration can be measured using the following code:

```
>    dur <- duration(cashflow,maturity, by[,"Yield"])
```

It returns duration in years, modified duration, and weights for all bonds in the portfolio. If you want to look at the portfolio composition, you can see the third column of the output matrix. The third column is weights for your investment and you would see that the sum of the weights is equal to 1:

```
> sum(dur[,3])
[1] 1
```

Credit spread

Credit risk is one of the major problems for financial institutions. The major cause for this is credit quality, and credit spread values help to understand credit risk depending upon the credit quality. Credit spread is an important concept in institutional trading as credit spread depends upon the quality or rating of bonds. It is the difference in bond yield of two bonds with similar maturity but with different bond ratings. We are going to use the `CreditMetrics` package for this, which can be installed and imported to the R workspace using the following two commands:

```
> install.packages('CreditMetrics')
> library('CreditMetrics')
```

Credit spread is calculated using `cm.cs()`, which has just two parameters. The first parameter is the one-year migration matrix for some institution or government which issues credit and the second parameter is **loss given default** (**LGD**), which means maximum loss if the obligor of credit defaults. Normally, credit with rating `AAA` is on the top and considered as safe, and rating `D` is on the bottom and considered as default.

The following code is a vector of all credit ratings:

```
> rc <- c("AAA", "AA", "A", "BBB", "BB", "B", "CCC", "D")
```

The preceding code shows we have eight ratings. The transition matrix is the probability of going from one credit rating to another.

This code generates a matrix of such probabilities in an eight-by-eight matrix, with rating as index and column names:

```
> M <- matrix(c(90.81, 8.33, 0.68, 0.06, 0.08, 0.02, 0.01, 0.01,
+ 0.70, 90.65, 7.79, 0.64, 0.06, 0.13, 0.02, 0.01,
+ 0.09, 2.27, 91.05, 5.52, 0.74, 0.26, 0.01, 0.06,
+ 0.02, 0.33, 5.95, 85.93, 5.30, 1.17, 1.12, 0.18,
+ 0.03, 0.14, 0.67, 7.73, 80.53, 8.84, 1.00, 1.06,
+ 0.01, 0.11, 0.24, 0.43, 6.48, 83.46, 4.07, 5.20,
+ 0.21, 0, 0.22, 1.30, 2.38, 11.24, 64.86, 19.79,
+ 0, 0, 0, 0, 0, 0, 0, 100
+ )/100, 8, 8, dimnames = list(rc, rc), byrow = TRUE)
```

You can have a look at this matrix by typing the variable name, that is, `M`, on the command prompt, as shown here:

```
> M
          AAA      AA       A    BBB      BB       B    CCC        D
AA   0.9081  0.0833  0.0068  0.0006  0.0008  0.0002  0.0001  0.0001
AA   0.0070  0.9065  0.0779  0.0064  0.0006  0.0013  0.0002  0.0001
A    0.0009  0.0227  0.9105  0.0552  0.0074  0.0026  0.0001  0.0006
BBB  0.0002  0.0033  0.0595  0.8593  0.0530  0.0117  0.0112  0.0018
BB   0.0003  0.0014  0.0067  0.0773  0.8053  0.0884  0.0100  0.0106
B    0.0001  0.0011  0.0024  0.0043  0.0648  0.8346  0.0407  0.0520
CCC  0.0021  0.0000  0.0022  0.0130  0.0238  0.1124  0.6486  0.1979
D    0.0000  0.0000 -0.0000  0.0000  0.0000  0.0000  0.0000  1.0000
```

You can see in the preceding table that the last column has probabilities of default for bonds of all ratings; that means it is very unlikely bonds with AAA, AA, and A rating will default. However, the default probability increases as the bond rating deteriorates towards CCC. The last row has all zeros except for the last one, which means bonds which are default have zero probability of improving the rating. We can set the loss given default (`lgd`) parameter as `0.2` in the following code:

```
> lgd <- 0.2
```

As we have designed a transition matrix and set the `lgd` parameter, we can now use the `cm.cs()` function to generate credit spread.

The following code does this and calculates credit spread for all ratings respectively:

```
> cm.cs(M, lgd)
AAA              AA        A         BBB        BB          B         CCC
0.0000200   0.0000200   0.000120   0.000360   0.002122   0.010454   0.040384
```

The preceding results illustrate that credit spread is less for good credit rating bonds and it increases as we move toward the left or as the probability of default increases. The rightmost rating CCC has the highest spread of 4% because, as per above matrix M, the probability of default for CCC rating bonds is 19.79 % .Value at risk for this credit can be calculated using cm.CVaR(), which has nine parameters. The first two parameters are the same as for cm.cs(), that is, migration matrix and loss given default (lgd), and the remaining are exposure at default, number of companies, number of simulated random numbers, risk-free interest, correlation matrix, confidence level, and rating of companies.

All parameters are set as follows:

```
> ead <- c(4000000, 1000000, 10000000)      #  Exposure at default
> N <- 3              # Number of companies
> n <- 50000          # Number of simulated random numbers
>r <- 0.03                    # Risk free interest rate
> rating <- c("BBB", "AA", "B")          # Rating of selected companies
> firmnames <- c("firm 1", "firm 2", "firm 3")
> alpha <- 0.99          # Confidence interval
# Correlation matrix
> rho <- matrix(c( 1, 0.4, 0.6, 0.4, 1, 0.5, 0.6, 0.5, 1), 3, 3, dimnames =
list(firmnames, firmnames), byrow = TRUE)
```

Credit value at risk can be used in the following line of code, where the parameters are as defined previously:

```
> cm.CVaR(M, lgd, ead, N, n, r, rho, alpha, rating)
     1%
3993485
```

This credit VaR number is annualized, which means there is a 1% chance that this portfolio of three companies might lose this value in the next year. This output is based on simulated prices. Simulated prices change in every run so cm.CVaR() output might also change every time you execute the preceding code. ca.gain(), which requires all the parameters as cm.CVaR() except alpha, is used to calculate simulated profit and loss and can be used like the following code:

```
> pnl <- cm.gain(M, lgd, ead, N, n, r, rho, rating)
```

Credit default swaps

In brief, a **credit default swap** (**CDS**) is used to transfer the credit risk of a reference entity (corporate or sovereign) from one party to another. In a standard CDS contract, one party purchases credit protection from another party, to cover the loss of the face value of an asset following a credit event. A credit event is a legally defined event that typically includes bankruptcy, failure-to-pay, and restructuring. The protection lasts until some specified maturity date. To pay for this protection, the protection buyer makes a regular stream of payments, known as the premium leg, to the protection seller. This size of these premium payments is calculated from a quoted default swap spread, which is paid on the face value of the protection. These payments are made until a credit event occurs or until maturity, whichever occurs first. The issuer of the CDS derivative has to price it before selling. We will be using the `credule` package for this.

These two codes are used for installing this package and loading it into the R workspace:

```
> install.packages('credule')
> library('credule')
```

`priceCDS()` calculates the spread of several CDSs of different maturities from a yield curve and credit curve. Here, we are going to define parameters which will be used for pricing CDSs. The yield curve vector is defined below and is the tenor of each yield curve in years:

```
>yct = c(1,2,3,4,5,7)
```

Here, the vector is defined as yield curve discounted rate, which is going to be the second parameter in the pricing CDS function:

```
> ycr = c(0.0050,0.0070,0.0080,0.0100, 0.0120,0.0150)
```

The following two lines of code define the tenor of the credit curve in years and survival probability for a tenor:

```
>cct = c(1,3,5,7)
>ccsp = c(0.99,0.98,0.95,0.92)
```

Next is the maturity of the CDS in years, which we are going to price:

```
>tenors = c(1,3,5,7)
```

Another parameter is defined here, which is recovery rate in case of default:

```
>r = 0.40
```

We have successfully defined mandatory parameters. The next line does the job of pricing the CDS of multiple tenors:

```
> priceCDS(yct,ycr,cct,ccsp,tenors,r)
  tenor      spread
      1 0.006032713
      3 0.004057761
      5 0.006101041
      7 0.007038156
```

The preceding function returns a DataFrame where the first column is tenors and the second column is spreads for **credit default swaps** (CDS) for a given tenor. If you would like to use the bootstrap technique to understand the probability distribution of credit default swaps then you can use `bootstrapCDS()`, which has yield curve tenor, yield curve rates, CDS tenor, CDS spread, and recovery rates. We are going to define the `cdsSpread` parameter, as all other parameters have already been defined above, which we will use in `bootstrapCDS()`:

```
> cdsSpreads = c(0.0050,0.0070,0.0090,0.0110)
```

The following command gives the bootstrap credit curve for credit default swap spreads for different maturities:

```
> bootstrapCDS(yct,ycr,cct,ccsp,r)
  tenor      survprob       hazrate
1       1 0.187640397   1.673228e+00
2       3 0.007953847   1.580436e+00
3       5 0.007953847   2.081668e-15
4       7 0.007953847   4.579670e-15
```

The output of the preceding command generates three columns. The first is the tenor, the second column is survival probability for each tenor, and the last column is hazard rate, that is, the intensity of Poisson distribution, for each tenor.

Interest rate derivatives

We will use the GUIDE package to calculate the price for interest rate derivatives:

```
> install.packages("GUIDE")
> library(GUIDE)
```

The following command will open a pop-up window which requires all the parameters. Once you supply the required parameters in the pop-up window, it generates the interest rate derivative price:

```
>irswapvalue()
```

Parameters to be supplied in the pop-up window are as follows:

- **Notional:** To be entered in decimals
- **Fixed rate**: Entered in decimals, for example, 0.05 for 5%
- **Last spot rate**: Entered in decimals, for example, 0.05 for 5 per cent
- **Months for first payment**: Enter 3 for 3 months
- **Spot rates**: Enter with comma separation, for example, 0.054, 0.056, 0.058
- **Frequency of spot rates**: Chosen from continuous/quarterly/semi-annual/annual
- **Settlement frequency**: Chosen from quarterly/semi-annual/annual

Exotic options

Asian, barrier, binary, and lookback options are a few exotic options. Exotic options are quite different than normal American or European options, or vanilla options, and have a few new features which make it quite complex to price. An American or European `call` or `put` option is considered as a non-exotic or vanilla option. Exotic options are complex because of a few features:

- The way it gets settled varies depending on the moneyless of the option at the time of maturity. It can be settled in cash as well as stock options.
- It could also involve foreign exchange rates.
- Payoff at the time of maturity depends not just on the underlying stock price but on its value at several times during the contract life.

We will be using the `fExoticOptions` package to price various types of exotic options. For this, the following two lines of code are used to install and load this package into the R workspace:

```
> install.packages('fExoticOptions')
> library(fExoticOptions)
```

Asian options can be priced in different ways. Here are a few functions to price Asian options. `GeometricAverageRateOption()` prices Asian options based on geometric average rate options.

Here is a code with the Asian `call` option pricing function using geometric average rate option. The first parameter is the `call` (`"c"`) option and other parameters are stock price (`110`), exercise price (`120`), time to maturity (`0.5`, that is, 6 months), risk-free interest rate (`3%`), cost of carry (`5%`), and volatility (`10%`):

```
> price <- GeometricAverageRateOption("c", 110, 120, 0.5, 0.03, 0.05, 0.1)
> price
Title:
 Geometric Average Rate Option
Call:
 GeometricAverageRateOption(TypeFlag = "c", S = 110, X = 120,
     Time = 0.5, r = 0.03, b = 0.05, sigma = 0.1)


Parameters:
 Value:
 TypeFlag c
 S          110
 X          120
 Time       0.5
 r          0.03
 b          0.05
 sigma                    0.1
Option Price:
 0.06067219
Description:
 Sun Jan 15 01:00:34 2017
```

You can calculate the price for Asian `put` options as well by replacing `c` with `p`. `TurnbullWakemanAsianApproxOption()` also calculates the Asian option price and is based on Turnbull and Wakeman's approximation. It uses two new parameters (`SA`), time and `tau` in addition to parameters used in previous functions. `SA` and time are used. Here is the code:

```
> TurnbullWakemanAsianApproxOption(TypeFlag = "p", S = 100, SA = 102, X =
120, Time = 0.50, time = 0.25, tau = 0.0, r = 0.03, b = 0.05, sigma =
0.1)@price
[1] 18.54625
```

However, there is another technique to calculate the Asian option price by using
`LevyAsianApproxOption()`, which uses Levy's approximation to price Asian options and
use all parameters used in `TurnbullWakemanAsianApproxOption()` except `tau`:

```
> LevyAsianApproxOption(TypeFlag = "p", S = 100, SA = 102, X = 120, Time =
0.50, time = 0.25, r = 0.03,  b = 0.05, sigma = 0.1)@price
[1] 18.54657
```

There are many functions to calculate the price for barrier options as well. Standard barrier
option, double barrier option, and lookback barrier option are a few of them. There are four
types of single barrier options.

The type flag `cdi` denotes a down-and-in call, `cui` denotes an up-and-in call, `cdo` denotes a
down-and-out call, and `cuo` denotes an up-and-out call.

The following command calculates the standard barrier option price using
`StandardBarrierOption()`, which requires two additional parameters in
`GeometricAverageRateOption()` and these additional parameters are barrier value and
rebate value.

The first parameter is option type, which is a down-and-out call in the following command:

```
>  StandardBarrierOption(TypeFlag = "cdo", S = 100, X = 90, H = 95, K = 3,
Time = 0.5,  r = 0.08, b = 0.04, sigma = 0.25)@price
[1] 9.024584
```

In the preceding command, `H = 95` is barrier value and `K=3` is rebate. Double barrier
option requires lower (`L`) and upper (`U`) bounds along with curvature of lower and upper
bounds, that is, `delta1` and `delta2`. It also has four types of options.

The type flag `co` denotes an up-and-out-down-and-out call, `ci` denotes an up-and-in-down-
and-in `call`, `po` denotes an up-and-out-down-and-out `put`, and `pi` denotes an up-and-in-
down-and-in call. We will use `co` type option in the following command along with other
parameters to calculate the double barrier option price:

```
>  DoubleBarrierOption(TypeFlag = "co", S = 100, X = 100, L = 50,U = 150,
Time = 0.25,  r = 0.10, b = 0.10, sigma = 0.15,delta1 = -0.1, delta2 =
0.1)@price
[1] 4.351415
```

The option comes into existence if it is a knock-in barrier or becomes worthless if it is a knocked-out barrier. Lookback barrier is another type of barrier option and it also has four types, `cuo` denotes an up-and-out call, `cui` denotes an up-and-in call, `pdo` denotes a down-and-out put, `pdi` denotes a down-and-in put.The option's barrier monitoring period starts at time zero and ends at an arbitrary date before expiration. If the barrier is not triggered during this period, the fixed strike lookback option will be kicked off at the end of the barrier tenor.

The following line of code calculates the lookback barrier, that is, `cuo`, option price:

```
> LookBarrierOption(TypeFlag = "cuo", S = 100, X = 100, H = 130,time1 =
0.25, Time2 = 1, r = 0.1, b = 0.1, sigma = 0.15)@price
[1] 17.05969
```

Barrier options are another kind of exotic option, which are also called digital options. Unlike standard European-style options, the payout for binary options does not depend on how much it is in the money but rather whether or not it is on the money. The option's payoff is fixed at the option's inception and is based on the price of the underlying asset on the expiration date. Gap option, cash or nothing, and two asset cash or nothing are a few of the binary options. The payoff on a gap option depends on the usual factors of a plain option, but is also affected by a `gap` amount of exercise prices, which may be positive or negative. The following commands calculate gap option, which is one of the binary options, price using `GapOption()` and the `X1` and `X2` parameters in this function are two exercise price which create gap option, and all other parameters are as usual:

```
> GapOption(TypeFlag = "c", S = 50, X1 = 50, X2 = 57, Time = 0.5,r = 0.09,
b = 0.09, sigma = 0.20)
```

`CashOrNothingOption()` calculates the price for the cash or nothing option and for this option, a predetermined amount is paid at expiration if the asset is above for a call or below for a put at strike level. The amount independent of the path is taken. These options require no payment of an exercise price. The exercise price determines whether or not the option returns a payoff. The value of a cash-or-nothing `call` (`put`) option is the present value of the fixed cash payoff multiplied by the probability that the terminal price will be greater than (less than) the exercise price. The following line has `S` as stock price, `X` as exercise price, and `K` as cash amount to be paid at expiry if the option expires in the money:

```
> CashOrNothingOption(TypeFlag = "p", S = 100, X = 80, K = 10,Time = 9/12,
r = 0.06, b = 0, sigma = 0.35)
```

Two Asset Cash or Nothing options are building blocks for constructing more complex exotic options and there are four types of two asset cash or nothing options. The first two situations are: a Two Asset Cash or Nothing call which pays out a fixed cash amount if the price of the first asset is above (below) the strike price of the first asset and the price of the second asset is also above (below) the strike price of the second asset at expiration. The other two situations arise under the following conditions: a Two Asset Cash or Nothing down-up pays out a fixed cash amount if the price of the first asset is below (above) the strike price of the first asset and the price of the second asset is above (below) the strike price of the second asset at expiration.

The following function does the job of calculating the two asset cash or nothing option price:

```
> TwoAssetCashOrNothingOption(TypeFlag = "c", S1 = 100, S2 = 100,X1 = 110,
X2 = 90, K = 10, Time = 0.5, r = 0.10, b1 = 0.05,b2 = 0.06, sigma1 = 0.20,
sigma2 = 0.25, rho = 0.5)@price
[1] 2.49875
```

Here:

- TypeFlag : Option type "c" for call "p" for put
- S1, S2: Stock price for two assets
- X1, X2: Two exercise prices
- K: Cash amount to be paid at expiry
- Time: Time to expiry
- r: Risk-free interest rate
- b1, b2: Cost of carry for two assets
- sigma1, sigma2: Two asset volatility
- rho: Correlation between two assets

There is much more detail available about all other type of exotic options and for more details about exotic options, you should look at the PDF file with the name fExoticOptions which you can download from the Web.

Questions

1. What are the packages to be used for option, bond, and exotic options pricing?
2. Which functions will you use to calculate the option price using the Black-Scholes and Cox-Ross-Rubinstein methods?
3. How does the CRR price converge to the binomial price and which command would you use to calculate Greeks?
4. Write a command to calculate implied volatility.
5. How would you prepare a `cashflow` and `maturity` matrix to the form which would be used in bond pricing function, and which function would be used for bond pricing?
6. What are the functions to be used for credit spread and credit default swaps?
7. What are the Asian option types, barrier option types, and digital option types?
8. What are the functions you would use for the options in question 7?

Summary

This chapter used derivative pricing only in terms of implementation in R, and various packages such as `foptions`, `termstrc`, `CreditMetrics`, `credule`, `GUIDE`, and `fExoticOptions` to price options, bonds, credit spreads, credit default swaps, and interest rate derivatives, and different types of exotic options were used. Derivative pricing is crucial in derivative trading and it is very important to learn it.

This chapter also covered the Black-Scholes and Cox-Ross-Rubinstein methods, along with Greeks and implied volatility for options. It also explained bond price and yield curves. It also used functions which explain how credit spread, credit default swaps, and interest rate derivatives are priced. Toward the end, it covered various types of exotic options. It used data given in relevant packages and implemented functions.

Index

A

algorithmic trading 129
ANOVA 79, 80
apply() function 31
arithmetic expression 21, 22
arrays 14
as.xts
  used, for constructing xts 107
assignment operator 23
atomic objects 11
autocorrelation 51
autoregressive integrated moving average
  (ARIMA) 113, 115, 116, 118, 119
autoregressive model (AR) 110, 111

B

Basel regulation 216
Black-Scholes model 244
Bollinger 133
bond pricing 250, 252, 253
boxplot
  outliers, detecting 64, 65
break statement 31

C

capital asset pricing model (CAPM) 155, 156
Chevron corporation (CVX) 142
classification
  for variable selection 83
co-integration based pairs trading 151, 152, 154
code expressions
  assignment operator 23
  expressions 21
  keywords 24
  symbols 23
  variables, naming 24

writing 21
coefficient of determination
  about 72, 78
  confidence interval 78
Comprehensive R Archive Network (CRAN)
  about 10
  packages, installing 10
conditional expression 22, 23
constant expression 21
control statements, loops
  about 31
  break 31
  next 32
correlation based pairs trading 147, 148, 150
correlation
  about 51
  autocorrelation 51
  cross-correlation 53
  partial autocorrelation 52
Cox-Ross-Rubinstein model 245, 247
credit default swap (CDS) 256, 257
credit risk 217, 219, 221, 222
credit spread 253, 254, 255
cross-correlation 53
CSV format file
  reading 17
  writing 17
cumulative distribution function (CDF) 211
currency risk 215

D

data types
  about 10, 11, 12
  arrays 14
  CSV format file, reading 17
  CSV format file, writing 17
  databases 20

DataFrames 15, 16
  exporting 16
  importing 16
  lists 13, 14
  matrix 14
  vectors 12, 13
  web data 19
  xlsx package 18, 19
data
  converting, to time series 101, 102
DataFrames 15, 16
decision tree 194, 195
deep neural network 183, 184, 185
dependent variable 70
directional trading 130, 132, 140
discrete wavelets transformation (DWT) 87
distance-based pairs trading 141, 142, 144, 147
dlnorm 39
Dow Jones Index (DJI) 130, 137, 169
Dow Jones Industrial Average (DJIA) 85
dynamic conditional correlation (DCC) 125
dynamic rebalancing
  about 228
  periodic rebalancing 228, 229, 232

E

errors
  normality distribution 75
exchange-rate risk 215
exotic options
  about 258, 261, 262
  features 258
expected shortfall (ES) 210
exponential GARCH (EGARCH) 122
exposure at default (EAD) 217
expressions
  about 21
  arithmetic expression 21, 22
  conditional expression 22, 23
  constant expression 21
  functional call expression 23
extreme value theory (EVT) 43, 45
Exxon Mobil (XOM) 142, 154

F

factors 15
Fast Fourier transformation (FFT) 91, 93
feature selection
  about 81
  irrelevant features, removing 81
for loop 30
fraud detection 223, 225
function
  about 24
  arguments 25
  body 25
  constructing, with argument 26
  constructing, without argument 26
  name 25
  R programs, executing 27
  R script, sourcing 27, 28
  return value 25
  saved file, executing through R Window 27
functional call expression 23

G

generalized autoregressive conditional
    heteroscedasticity (GARCH)
  about 120
  distribution model 121
  mean model 121
  variance model 121
generalized extreme value (GEV) 43
generalized Pareto distribution (GPD) 43
genetic algorithm (GA) 236, 238, 240
Greeks 248, 249
grid testing 233, 236
GUIDE package 257

H

hedging
  about 215
  currency risk 215
  short hedge 215
Hilbert transformation 93, 95, 96
historical VaR 211, 213
hypothesis testing
  about 54

lower tail test, of population mean with known
  variance 54, 55, 56
lower tail test, of population mean with unknown
  variance 58, 59
two tailed test, of population mean with unknown
  variance 60, 61
two-tailed test, of population mean with known
  variance 57, 58
upper tail test, of population mean with known
  variance 56, 57
upper tail test, of population mean with unknown
  variance 59, 60

I

if statement 29
if...else statement 29
implied volatility 250
independent variable 70
interest rate derivatives
  calculating 257

K

K means algorithm 186, 187, 188
K nearest neighborhood 188, 189, 191
keywords 24
kurtosis
  computing 50

L

liability management 225
linear filters 108
linear model 63
lists 13, 14
local outlier factor (LOF) 65
LOF algorithm
  outliers, detecting 65, 66
logistic regression neural network 168, 169, 172,
  174
lognormal distribution
  about 39
  dlnorm 39
  plnorm 40
  qlnorm 42
  rlnorm 42
loops

about 28
apply() function 31
control statements 31
for loop 30
if statement 29
if...else statement 29
sapply() function 31
while loop 30
loss given default (LGD) 217, 253

M

market risk 203
matrix 14
maximal overlap discrete wavelet transform
  (MODWT) 89
maximum likelihood estimation (MLE) 61, 62
mean
  computing 48
measure of central tendency 48
measure of summary statistics 48
median
  computing 49
mode
  computing 49
moment
  computing 49
momentum trading
  about 130, 132, 140
  pairs trading 140
Monte Carlo simulation 213, 214
moving average (MA) 111, 112, 113
moving average convergence divergence (MACD)
  133
multi factor model
  about 157, 158, 160, 161
  URL 157
multicollinearity 78
multiresolution analysis (MRA) 89
multivariate linear regression
  about 76
  coefficient of determination 78

N

neural network 175, 176, 178, 180, 181
next statement 32

normal distribution
  about 36
  norm 36
  pnorm 38
  qnorm 38
  rnorm 38
normality distribution
  of errors 75
normalization 67

O

objects 10
option pricing
  about 243
  Black-Scholes model 244
  Cox-Ross-Rubinstein model 245, 247
  Greeks 248, 249
outliers
  about 64
  detecting, with boxplot 64, 65
  detecting, with LOF algorithm 65, 66

P

packages
  installing 9
  installing, from CRAN 10
  installing, manually 10
pairs trading
  about 140
  co-integration based pairs trading 151, 152, 154
  correlation based pairs trading 147, 148, 150
  distance-based pairs trading 141, 142, 144, 147
parameter estimation
  about 61
  linear model 63
  maximum likelihood estimation (MLE) 61, 63
parametric VaR 209
partial autocorrelation 52
peaks over threshold (POT) 43
periodic rebalancing 228, 229, 232
plnorm 40
pnorm 38
poisson distribution 42
portfolio
  constructing 162, 163, 164

reference link 163
  risk, managing 205, 206, 208
predictor variable 70
probability distributions
  about 35
  extreme value theory (EVT) 43, 45
  lognormal distribution 39
  normal distribution 36
  poisson distribution 42
  uniform distribution 43
probability of default (PD) 217

Q

qlnorm 42
qnorm 38

R

R
  downloading 8, 9
  installing 8, 9
  need for 7, 8
  saved file, executing 27
  script, sourcing 27, 28
  URL 8
random forest 197, 198, 200
random sampling 46
rlnorm 42
rnorm 38

S

sampling
  about 46
  random sampling 46
  stratified sampling 47
sapply() function 31
short hedge 215
simple linear regression
  about 70
  coefficient of determination 72
  confidence interval 73
  normality distribution, of errors 75
  residual plot, plotting 74
  scatter plot, plotting 71
  testing 73
skewness

computing 50
standardization 67
statistical distributions 43
statistics
    about 48
    kurtosis 50
    mean 48
    median 49
    mode 49
    moment 49
    skewness 50
    summary 49
stepwise variable selection
    about 82
    by classification 83, 84
strata 47
stratified sampling 47
summary
    computing 49
support vector machine 192, 193
symbols 23

T

time series data
    cycles (Ct) 100
    residuals 100
    seasonal effects 100
    trend 100
time series
    about 100
    data, converting 101, 102

U

uniform distribution 43

V

VaR
    about 209
    historical VaR 211, 213
    Monte Carlo simulation 213, 214
    parametric VaR 209
variables
    naming 24
    ranking 84
vector GARCH (VGARCH) 123
vectors 12, 13

W

walk forward testing 232
wavelet analysis 85, 87, 91
Wavelet transformation (WT) 85
while loop 30

X

xlsx package 18, 19
xts object
    about 107
    constructing, from scratch 108
    constructing, with as.xts 107

Z

zoo object
    about 103
    advantages 105
    constructing 103
    data, subsetting 105
    disadvantages 106
    external file, reading 104
    merging 105
    plotting 106